Cuban
Revolution
Reader

Cuban Revolution Reader

A Documentary History
of 40 Key Moments of
the Cuban Revolution

Edited by Julio García Luis

OCEAN PRESS
Melbourne • New York

www.oceanbooks.com.au

Cover design by David Spratt

Copyright © 2001 Ocean Press
Copyright © 2001 Julio García Luis

ISBN 1-876175-10-9

Printed in Australia

First printed 2001

Published by Ocean Press
Australia: GPO Box 3279, Melbourne, Victoria 3001, Australia
  • Fax: (61-3) 9329 5040 • E-mail: info@oceanbooks.com.au
USA: PO Box 1186, Old Chelsea Station, New York, NY 10113-1186, USA

Library of Congress Catalog Card No: 00-112186

OCEAN PRESS DISTRIBUTORS
United States & Canada: LPC Group,
    1436 West Randolph St, Chicago, IL 60607, USA
Britain and Europe: Global Book Marketing,
    38 King Street, London, WC2E 8JT, UK
Australia and New Zealand: Astam Books,
    57-61 John Street, Leichhardt, NSW 2040, Australia
Cuba and Latin America: Ocean Press,
    Calle 21 #406, Vedado, Havana, Cuba
Southern Africa: Phambili Agencies,
    PO Box 28680, Kensington 2101, Johannesburg, South Africa

www.oceanbooks.com.au

CONTENTS

CHRONOLOGY

1952
March 10   Fulgencio Batista takes power in military coup

1953
July 26   Fidel Castro leads the attack on the Moncada Barracks in Santiago de Cuba

1956
December   Landing of the *Granma*

1959
January 1   Batista flees, Fidel Castro arrives in Havana January 8
April 15-26   Fidel Castro visits the United States
May 17   First Agrarian Reform Law
October 28   Disappearance of Camilo Cienfuegos in air accident

1960
February   Visit of Soviet Foreign Minister Anastas Mikoyan to Cuba
March 4   Explosion on *La Coubre*, Havana harbor
March 17   CIA plans for overthrowing Fidel Castro approved by President Eisenhower
May 8   Cuba and the Soviet Union establish diplomatic relations
June 7   U.S. oil companies that refuse to refine Soviet oil are nationalized
July 8   Cuba's U.S. sugar quota is suspended, Soviet Union agrees to buy Cuban sugar
August 6   Cuba nationalizes U.S. companies
August 28   U.S. imposes economic embargo against trade with Cuba
September 2   First Declaration of Havana
September 26   Fidel Castro addresses the United Nations in New York
October 14   Large commercial and industrial enterprises in Cuba are nationalized

1961
January 3   U.S. breaks diplomatic relations with Cuba
April 15   Bombing raid on Cuban air fields
April 16   Fidel Castro proclaims socialist character of the revolution
April 17-19   Bay of Pigs invasion
August 8   Che Guevara denounces the Alliance for Progress at Punta del Este
December 22   Cuba is declared a Territory Free of Illiteracy

1962

January	Organization of American States expels Cuba
February 4	Second Declaration of Havana
February 7	Economic blockade against Cuba is imposed by President Kennedy
March 12	Ration system is established in Cuba
March 14	Operation Mongoose initiated
October 22-28	Missile Crisis

1963

October 4	Hurricane Flora devastates Cuba
December 20	Cuba initiates campaign of solidarity with Vietnam

1965

April	Che Guevara leaves on the mission to Africa
October 3	Cuban Communist Party's first Central Committee meeting

1966

January	First conference of Tricontinental held in Havana
November	Che Guevara's mission to Bolivia begins

1967

October 9	Che Guevara is assassinated in Bolivia

1968

October 10	Cuba celebrates 100 years of struggle for independence

1969

July 26	Fidel Castro announces the 10-million-ton sugar harvest

1972

July 11	Cuba joins the CMEA (socialist trading bloc)

1974

January	Premier Brezhnev visits Cuba

1975

February 14	Introduction of the Family Code
November 5	As part of Operation Carlota Cuba sends troops to support Angolan independence against South African invasion
December 17	First Congress of the Cuban Communist Party

1976

February 26	Cuba adopts a new socialist constitution
October 6	Cubana airlines plane bombed in Barbados
December 2	Institution of People's Power

1979

January 1	Cuban Americans are permitted to visit Cuba. More than 100,000 visit Cuba during this year
March 13	Revolution in Grenada
July 19	Victory of the Sandinistas in Nicaragua
September	Fidel Castro is elected chair of the Nonaligned Movement at its sixth summit

1980
April — Mariel emigration crisis

1981
January 20 — Formation of the Territorial Troop Militia

1985
May 19 — Radio Martí broadcasts begin
August 3-7 — Conference in Havana on the debt crisis in Latin America

1986
April 19 — Fidel Castro announces the rectification campaign

1988
March 23 — Victory against South Africa at Cuito Cuanavale, Angola

1989
June/ — Trials against corruption
September
December 7 — Cuba honors heroes of internationalist missions

1992
January 1 — First year of the "special period" declared

1994
August — Rafters' crisis leading to new migration agreement between the United States and Cuba

1996
February — President Clinton signs Helms-Burton Bill into law

1998
January 21-25 — Pope John Paul II visits Cuba

Editor's Preface

Relic from the Cold War or Herald of the Third Millennium?

The Cuban Revolution, one of the events that has defined the shape of the 20th century, is now 40 years old. Throughout those years, the propaganda of its enemies has sought to depict it first as a satellite, a tool of Soviet policy in Latin America and Africa, and then, after the collapse of the Soviet Union and the community of nations created when Central and Eastern Europe were liberated from Nazism, as a kind of tenacious relic left over from the Cold War. But the very fact of Cuba's survival, which defied all logic, rules out these simplifications.

Anyone can understand that the continued existence of revolutionary Cuba in today's world is a consequence of something much more profound than any individual's whim or the Numantian stubbornness that was referred to years ago as a synonym of hopeless, suicidal determination. Nor is its survival explained by the understandable reaction to the stupidity of U.S. policy toward Cuba, expressed in this latest stage in the Torricelli and Helms-Burton Acts.

Nearly 40 years ago, Che Guevara proposed the thesis that Cuba was an historical exception. His reasoning is still valid.

Thus, on arriving at this anniversary, which brought us to the threshold of a new century and a new millennium, it could be said that the greatest moments of the Cuban Revolution may not be these 40 moments that we have selected as being symbolic and incorporated in this book. Perhaps the greatest moments still lie in the future, in the difficult new era awaiting us in the coming decades and in which we have already begun to live.

Some texts written outside Cuba and even certain reflections from inside Cuba contain hints of something akin to belated remorse over the fact that the Cuban Revolution entered into the sphere of influence of and became somewhat dependent on the Soviet Union. According to this thesis, it would have been better for Cuba if those links hadn't existed. Those who argue this say that we wouldn't have received the dangerous burden of a dogmatized Marxism; the experience of highly centralized and bureaucratic economic management; backward technologies; tendencies toward gigantism, excessive consumption of electric power and indifference to the environmental effects of investment projects; a formalistic concept of democracy; and a cultural policy based on scholastic models.

Naturally, it is easy to speculate with hindsight about what the course of history might have been, but the indispensable conclusions that the country should draw from these four decades are one thing, and the desire to replace history with abstractions is something very different.

Cuba didn't choose — nor could it choose — the world in which the revolution took place. Naturally, it would have been much better if the Soviet Union, which was to become its main economic, political and military partner, hadn't so early lost Lenin, the true leader of its socialist revolution; that it hadn't experienced the mistakes and crimes of Stalinism; that it hadn't had to pay the terrible price of the war; and then, in conditions in which a political bureaucracy was more interested in looking after its own interests than in achieving socialist ideals, was unable to complete the rectification of those deformations. It would have been much better if the enemy's blockade hadn't forced it to compete in an arms race that drained its resources.

But, accepting reality as it was, Cuba had the unplanned good fortune of achieving its people's victory when the balance of power in the world offered it at least minimal conditions for survival.

The existence of the Soviet Union — whatever its historical tragedies and mistakes — constituted a decisive advantage in the consolidation of the Cuban people's militant self-determination and their right to defend their independence and revolution at whatever cost. Moreover, the Soviet Government of that period, headed by Nikita S. Khrushchev, still had some Bolshevik daring, an ethic of solidarity and the political will to take the risks that the defense of Cuba implied. These facts constituted important factors in those circumstances which determined whether or not the Cuban people could be crushed.

To think that Cuba had options, that it could choose between one thing and another, is simply ridiculous. The country lacked the required critical mass, economic clout and military strength to break away from the forces of the bipolar world.

The real alternative faced by Cuba was between sovereignty and the ruthless re-establishment of U.S. rule, between the revolution and the counterrevolution, between the advancement and deepening of the process toward socialism and an unimaginable regression in history. Che summed it up concisely: "Socialist revolution or caricature of revolution." And, when considered realistically, this challenge placed Cuba in the camp of the only allies it could count on. Soviet solidarity was a privilege, and we Cubans, who shouldn't be ungrateful, should always recognize this, even if now we can do so only in our hearts.

The foregoing, of course, doesn't exonerate us from the need to analyze why, in certain circumstances, those relations between our small, underdeveloped country and that great economic and military power — relations that, objectively, implied some degree of dependence — tended to lean excessively toward unjustified influences and were unnecessarily copied. These influences weren't sifted and subjected to the critical scrutiny that should accompany the importation of any experience.

Without pretending to exhaust such a vast topic, I would say that the Cuban Revolution inherited the old [Cuban] Communists' defensive approach toward the Soviet Union — an approach that was one of the unquestionable creeds of that party, which had so many merits and so many outstanding members. However, it now seems amazing that later, when the Soviet party was in power and had so many resources and possibilities, it did so little to replace that defense with a more serious, documented and scientific study of the realities and internal contradictions that existed in the country that was our main ally.

It seems undeniable that the preponderant role played by the Soviet Union — when it supplied us with the weapons we needed for our defense, bought the sugar that the United States rejected, and sent us oil and food when a deadly trap had been laid for Cuba — to some extent placed it beyond criticism and investigation.

In addition, a more balanced relationship would have been difficult to conceive of without lesser economic dependence. Unfortunately, Cuba's economy was extremely vulnerable and very dependent on foreign trade; and Cuba was a net importer of food and energy — the historical result of the slave plantation economy that had developed from the end of the 18th century on. A single-crop system, a single export product, submission to the U.S. market and the profound structural deformities were the features of this reality.

Cuba couldn't limit itself to changing trading and financial partners. It had to try to effect basic changes, and that was what it did, starting with the Agrarian Reform. That was what undeniably lay behind the effort to bring in an enormous sugarcane harvest in 1970. The setback of that effort, the defects that later hindered the country in its attempts to increase and diversify its export capacities, the harsh blockade and the unfavorable circumstances of the world economy led to Cuba's becoming even more dependent.

It was difficult for a country that purchased 72 percent of Cuba's exports, dominating all of its main economic sectors, not to influence, consciously or not, many other spheres, even while maintaining a policy of respect for Cuba's independent decisions.

There are plenty of examples showing that Cuba never relinquished its sovereign prerogatives or behaved like a satellite country. When a point of principle was reached, the leaders of the revolution never hesitated to face the consequences of a quarrel with Moscow. However, it is obvious that the Soviet Union's significance for Cuba's continued survival and defense made it necessary to keep its positions in mind and to coordinate the policies of the two countries as much as possible.

Cuba didn't make a mistake when it availed itself of the advantages of its relations with the Soviet Union to confront the U.S. blockade and consolidate the country's development and defense.

The mistakes that were made — and there were some — were made by those who, in certain situations, thought that the safest, surest path was that of imitating methods and formulas that were already obsolete in the Soviet Union itself; those who ignored Martí's warning that the government in each new republic should reflect the nature of the country; and Mariátegui's foresight in saying that, in Latin America, socialism couldn't be a copy but must rather be a heroic creation.

The inglorious collapse of the Soviet Union and of the socialist experience stemming from the October Revolution created a completely new strategic situation in the world. This counter-balance had previously offset the imperialists' drive for expansion and domination and had served as a premise for the struggles of so many peoples against colonialism and other forms of oppression. Without going into what the disappearance of this balance meant for all humankind, for Cuba the loss of its main ally, its markets, its fair prices, its financing and its supplies of arms constituted a life-or-death challenge.

The blockade was doubled. For the second time in 30 years, Cuba had to restructure and redirect its entire economy. In slightly over two years, it lost 35 percent of its Gross Domestic Product, and its import capacity — a decisive index in our case — was reduced from US$8.139 billion in 1989 to US$2.236 billion in 1992. In the political and theoretical spheres, the situation seemed to take Cuba back to the polemic the Bolsheviks had with their adversaries in 1903 about whether or not it was possible for socialism to triumph in a single country.

The Cuban leaders, headed by Fidel Castro, thus had to confront a new problem that was unprecedented in the history of the revolutionary movement, with the aggravating factor that, this time, it wasn't an immense country rich in natural resources, such as Russia, facing the imperialist powers at the beginning of the 20th century, but was rather a tiny, relatively poor island confronting the designs of the strongest military and political power of all time.

Once more in the life of the Cuban nation, the determining factor wasn't theoretical analysis or the cool calculation of probabilities. Cuba overcame that terrible trial — is overcoming it — because it drew on its history, sense of duty and honor, and the ethics that constitute the essence of the Cuban spirit.

Paradoxically, this may be a new example of every cloud having a silver lining.

The disappearance of the Soviet Union — a misfortune that seemed inconceivable some years ago — has brought Cuba not only dangers and challenges but also the opportunity to review its own experiences, free itself from foreign elements, return to some extent to its original values and — in short — begin anew. The task is not an easy one, because the pincers of the U.S. blockade squeeze tighter than ever before. In addition, in order to enable its economy to recover in the present conditions, Cuba must allow capitalist formulas to be applied — in however limited a way — within its territory, open areas to market influences and undertake reforms in its economic structure, accepting the social costs and ideological risks this implies.

This isn't a case of Caribbean rationalization in the sense that everything that happens is a good thing. Naturally, it would have been much better if the Soviet Union had found a way out of the bog in which it was mired that would have preserved that socialist nation's enormous achievements.

Did any such way out exist? Probably yes. The peoples of the Soviet Union had the traditions, patriotism and moral reserves for regenerating their society. The catastrophe wasn't fatal; it was the leadership that failed. Opportunism, political primitivism and personal ambition prevailed. The lack of true democracy, inveterate isolation and a lack of information facilitated the rise of confusion and demoralization. Bureaucracy wound up by taking over the government. The workers and the people as a whole were pitilessly sacrificed.

A complete analysis of this phenomenon has yet to be made, but it is important for the Cuban Revolution to examine more deeply and fully all that happened there, since the Soviets' ideas and practice permeated many spheres of this country.

The responsibility and possibility for making a valuable contribution to the reconstruction of the peoples' alternatives to modern capitalism — that is, neoliberal globalization — have fallen, unsought, to the Cuban Revolution.

People are now beginning to see more clearly that the true meaning of Cuba's resistance in these years hasn't been just to protect the independence, social justice and right to self-determination of the Cuban people — which, in itself, would have been of tremendous value. More importantly, it also lies in Cuba's role in saving the hope, idea and prospects of socialism and the new development of revolutionary thought.

Parodying the classical judgment of history that *latifundism* was Rome's downfall, it may be said that corruption was the downfall of the Soviet Union. Even though that country was a strategic nuclear force, the internal decay of its values, its spiritual aging, left it without solutions for its own future as well as the present and future problems of humanity. Cuba was not exempt from negative internal phenomena, which were, above all, the consequence of its lack of social development. However, Cuba has a revolution that now, 40 years after its triumph, still maintains its links with the masses and retains their support, ensures communication between the leaders and the people, upholds administrative honesty, rejects caste privileges and implements a principled policy.

It is only fair to recognize that serious Marxist-Leninist thought existed in the Soviet Union, as well, which tried to develop in accord with the times and influence reality, but bureaucratic sway over intellectual and scientific creativity suffocated it. Cuba's circumstances in this sphere — apart from occasional mistakes — have been incomparably more advantageous.

Cuba has an eminently advanced, patriotic and socialist culture, which is both its shield for defending the island against constant informational and psychological siege by its enemies and its sword for taking the offensive and making progress in the decisive terrain of the struggle of ideas.

This culture — forged at one of the crossroads of the Western world, heir to the values it created and a participant in the codes and agendas of its intellectual debate (even though, on occasion, resentfully, because of certain isolation) — has greater possibilities than others for communicating with political forces and with thinking men and women all over the world. It is also this culture that helps Cuba to delve deeper into current world problems and to discern the solutions required by the fast-approaching future.

In political and theoretical terms, this culture is alien to any kind of sectarian narrowness. The Cuban Revolution's — and especially Fidel Castro's — understanding of Marxism-Leninism has nothing to do with dogma and the mechanical transposition of concepts. Revolutionary thought in Cuba is considered to be a combination of the basic ideas of Marx, Engels and Lenin with the dialectical method inherent to that universal theory; the legacy of José Martí and the other essential experiences, traditions and values of the Cuban national liberation movement; and, above all, the present development of that thought in the praxis of the struggle to transform the country.

If we add to these conditions the tremendous esteem in which Cuba is held in the rest of Latin America, the Caribbean and throughout the world; the respect with which people listen to its leaders' views in all international forums; and the ability of its leaders to get people to meet and unite, it is clear that, in these circumstances, no other country or revolutionary process can presently play the role assumed by Cuba.

This doesn't mean that Cuba should seek to set itself up as a new "model" or as a new "center" of the world revolutionary movement. In the coming years, keeping pace with irreversible technological changes, the world will become ever more closely knit and interdependent, but, along with the increasing need for more integrated action, there will also be the prospect of great diversity. Each country and region will seek its own formulas. There won't be any "models" or "centers" to be imitated or to tell others what they should do.

Cuba's most important role in that world will be that of setting an example of firmness and resistance, of showing that there is an humane developmental alternative to neoliberal capitalism, promoting sustainable and rational environmental policy, and especially of establishing itself as a force for promoting and spreading the new revolutionary thinking that is needed for rising above this phase of history.

It is not fate that Cuba should make these important contributions; it is simply a possibility. In the past, we heard it said that socialism was irreversible; now, we know that that is only true when a principled line is followed and that subjective mistakes can lead to the failure of any revolutionary process.

The possibility of the Cuban Revolution serving as the standard-bearer of these ideas requires that the internal unity of the people and of their political vanguard be constantly strengthened. The Communist Party of Cuba, with its 800,000 members, is the heart of this cohesion and represents the force par excellence of example, morale and intelligent action for solving or explaining all problems. The party and all the other social organizations and institutions have the task of doing ever more effective ideological work, because Cuban society must develop its virtues while in open contact with all kinds of ideological contaminants and influences.

Together with this, economic efforts are now of decisive importance. We no longer have trading partners who will underwrite the deficits of our balance of payments; the blockade continues, like a monster octopus, to plague our operations in all parts of the world; and some effects of globalization are creating additional difficulties for us. Cuba's only solution lies in its capacity to increase its economic efficiency; master the art of good administration; and, in short, obtain the hard-currency income required to meet the country's needs, including the basic one of feeding its people.

Never before could Cuba make such an essential and timely contribution to humanity, which seems to be on the brink of a global crisis of incalculable proportions.

This crisis is defined by the fact that four-fifths of the world's population now live in conditions of poverty or physical hunger. Although the population is growing quickly, especially in the underdeveloped world, the means required for providing food, clothing, shelter and medicine are not increasing. The scientific-technological progress of industrialized countries is amazing and could ensure a decent life for every man and woman in the world, but it has a diametrically opposite effect. Even though the possibilities for communication, information and the transmission of knowledge are extraordinary, isolation and marginalization prevail.

Moreover, environmental destruction — due to the selfishness of the consumer societies and the devastating impact on those who are struggling at the extreme limits of survival — has, in several fields, already passed the point of no return.

Capitalism, with its incurable blindness, is dragging our planet to the brink of a catastrophe. This is no science fiction movie and is not something to be faced in the distant future — it is already happening to the 40 million people, especially children, who die of hunger and curable diseases each year.

A global crisis calls for global thinking and a global strategy. Recently, in a manner consistent with his ideas on solidarity, the unity of the exploited peoples and their joining forces to attain their legitimate rights, Fidel Castro has been outlining the key elements of what could be a new revolutionary approach for the beginning of the 21st century.

The first thing that should be clearly understood is the need to avoid confusing globalization — which is an objective phenomenon and consequence of the age-old development of the productive forces and of human knowledge and which implies new opportunities and possibilities for the peoples of the world — with the model that dominant capitalism has imposed: neoliberal globalization, which turns the market into an all-powerful god, turns its back on human beings, tramples them underfoot and subordinates everything to super-exploitation and super-profits.

As Fidel Castro has said, "The most important stage in the history of humanity is beginning now." In his view, in line with the world situation and the changes that have been wrought — including the strong claim by the United States to political and military unipolarity — the violent revolutionary methods appropriate to the 19th century and to the first half of the 20th century are not the most advisable now.

Naturally, an isolated revolution may appear where oppression, repression and hunger become unbearable. Those who see all other paths closed to them and resort to rebellion cannot be criticized. But imperialism now has greater means than ever before for crushing any attempt to attain or retain power by force of arms. The international financial institutions serve its interests. The United States even uses the Security Council of the United Nations selectively and undemocratically to serve its own superpower interests by intervening and punishing governments it doesn't like.

The globalized world needs a world government that will establish order in the present chaos, contribute to a better distribution of resources, protect the environment and promote international cooperation and democratic participation by all countries — a government that is a far cry from the gross caricature that the United States is imposing unilaterally and abusively on the world community.

In the mid-1980s, the poor countries — many of which were victims of division, submissiveness and false promises — lost their great opportunity to solve the foreign debt crisis.

The same situation is being repeated now, at a higher level. During the past 15 years, far from being alleviated, the economic problems of these peoples have multiplied. The crisis is no longer simply financial; now, it is also political, spiritual, medical and ecological. It no longer affects the Third World countries alone but includes growing masses within the industrialized countries themselves, as well.

At the same time, the transnationalization of the economy and the prevailing speculative flows in what has been called a "casino economy" are showing signs of what may well become a great global crisis, one unprecedented in the world in its scope and implications. The strong north winds of the storm have begun to sweep through Asia — which, only recently, the experts of neoliberalism had considered to be the area of most dynamic end-of-the-century and beginning-of-the-next-century growth.

Thus, while entailing serious dangers and threats for all humankind, neoliberal globalization — like the foreign debt crisis in the past — is also placing a very powerful weapon in the hands of governments and peoples.

The objective, material premises for taking advantage of this opportunity take shape relatively rapidly. However, there are still inadequate subjective conditions in terms of ideas, programs, organization, leadership and determination to act in a united, coordinated way.

It is hardly strange that this should be so in a world in which the ruling powers — especially the United States — have imposed and keep reinforcing a virtual spiritual and informational dictatorship as part of their totalitarian plan to establish a single mindset. In this same context, the revolutionary and other progressive forces are barely beginning to recover from the confusion, despair and fatalism that stemmed from the collapse of the socialist community formed around the Soviet Union.

This explains Fidel Castro's statement to the effect that, at this moment, the Cuban Revolution's main role — and his own — is to work to create awareness among the peoples of all latitudes to understand the problems they face; to carry this message to political figures, thinkers and spiritual leaders; and to mobilize public opinion.

In today's world, the importance of ideas is growing; the possibilities for spreading the truth are multiplying. No one's voice is weak if they are determined to be heard.

Achieving true, socialist, human globalization implies, above all, joining forces to confront the unipolar appetites of U.S. imperialism, its hegemonism, its policy of ruling the entire planet. In these circumstances, socialism cannot be an immediate goal. Intermediary stages will probably be required — in which multipolarism is strengthened, various formulas of regional integration gain ground, the unity and coordination of peoples and governments assert the right to full and multilateral negotiations, and the United Nations is effectively democratized.

The important thing is for such thinking to help hold us on course in the medium and long term. Therefore, it isn't a matter of just any old method of thought. It should constitute a higher synthesis of the best and most advanced principles of human integrity.

The revolutionary concepts of Marx, Engels and Lenin and the lessons learned by the international communist movement in the past century and a half will have a prominent place in it. It will also include the patriotic and humanistic traditions of each nation and, unquestionably, the ethics and aspirations of the great universal religions to spiritual improvement. The theories and analyses of environmental protection will be included, as will the other great contemporary contributions of the social and natural sciences. The new political movements, the new forms of association of the masses that are emerging from the present socioeconomic crisis, will also add their experiences to this thinking.

If this new universalism manages to slough off old, sectarian models; if the peoples and all the other social forces learn to unite; and if the countries and governments set aside what now divides them, a new era will be ushered in for all humankind. Cuba is speaking out for these goals. Now, 40 years after the triumph of its revolution, it pledges its best, most determined efforts to achieving them. Cuba is advancing, stepping into the breach. The real history of humanity may well be beginning. Great moments await us.

Julio García Luis
Havana, 1998

1

TRIUMPH OF THE REVOLUTION

January 1, 1959

The last few hours of the Batista dictatorship ran out on the night of December 31, 1958. The end of the war was imminent because of the Rebel Army's sudden offensive on all fronts. A revolutionary force of fewer than 3,000 armed men had pushed the 80,000 members of the repressive bodies of the terrorist regime that had taken power on March 10, 1952, to the brink of collapse.

In Oriente Province, the main scene of the rebel campaign, the combined forces of the First, Second and Third Fronts, under Fidel Castro's direct command, set about launching an attack on Santiago de Cuba, the second largest city in the country. Most of the towns in Oriente Province had already been liberated, and the military garrisons that hadn't yet surrendered were being besieged.

At the same time, Che Guevara was winding up his brilliant offensive in Santa Clara, in centrally located Las Villas Province, cutting the island in two, and Camilo Cienfuegos, on the northern front, was completing his 10-day attack on the Yaguajay Garrison. Other rebel forces and groups were active in Camagüey, Matanzas, Havana and Pinar del Río Provinces. The demoralization and collapse of Batista's army was an undeniable fact.

In the early morning hours of January 1, 1959, Batista and his main accomplices went straight from the New Year's Eve party at Camp Columbia to planes that were to take them to the Dominican Republic.

General Eulogio Cantillo, who had been Chief of Operations in the eastern region, played a role in these events. General Cantillo broke the promises he had made to the commander of the Rebel Army during an interview they had had some days earlier, in which he had acknowledged that the Batista regime had lost the war and, in an effort to help end it, had agreed to have the troops in Santiago de Cuba rebel on the afternoon of December 31. In spite of Fidel Castro's warnings, Cantillo went to Havana, placed himself at the service of the plans that the U.S. Embassy had hurriedly slapped together to prevent a revolutionary victory, facilitated Batista's flight, became temporary head of the Armed Forces and carried out a fleeting coup.

Instructions from General Headquarters to all Rebel Army Commanders and the people[1]

No matter what news comes from the capital, our troops should not cease firing at any time.

Our forces should continue their operations against the enemy on all battle fronts.

Agree to parleys only with garrisons that want to surrender.

It seems that there has been a coup in the capital. The Rebel Army doesn't know the conditions in which it came about.

The people should be very alert and heed only those instructions that come from General Headquarters.

The dictatorship has collapsed as a result of the crushing defeats dealt it in the last few weeks, but this doesn't mean that the revolution has already triumphed.

Military operations will continue unchanged until an express order to the contrary is received from this Headquarters. Such an order will be issued only when the military elements that have rebelled in the capital place themselves unconditionally under the orders of the revolutionary leadership.

Revolution, yes! Military coup, no!

A military coup behind the backs of the people and the revolution, no, because it would only serve to prolong the war.

A coup that enables Batista and the other criminals to escape, no, because it would only serve to prolong the war.

A Batista-style coup, no, because it would only serve to prolong the war.

Stealing the people's victory, no, because it would only serve to

---

[1] This address was read over Radio Rebelde from the city of Palma Soriano on January 1, 1959. Fidel Castro, *La Sierra y el Llano* (The Mountains and the Plains) (Havana: Casa de las Américas, 1969), 305-6.

prolong the war until the people have achieved total victory.

After seven years of struggle, the people's democratic victory must be absolute, so there will never be another coup like that of March 10 [1952] in our homeland.

No one should allow themselves to be confused or deceived.

You are ordered to stay on the alert.

The people — and especially the workers throughout the Republic — should keep tuned to Radio Rebelde, make preparations for a general strike in all workplaces and begin it when they receive the order, if it is needed to resist a counterrevolutionary coup attempt.

The people and the Rebel Army must be more united and firmer than ever before, so the victory that has cost so many lives may not be snatched away.

Fidel Castro
Commander in Chief

Call for a Revolutionary General Strike[2]

To the people of Cuba, especially all workers:

A military junta in complicity with the tyrant [Batista] has seized power to ensure his flight and that of the main murderers and to try to halt the revolutionary impetus, to snatch victory from us.

The Rebel Army will continue its sweeping campaign, accepting   •
only the unconditional surrender of the military garrisons.

The workers and other people of Cuba should immediately make preparations for a general strike, to begin throughout the country on January 2, supporting the revolutionary forces and thus guaranteeing the total victory of the revolution.

Seven years of heroic struggle, with thousands of martyrs whose blood was shed throughout Cuba, cannot be ignored. The same people who, up until yesterday, were accomplices of and responsible for the dictatorship and its crimes want to continue to give the orders in Cuba.

Cuban workers, guided by the workers' section of the July 26 Movement,[3] should take over all of the pro-Mujal[4] unions and

---

[2] This "Call for a Revolutionary General Strike" was also read over Radio Rebelde from Palma Soriano on January 1, 1959. Fidel Castro, *El pensamiento de Fidel Castro* (The Thought of Fidel Castro) (Havana: Editora Política, 1983), vol. I, book 2, 451.

[3] The United National Workers' Front (Frente Obrero Nacional Unido, FONU), that had been formed in November 1958, grouping all of the workers' organizations that opposed the dictatorship, responded to this call.

organize themselves in the factories and other workplaces to bring the country to a halt at dawn.

Batista[5] and Mujal have fled, but their accomplices still control the army and the unions.

A coup to betray the people, no. That would only prolong the war.

The war will not have ended until the forces at Camp Columbia have surrendered. This time, nothing and nobody can prevent the triumph of the revolution.

Cubans, for freedom, democracy and the complete triumph of the revolution, join in the revolutionary general strike in all of the territories still to be liberated.

...This time, it really is a revolution![6]

(Excerpts from the address by Fidel Castro in Céspedes Park, Santiago de Cuba, on January 2, 1959)

I am not going to beat around the bush: General Cantillo has betrayed us... Of course, we had always said that they shouldn't try any little last-minute military coup to solve things, because, if there is a military coup behind the people's backs, our revolution will keep on advancing. This time, the revolution won't be frustrated. This time, for Cuba's good fortune, the revolution will really develop in full.

It won't be like what happened in 1895, when the North Americans came and took over the country; they intervened at the last minute, and then they didn't let even Calixto García,[7] who had fought for 30 years, enter Santiago de Cuba. It won't be like what happened in 1933, when Mr. Batista came along just when the

---

[4] Eusebio Mujal Barniol led the attack on labor unions under the administrations of Ramón Grau San Martín and Carlos Prío and seized control of the Confederation of Cuban Workers (Confederación de Trabajadores de Cuba, CTC). When Batista carried out his 1952 coup, Mujal became one of his main yes-men.

[5] Fulgencio Batista y Zaldívar (1901-73) took part in the September 4, 1933, military coup as a sergeant and stenographer. Turned into a tool of the reaction and imperialism, he overthrew the Grau-Guiteras Administration in 1934 and wielded power in Cuba until 1944. On March 10, 1952, he instigated another coup and installed a bloody tyranny. He fled from Cuba with a group of his accomplices on January 1, 1959.

[6] Fidel Castro, *El pensamiento de Fidel Castro* (The Thought of Fidel Castro) (Havana: Editora Política, 1983), vol. I, book 1, 3.

[7] Calixto García Iñiguez (1839-98), Major General of the Cuban Liberation Army. He took part in all three of Cuba's wars of independence in the 19th century: the Ten Years' War, the Little War and the War of 1895 — in which, after the death of Antonio Maceo, García became second in command of the Liberation Army.

people were beginning to think that the revolution would triumph, and betrayed the revolution, seized power and installed a terrible dictatorship. It won't be like what happened in 1944, when, just as the masses of the people got excited, thinking that, at last, they had come to power, it turned out that it was thieves[8] who were installed. No thieves, no traitors, no interventionists — this time, it really is a revolution!...

The time factor is very important in everything. The revolution cannot be made in a day, but you may be sure that we will bring about the revolution; you may be sure that, for the first time, the Republic really will be completely free, and the people will have what they deserve.

---

[8] The reference is to the Authentic (Auténtico) Party administrations of Ramón Grau San Martín (1944-48) and Carlos Prío Socarrás (1948-52), which were characterized by graft and corruption.

2

FIDEL ENTERS HAVANA

January 8, 1959

Between January 1 and January 8, 1959, there was a dizzying succession of events, many of them occurring at the same time. They constituted the most radical turn in all of Cuba's history. The neocolonial government and its repressive forces — established when independence was thwarted in 1898 — were dismantled, and a new, revolutionary government was created.

Caught off guard by the speed of the dictatorship's collapse, the United States took hasty action to try to save Batista's Army, which had always been the kingpin in its domination of the island.

On January 1, in cahoots with the U.S. Embassy, the leaders of the coup sent a plane to the Isle of Pines (now the Isle of Youth) to bring back Colonel Ramón Barquín,[1] who was serving a prison term there for having been involved in the "conspiracy of the pure," in which a group of military officers who were opposed to Batista had tried to overthrow him in 1956. Eulogio Cantillo handed over command of the Army to Barquín, who was trusted by the CIA and who tried to make changes in the army's officers.

In Santiago de Cuba, Fidel Castro stated that he did not recognize Barquín's authority and that he would speak with only one person at Camp

---

[1] Colonel Ramón Barquín had been Military Attaché at the Cuban Embassy in Washington and had been sent to prison for having taken part in the 1956 military conspiracy against Batista.

Columbia — Major Camilo Cienfuegos[2] — once he had taken charge of the Camp.

To thwart the U.S. Embassy's maneuver, Fidel called a revolutionary general strike and ordered Majors Ernesto Che Guevara[3] and Camilo Cienfuegos, heading the "Ciro Redondo" and "Antonio Maceo" rebel columns, to advance quickly from the central part of the country toward the capital. Once there, Che was to occupy the La Cabaña Fortress, headquarters of the artillery, and Camilo, Camp Columbia, headquarters of the Army. They achieved this, the enemy garrisons along the Central Highway surrendering to them one after another without putting up any resistance.

After addressing the people of Santiago de Cuba early on the morning of January 2, Fidel Castro set out for Bayamo — where the operations troops of Batista's Army in Oriente Province had their main base — with a mixed force composed of rebel combatants and soldiers from the deposed regime who had joined them. More men joined the rebels in Bayamo, and the Column of Freedom, headed by Fidel Castro and composed of 1,000 rebels and 2,000 soldiers from Batista's defeated Army, began its march to Havana on January 3.

On January 4, after the attempted coup had been exposed and the revolutionary forces had control of all the weapons and military installations in the country, the people were called on to end the strike and go back to work.

During those days, the local governments were dissolved in all of the municipalities and provinces, and new, revolutionary authorities were named.. Leadership of the labor unions was placed in the hands of their legitimate class leaders. For their part, the old political parties disappeared from the scene. On January 5, Dr. Manuel Urrutia Lleó[4] took office as

---

[2] Camilo Cienfuegos Gorriarán (1932-59). He returned to Cuba from Mexico aboard the *Granma*. As a major in the Rebel Army, he led the "Antonio Maceo" Invasion Column 2 to the northern part of Las Villas Province and, with it, took part in the final offensive against the dictatorship. Appointed head of the Rebel Army in 1959, he died in a plane accident on October 28, 1959, while returning to Havana from Camagüey, where he had gone to handle the tricky political situation created by Hubert Matos's treachery.

[3] Ernesto "Che" Guevara de la Serna, (1928-67). An Argentine doctor, he came to Cuba from Mexico aboard the *Granma*. He was a major in the Rebel Army and head of Column 4 in the Sierra Maestra and of the "Ciro Redondo" Invasion Column 4, with which he went to Las Villas Province. A distinguished political leader, theoretician, economist and military chief, he was minister of industry and president of the National Bank. He headed a contingent of internationalists who went to help the national liberation forces in the Congo, Africa. Wounded and taken prisoner in Bolivia, he was murdered on October 9, 1967.

[4] Manuel Urrutia Lleó, a judge in the Santiago de Cuba Court. His worthy attitude in the trial following the events of November 30, 1956, led the revolutionary movement

President of the Republic; he quickly named a cabinet of ministers.

On January 8, Fidel Castro entered Havana. This marked the consolidation of the people's triumph. Fidel Castro visited the cabin cruiser Granma, *which was tied up at a dock in the bay, and then went to the Presidential Palace, where he addressed the people who thronged the terrace on the northern side of the building. That night, a mass meeting was held at Camp Columbia (later renamed Liberty School City) in which Fidel addressed all the people of Cuba over radio and television.*

We will never defraud the people

(Excerpts from the address by Fidel Castro at Camp Columbia, a military fortress in Havana, on January 8, 1959)

I know that my speaking here this evening presents me with an obligation that may well be one of the most difficult ones in the long process of struggle that began in Santiago de Cuba on November 30, 1956.

The revolutionary combatants; the army soldiers, whose fate is in our hands; and all the rest of the people are listening.

I think that this is a decisive moment in our history. The dictatorship has been overthrown and there is tremendous joy, but there is still much to do. We shouldn't fool ourselves, thinking that everything will be easy from now on, because everything may turn out to be more difficult.

The first duty of all revolutionaries is to tell the truth. Fooling the people, promoting illusions, always brings the worst consequences, and I believe that the people should be warned against excessive optimism.

How did the Rebel Army win the war? By telling the truth. How did the [Batista] dictatorship lose the war? By deceiving the soldiers.

When we were dealt a setback, we said so over Radio Rebelde; we criticized the mistakes of any officer who committed them, and we warned all the comrades so the same thing wouldn't happen with another unit. That didn't happen with the Army's companies. Several units made the same mistakes, because nobody ever told the officers and soldiers the truth.

That's why I want to start — or, rather, continue — using the same system: that of always telling the people the truth.

---

to propose him as President of the Republic. He took office on January 5, 1959, but the positions he took obstructing revolutionary measures led him to resign on July 17 that same year. He left the country and went to the United States. He died in 1981.

We have advanced, perhaps quite a long way.

Here we are in the capital, at Camp Columbia. The revolutionary forces appear to be victorious. The government has been constituted and recognized by many countries. It seems that we have achieved peace, yet we shouldn't be too optimistic.

While the people laughed and celebrated today, I worried; the larger the crowd that came to welcome us and the greater the people's joy, the more worried I was, because the greater was our responsibility to history and to the Cuban people.

The revolution no longer has to confront an army ready for action. Who might be the enemies of the revolution now and in the future? Who, in the face of this victorious nation, might be the enemies of the Cuban Revolution in the future? We ourselves, the revolutionaries.

As I always told the rebel combatants, when we aren't confronting the enemy, when the war is over, we ourselves will be the only enemies the revolution can have. That's why I always said and still say that we should be more rigorous and demanding with the rebel soldiers than with anyone else, because the success or failure of the revolution depends on them...

The first thing that those of us who have carried out this revolution have to ask ourselves is why we did so. Was it out of ambition, a lust for power or any other ignoble reason? Were any of the combatants for this revolution idealists who, while moved by idealism, sought other ends? Did we carry out the revolution thinking that, as soon as the dictatorship was overthrown, we would benefit from being in power? Did any of us do what we did simply to jump on the bandwagon? Did any of us want to live like a king and have a mansion? Did any of us become revolutionaries and overthrow the dictatorship in order to make life easy for ourselves? Did we simply want to replace some ministers?

Or, did we do what we did out of a real spirit of selflessness? Did each of us have a true willingness to make sacrifices? Was each of us willing to give their all without any thought of personal gain? And, right from the start, were we ready to renounce everything that didn't mean continuing to carry out our duty as sincere revolutionaries?

Those are the questions we must ask ourselves, because the future of Cuba, ourselves and the people is largely dependent on this examination of conscience.

When I hear talk of columns, battlefronts and troops of whatever size, I always think, here is our firmest column, our best troops —

the only troops that, alone, can win the war: the people!

No general or army can do more than the people. If you were to ask me what troops I preferred to command, I would say, I prefer to command the people, because the people are invincible. It was the people who won this war, because we didn't have any tanks, planes, cannon, military academies, recruiting and training centers, divisions, regiments, companies, platoons or even squads.

So, who won the war? The people. The people won the war.

It was the people who won this war — I'm saying this very clearly in case anyone thinks they won it or any troops think they won it. Therefore, the people come first.

But there is something else: the revolution isn't interested in me or in any other commander or captain individually; the revolution isn't interested in any particular column or company. What it is interested in is the people.

It was the people who won or lost. It was the people who suffered from the horrors of the last seven years, the people who must ask themselves if, in 10, 15 or 20 years, they and their children and grandchildren are going to continue suffering from the horrors they have been suffering from ever since the establishment of the Republic of Cuba, crowned with dictatorships such as those of Machado and Batista.

The people want to know if we're going to do a good job of carrying out this revolution or if we're going to make the same mistakes that previous revolutions made — and, as a result, make them suffer the consequences of our mistakes, for every mistake has terrible consequences for the people; sooner or later, every political mistake takes its toll.

Some circumstances aren't the same. For example, I think that, this time, there is a greater chance than ever before that the revolution will really fulfill its destiny. This may explain why the people are so very happy, losing sight a little of how much hard work lies ahead...

What do the people want? An honest government. Isn't that right? (*exclamations of "Yes!"*) There you have it: an honorable judge as President of the Republic. What do you want? That young men whose slates are clean be the ministers of the Revolutionary Government? (*exclamations of "Yes!"*) There you have them: analyze each of the ministers of the Revolutionary Government, and tell me if there are any thieves, criminals or scoundrels among them. (*exclamations of "No!"*)...

It's necessary to talk this way so there will be no demagogy, confusion or splits and so the people will be immediately aware of it if anybody becomes ambitious. As for me, since I want the people to command and I consider the people to be the best troops and prefer them to all the columns of armed men put together, the first thing I will always do, when I see the revolution in danger, is call on the people.

We can prevent bloodshed by speaking to the people. Before there is any shooting here, we must call on the people a thousand times and speak to the people so that, without any shooting, the people will solve the problem. I have faith in the people, and I have demonstrated this. I know what the people are capable of, and I think I have demonstrated this, too. If the people here want this, no more shots will be heard in this country. Public opinion has incredible strength and influence, especially when there is no dictatorship. In eras of dictatorships, public opinion is nothing, but, in eras of freedom, public opinion is everything, and the military must bow to public opinion. How am I doing, Camilo? (*exclamations of "Long live Camilo!"*)

The important thing, or what I still have to tell you, is that I believe that the actions of the people in Havana today, the mass meetings that were held today, the crowds that filled the streets for kilometers — all of that was amazing, and you saw it; it will be in the movies and photos — I sincerely think that the people went overboard, for it's much more than we deserve. (*exclamations of "No!"*)

Moreover, I know that there never will be such a crowd again, except on one other occasion: the day I'm buried. I'm sure that there will be a large crowd then, too, to take me to my grave, because I will never defraud our people.

3

FIRST AGRARIAN REFORM LAW

May 17, 1959

The signing of the first Agrarian Reform Law in the camp at La Plata, in the Sierra Maestra Mountains, four and a half months after the taking of power was the most decisive step the revolution took in the national liberation stage and the event that led the U.S. Government to use any and all means to try to overthrow the new power in Cuba.

Agrarian Reform was absolutely necessary for undertaking any program of socioeconomic development, even within the capitalist relations that still prevailed on the island at the time.

Part of the agrarian problem was caused by the fact that Cuba's main material resource — the land — had been expropriated. This expropriation had started with the U.S. intervention in 1898 and continued with attacks by large U.S. sugar and cattle companies — joined by the Cuban oligarchs — who took over most of the land that had been owned by the government.

The fact that, prior to the Agrarian Reform Law, 1.5 percent of the landowners possessed more than 46 percent of the arable land in Cuba is proof of this.

The other aspect of Cuba's agrarian problem was the terrible deprivation of those who worked the land. Around 150,000 farm families were sharecroppers, tenant farmers and squatters, working land that didn't belong to them. Another 200,000 families living in the countryside had no land at all, obtaining sporadic employment as day laborers.

The first Agrarian Reform Law set a limit of 402 hectares of land for each individual owner, though more was allowed in exceptional cases. The law made the farmers who worked small and medium-sized plots the owners of the land they worked, freeing them from rent payments. Even though it was not a socialist law and left an important stratum of rural bourgeoisie (who owned around 1.7 million hectares), in Cuba's conditions it meant a radical challenge to the control held up until then by the United States and the Cuban oligarchy. In its application, the Cuban government had the foresight not to carve up the large landholdings that were expropriated — instead, it promoted the creation of cooperative farms and agricultural enterprises that could apply technologies of large-scale production.

That law was complemented by a second Agrarian Reform Law, which set the maximum amount of land that could be owned by any individual at 67 hectares.

✳

Agrarian Reform Law
Chapter I: On the Land in General

Article 1. Large landholdings are proscribed. The maximum amount of land that any individual or body corporate may own is 74 acres.[1] Land owned by an individual or body corporate in excess of this limit will be expropriated for distribution among the landless agricultural workers and farmers.

Article 2. The following land is exempted from the provisions of the preceding article:

a. Sugarcane areas whose yield is no less than 50 percent over the national average.

b. Cattle-raising areas that support at least the minimum number of head of cattle per acre established by the National Institute of the Agrarian Reform (Instituto Nacional de Reforma Agraria, INRA), in accord with the breed, age, birth rate, feeding system and yield in terms of beef (in the case of beef cattle) or milk (in the case of milk cattle). The possibilities of the production area concerned will be assessed by means of a physical-chemical analysis of the soil, humidity and rainfall.

c. Rice areas that normally yield at least 50 percent more than the average national production for the variety involved, in the opinion of the National Institute of the Agrarian Reform.

d. Areas used for one or several crops or animal husbandry,

---

[1] For the sake of synthesis and to present the most substantive aspects of the law, the introduction and articles on technical elements of the law are omitted. Text taken from *Las leyes de Reforma Agraria en Cuba* (Laws of the Agrarian Reform in Cuba) (Havana: 1964).

either with or without industrial activity, for whose efficient exploitation and rational economic yield it is necessary to maintain an amount of land greater than that established as the limit in Article 1 of this law.

In spite of the foregoing, in no case may an individual or body corporate own more than 247 acres.

Article 3. Land belonging to the Government, provinces and municipalities will also be subject to distribution...

Article 5. The order of procedure for expropriation, when applicable, and for the redistribution of land in each Agrarian Development Area will be as follows:

First: The Government-owned land and privately-owned land that is worked by tenant farmers, subtenants, small and/or medium peasant cane growers, sharecroppers and squatters.

Second: The excess land not protected by the exemptions set forth in Article 2 of this law.

Third: The rest of the land that may be encumbered...

Article 6. Land in the private domain up to a limit of 74 acres per person or entity will not be expropriated unless it is affected by contracts with small and/or medium peasant cane growers, tenant farmers, subtenants and/or sharecroppers or is occupied by squatters who have plots no greater than 12 1/3 acres, in which case it, too, will be subject to expropriation under the provisions of this law.

Article 7. Once the expropriations, adjudications and sales to tenant farmers, subtenants, small and/or medium peasant cane growers and squatters living on the farms have been carried out, the former owners of the land that was encumbered may retain the rest of the property up to the maximum amount authorized by the law.

Article 8. Land that was not registered in the real estate record offices prior to October 10, 1958, will be considered to belong to the Government...

Article 11. As of the promulgation of this law, sharecropping and/or any other contracts that stipulate that rents for rural properties will take the form of a share of their products are prohibited. Contracts for grinding sugarcane are not included in this concept.

Chapter II: On the Redistribution of Land and Compensation for Owners

Article 16. A "vital minimum" of five acres of fertile land that does not have irrigation, is far from any urban centers and is used for crops of average economic yield is established for a farm family of five people...

Article 17. The private land that may be expropriated under the provisions of this law and the Government-owned land will be granted in areas of undivided property to cooperatives recognized by this law or will be distributed among the beneficiaries, in plots of no more than five acres, whose ownership they will receive without prejudice to the adjustments that the National Institute of the Agrarian Reform may make to determine the "vital minimum" in each case...

Article 18. The land in the private domain that is worked by small and/or medium peasant cane growers, tenant farmers and subtenants, sharecroppers and/or squatters will be adjudicated free of charge to those who work it when the amount of that land doesn't exceed the "vital minimum." When those farmers work less land than the "vital minimum," the land required to complete that amount will be adjudicated to them free of charge, as long as it is available and the socioeconomic conditions of the region permit...

Article 22. The land that is available for distribution under the provisions of this law will be apportioned in the following order of priority:

a. Farmers who have been evicted from the land they worked.

b. Farmers living in the region where the land to be distributed is located and who lack land, or who work an area less than the "vital minimum."

c. Agricultural workers who work and habitually live on the land to be distributed.

d. Farmers from other regions, with preference given to those from neighboring regions, who lack land or who have an area less than the "vital minimum."

e. Agricultural workers from other regions, with preference given to those from neighboring regions.

f. Anyone else who makes a request, with preference given to those who show they have agricultural experience and/or knowledge.

Article 23. Within the groups mentioned in the preceding article, preference will be given to the following:

a. Combatants of the Rebel Army and/or their dependent relatives.

b. Members of the auxiliary bodies of the Rebel Army.

c. Victims of the war and/or of repression by the dictatorship.

d. The dependent relatives of people killed because of their participation in the revolutionary struggle against the dictatorship.

In every case, the heads of families will be given priority...

Article 30. The constitutional right of the owners adversely affected by this law to receive compensation for the property that is expropriated is recognized. The said compensation will be established in accord with the market value of the farms as set forth in the municipal tax assessment statements made prior to October 10, 1958...

Article 31. The compensation will be paid in *callable* bonds. For that purpose, an issue of bonds of the Republic of Cuba will be made in the amount, terms and conditions to be established. The bonds will be called Agrarian Reform bonds and will be considered public securities. The issue or issues will be made for terms of 20 years, with annual interest of no more than 4.5 percent. The amount required to cover the payment of interest, amortization and issuance expenses will be included in the national budget each year...

Chapter III: On Redistributed Agricultural Property

Article 33. The property received free of charge under the precepts of this law may not be made a part of the capital of civil corporations or business partnerships other than matrimonial partnerships and the agricultural cooperatives referred to in Chapter V of this law.

Article 34. Under the precepts of this law, the property referred to in the preceding article may not be transferred by any means other than inheritance or sale to the Government or exchange authorized by the authorities in charge of its application, nor may it be the subject of contracts of leasing, sharecropping, usufruct or mortgage...

Chapter IV: On Agrarian Development Areas

Article 37. Agrarian development areas will be established out of continuous, defined portions of Cuba's national territory in which, by resolution of the National Institute of Agrarian Reform, it is divided for the purposes of facilitating the implementation of the Reform...

Chapter V: On Agrarian Cooperation

Article 43. Whenever possible, the National Institute of Agrarian Reform will promote agricultural cooperatives. The agricultural cooperatives that the National Institute of Agrarian Reform establishes on the land it has by virtue of the precepts of this law will be under its direction, and it reserves the right to appoint their administrators in order to ensure their optimal development in the initial stage of this kind of socioeconomic organization and until the law grants them greater autonomy.

Article 44. The National Institute of the Agrarian Reform will help only the agricultural cooperatives that farmers and/or agricultural workers form in order to exploit the soil and gather its fruits by means of the personal efforts of their members, according to the internal regime regulated by the Institute. In the cases of those cooperatives, the National Institute of Agrarian Reform will see to it that they are located on land appropriate for their purposes and act only if they are willing to accept the Institute's help and abide by its technical guidance.

Article 45. Other forms of cooperation may include one or several of the following: material resources, tools, credit, sales, the preservation of products, buildings to be used communally, other installations, reservoirs, irrigation, the industrial processing of by-products and residues and as many facilities and useful means as may contribute to the improvement of the cooperatives, in accord with the regulations, resolutions and instructions issued by the National Institute of Agrarian Reform.

Article 46. The National Institute of Agrarian Reform will mobilize all of the funds needed to promote the cooperatives, facilitating long-term credits for this purpose. These credits will be amortized with minimum interest. The Institute will also provide short-term credits for the functioning of the cooperatives, adapting systems of financing to the economic prospects of the enterprises and always guaranteeing a decent family income right from the start...

Chapter VI: On the National Institute of Agrarian Reform
Article 48. The National Institute of Agrarian Reform is created as an autonomous entity with its own legal status for the application and enforcement of this law.

The National Institute of Agrarian Reform will be governed by a President and an Executive Director, who will be appointed by the Council of Ministers...

Chapter VIII: On Forestry and Soil Conservation
Article 55. The Government will reserve forested areas in the land it owns to be made into national parks, in order to maintain and develop its forests. Those who have been given title to land by virtue of the application of this law should strictly comply with the forestry

laws and apply soil conservation when working their crops. Violation of these provisions will result in the loss of their right to the property acquired free of charge from the Government, without prejudice to the compensation to which they are entitled for improvements, which will be deducted from the amount corresponding to the damage occasioned...

Article 58. The tenant farmers, subtenants and/or squatters on rural properties that are to be used exclusively for recreational and/or residential purposes are excluded from the benefits of this law...

Article 62. The presumptive beneficiaries recognized in this law may not be evicted from the land they are using while the land to be encumbered by the Agrarian Reform is being distributed...

Final Provisions
First: Ownership of the summit of Turquino Peak and a strip of land stretching 5,000 feet (1,500 meters) west of it is reserved for the Government, to be made available to the Rebel Army so a Rebels' House, a botanical garden and a small museum may be built there. The museum, on the struggle against the dictatorship, will help to preserve the loyalty to principles and unity of the combatants in the Rebel Army...

Availing myself of the constituent powers of the Council of Ministers, I declare this law to be an integral part of the Constitution of the Republic, to which it is added.

Consequently, this law has constitutional force and standing.

Therefore, I order that this law be carried out and implemented throughout the country.

La Plata, Sierra Maestra, May 17, 1959, Year of Liberation
Fidel Castro Ruz
Prime Minister of the Revolutionary Government

4

LAST SPEECH OF CAMILO CIENFUEGOS

October 26, 1959

In the conditions prevailing during the first year after the triumph of the revolution — when there was still a lot of confusion and political prejudice stemming from the McCarthy period and when reactionaries both inside and outside Cuba were trying to undermine the people's unity on all fronts — one of the most dangerous and complex moments was the betrayal by Major Hubert Matos Benítez,[1] head of the Rebel Army in Camagüey.

Matos, an educated though arrogant and ambitious man, had a contradictory course in the revolutionary movement. After the January 1 victory, when he was named military chief of Camagüey, he sided politically with the sugar and cattle oligarchs, who had one of their strongest bases in that territory. After the adoption of the Agrarian Reform Law, they launched an intensive reactionary, anticommunist campaign that, as was frequently the case in that period, claimed that Marxists had "infiltrated" the ranks of the Rebel Army and demanded that the ideological direction of the revolution be defined and that a statement be made about how far it would go.

---

[1] By the end of the revolutionary war Hubert Matos Benítez was a major in the Rebel Army and head of the "Antonio Guiteras" Column 9. Appointed Military Chief of Camagüey after the triumph of the revolution, he was arrested and sentenced to 20 years in prison for the crime of treason. After serving his sentence, he became the ringleader of a counterrevolutionary organization outside Cuba.

As the culmination of this maneuver, Matos wrote a letter of resignation to Fidel Castro. Far from private, it was first shown to other officers and leaders of various organizations in the province. Its real purpose was to get them to adopt a seditious attitude and to create an internal and international crisis for the revolution.

Because of Camilo Cienfuegos's courage, proven loyalty and fine political sense, Fidel Castro appointed him to go to Camagüey. He was instructed to arrest the traitor and take immediate measures to halt the plot. When Fidel arrived in the province a few hours later, he would join him in the task of mobilizing the people of Camagüey and explaining to them the real meaning of what was going on.

Those tense days, beginning on October 21, highlighted the exceptional abilities of Camilo Cienfuegos, not only as a guerrilla leader but also as a political figure of the revolution noted for directness, frankness and clarity of thinking.

Referring to Matos's demand that Fidel state exactly how far he was going to take the Cuban Revolution, Camilo said, "It isn't necessary to say where Fidel Castro is going to take the Cuban Revolution. This revolution will go as far as it can. This revolution will reach its goals. As in the days of the war, this revolution has only two choices: to win or to die... If you ask me how far I'm going, I'll tell you that I'll be with this revolution all the way. We're going to have real social justice; we're going to take the farmers and workers out of the misery to which they've been subjected by the interests now serving the forces of the counterrevolution..."[2]

On October 26, Camilo Cienfuegos addressed a gathering in Havana. It was to be his last speech.

He returned to Camagüey to continue the work of repairing the damage done by the plot. Two days later, while he was flying back to Havana to report on his efforts, the small plane in which he was traveling was lost in a storm. Thus, Hubert Matos's betrayal cost the life of the man whom Che Guevara called "the best of all the guerrillas."

For every traitor who may appear, we will make new revolutionary laws

(Address given by Major Camilo Cienfuegos on the terrace of the Presidential Palace on October 26, 1959)[3]

The integrity, dignity and courage of the Cuban people in this

---

[2] William Gálvez, *Camilo, Señor de la Vanguardia* (Camilo, Gentleman of the Vanguard) (Havana: Editorial de Ciencias Sociales, 1979), 457-8.

[3] Ibid, 465-6.

enormous mass meeting in front of this now-revolutionary Palace of the Cuban people are as great and strong as the Sierra Maestra Mountains.

The Cuban people's support for the revolution, which was carried out for the Cuban people, is and always will be as great as the invincible Turquino Peak.[4]

This afternoon, you are showing that no deceitful, cowardly betrayals of this people and of this revolution matter. It doesn't matter that mercenary planes flown by war criminals and supported by powerful interests of the U.S. Government[5] have come, because, here, the people won't let themselves be confused by traitors and aren't afraid of mercenary planes, just as the Rebel [Army] troops weren't afraid of the dictatorship's planes when they were mounting an offensive.

This enormous mass meeting confirms the Cuban people's unbreakable faith in this government. I know that the people won't let themselves be confused by the campaigns launched by the enemies of the revolution. The Cuban people know that, for every traitor who may appear, we will make new revolutionary laws to benefit the people.

The Cuban people know that, for every traitor who appears, there will be 1,000 rebel soldiers who are willing to fight to the death defending the freedom and sovereignty that this nation has won. I can see the placards and hear the voices of the courageous people, saying, "Forward, Fidel — Cuba is with you!"

Now, the Rebel Army, the combatants who came out of the mountains, who didn't sell out to any interests, who can't be frightened, say, "Forward, Fidel — the Rebel Army is with you!" This mass meeting, these farmers, workers and students who have come to this Palace today, give us energy — energy to continue the revolution, to continue the Agrarian Reform, which nothing and nobody can stop. (*shouts of "No!"*) Today, you are showing that, just as 20,000 Cubans gave their lives to achieve this freedom and sovereignty, all of the people are willing to give their lives if necessary to keep from living on their knees.

Anyone who wants to halt this very Cuban Revolution will have

---

[4] The highest (1,960 meters) mountain in Cuba, Turquino Peak, in the Sierra Maestra Mountains, is one of the symbols of the Cuban Revolution.

[5] The reference is to the attacks on sugar mills made by planes coming from bases in the United States and, particularly, to the terrorist bombing of Havana that Pedro Luis Díaz Lanz, former head of the Cuban Air Force and a traitor, carried out on October 21, 1959, flying in from a base in Miami, Florida.

to kill all of the people to do so, and, if this should come to pass, the verses of Bonifacio Byrne[6] would become a reality:

> If my flag should ever be
> torn and full of rents,
> even the dead will leave their tombs
> and rise in its defense...

Neither the traitors nor all of the revolution's enemies and all the interests that try to confuse the people matter when the people don't allow themselves to be confused. The Cuban people know... that 20,000 Cubans died for this revolution — to put an end to abuses, other despicable actions, hunger and all of the agony which the Republic of Cuba experienced for more than 50 years.

The enemies of the revolution shouldn't think that we're going to stop, that this nation is going to stop; those who send planes and those who fly them shouldn't think that we are going to get down on our knees and bow our heads. (*shouts of "No!"*) We are going to bow our heads once and once only: on the day we reach Cuban soil, guarded by 20,000 Cubans, and tell them, "Brothers and sisters, the revolution has been carried out; your blood wasn't shed in vain!"

---

[6] Bonifacio Byrne, poet and patriot from Matanzas. He wrote these lines when, on returning from exile after the War of Independence, he saw the U.S. flag flying over Havana's Morro Castle.

5

EXPLOSION ON *LA COUBRE*

March 4, 1960

The year 1960 began with air incursions from Miami, with planes dropping bombs and incendiary materials on sugar mills, sugarcane fields and towns in Cuba in an attempt to disrupt the sugarcane harvest — Cuba's main source of income — and, at the same time, to create a climate of terror and instability.

On January 13, Allen Dulles, Director of the CIA, created a special task force for carrying out actions against the Cuban Government.

U.S. pilot Robert Ellis Frost died on February 18 when the plane he was flying in an attack against the España Sugar Mill, in Matanzas Province, exploded. Documents that were found on board confirmed that he had left U.S. bases three other times to make flights over Cuban territory.

Early on the afternoon of March 4, while the French steamship La Coubre *was being unloaded at the Pan American Dock in the port of Havana, an explosion occurred on board. Soldiers, firemen, policemen and other workers rushed toward the ship to help the victims, and then a second explosion killed or wounded even more people. It also completely destroyed the holds where the work of unloading had been in progress.*

The French ship, whose port of embarkation had been Antwerp, Belgium, was carrying arms and munitions that Cuba had purchased for its defense.

The toll was 75 dead and over 200 wounded, including many people who were badly mutilated. Investigations carried out by Cuba, which included taking some boxes of FAL rifle shells — some of which had exploded at the time of the disaster – up in a plane and dropping them, showed that the explosions couldn't possibly have been an accident.

The investigators became firmly convinced that it was an act of sabotage, with the boxes loaded in such a way that they would explode when moved.

The victims were buried on the next day, March 5. The long funeral cortege went along 23rd Street to Colón Cemetery, the largest in Havana. At its entrance, Fidel Castro addressed the indignant crowd. It was evening when he concluded, giving the Cubans their new catch cry of "Patria o muerte!" ("Homeland or death!")

Not only will we know how to resist but we can overcome any aggression

(Excerpts from the speech of Fidel Castro on March 5, 1960 at the burial of the victims from the ship La Coubre*)*[1]

Great have been our losses these 14 months; our dear and unforgettable comrades who are no longer amongst those of us who now follow their coffins; comrades who, in the course of duty, disappeared from our ranks; nonetheless, our ranks keep marching on, and our people remain standing on their own feet, and this is what matters! And what a powerful thing it is to see a people standing on its own feet, what a marvelous and impressive spectacle is a people standing on its own feet. What a spectacle, like this one today, to see people marching when some years ago it would have seemed to them like a dream, to see them marching as they were marching today. Who could have dreamed a few years ago that they would see workers' militias marching shoulder-to-shoulder with the university brigades; shoulder-to-shoulder with soldiers from the Rebel Army, shoulder-to-shoulder with members of the navy and the police; shoulder-to-shoulder with a column of peasants in their mambís hats, their ranks compact and soldierly, their guns on their shoulders; peasants from the mountains who have come to accompany us in this moment of sorrow today so that nobody would be left unrepresented, so that here, where ministers and citizens are one indistinguishable people, the whole nation has come together in all its generous, combative and heroic spirit!

Who could ever have dreamed that one day members of the

---

[1] In *El pensamiento de Fidel Castro* (The Thought of Fidel Castro), (Havana: Editora Política, 1983), vol. I.

military and workers would no longer be enemies; that one day military men, workers, students, peasants and the people would no longer be enemies; that one day intellectuals would march arm-in-arm with armed men; that one day, the power of labor, thought and the gun would march together, as they have marched today!

Once they marched separately, once they were enemies, once the country was split into different kinds of interests, dissimilar groups, dissimilar institutions, and today our country is one single spirit, our country is one single force, our country is one single group. Today peasants and soldiers, students and police, people and the armed forces, do not fight each other and die; today we all arise from the same yearning and the same aspiration: the people and the military are one and the same thing. Once they fought each other and now they fight together; once they marched along separate paths and today they march together. Today they die together, helping each other, giving their lives to save the lives of others, like beloved brothers...

Today I have seen — as I was saying before — our country as more glorious and more heroic, our people as more admirable, and worthy of being admired as a column returning from combat is admired, worthy of identifying with and expressing solidarity with.

What matters are not so much the empty spaces in our ranks; what matters is the presence of the spirit of those who remain on their feet. And it is not just once, but many times we have seen empty spaces in our ranks, in the ranks of our army. We see painful empty spaces, like those in the ranks of our people today; but the important thing is the firmness of the people, of a people still on its feet.

And thus, in saying farewell to our fallen today, to these soldiers and these workers, I have only one thought in saying goodbye, and this is the idea of what this struggle symbolizes and what our people symbolize today. May they rest in peace! Workers and soldiers together in their tombs. As they struggled together, so they died together and so are we prepared to die together.

And in saying goodbye to them, here at the entrance to the cemetery, we are aware that a promise is more than today's promise, for it is yesterday's promise and a promise forever. Cuba will never be intimidated, Cuba will never go back. The revolution will not be stopped, the revolution will not go back, the revolution will continue victoriously on its way, the revolution will continue on its march, yielding to nothing!...

Those who did not want us to receive these munitions are the enemies of our revolution, the same people who do not want our country to be able to defend itself, the ones who do not want our country to have what it needs to defend its sovereignty.

We know about the efforts that have been made to stop us from buying these arms, and amongst those most concerned that we should not receive these arms were employees of the U.S. Government. We can assert this without making any secret about it because, if this is a secret, it is one of those secrets that the whole world knows. It's not just what we say; it's what the British Government says. The British Government has declared that the U.S. Government was concerned that we should not acquire planes in England. The U.S. authorities have said it themselves, and their spokesmen have said it — that efforts should be made to prevent arms from being sold to Cuba. We have been struggling against these pressures and we have been struggling against these obstacles...

We will never be strong enough to attack anyone, not only because we don't have enough arms or men or resources but because we would never have the right to attack anybody. Yet we feel strong enough to defend ourselves, because we are defending what is right and we know how to defend that.

Then, why is it that they don't want us to have the resources we need? It is simply because they do not want us to be able to defend ourselves, so that we remain defenseless. And why do they want us to be defenseless? To break us, to make us submit, so that we can't resist their pressures, so that we can't resist their aggression. Do they, in fact, have the right to obstruct our efforts to acquire the means to defend ourselves, these authorities of a country that have not managed to prevent the systematic use of their own territory to launch bombing raids against us?...

If only these people, who are mentally unbalanced in the most elementary sense of the term, would dare to consider the possible consequences of an invasion of our territory, then they would discover the monstrous error of their ways — because we would be unstinting in our sacrifices! But if this should unfortunately occur, the misfortune would be still greater for those who attack us. Let them be in no doubt that here, in this land called Cuba, here, amongst these people who are called Cubans, they will have to fight us until the last drop of our blood has been shed, they will have to fight to the last remaining atom of our lives. We will never attack anybody and nobody will ever have anything to fear from us; but anybody who wants to attack us must know — make no mistake —

who the Cubans are today. We are not talking about 1899, we are not talking about the beginning of the century and we are not talking about 1910 or 1920 or 1930 — but the Cubans of this decade, the Cubans of this generation, the Cubans of this era. This is not because we are the best, but because we have had the good luck to be able to see more clearly, because we have had the good luck to receive the lessons and the example of history, the lesson for which our ancestors made so many sacrifices, the lesson that exacted so much humiliation and so much pain from the generations that have gone before us. Because we have had the good luck to receive this lesson, they will have to fight if they attack us, against this generation, to our last drop of blood. They will have to fight the guns that we have, the guns that we shall buy. We can buy weapons from anyone who will sell them to us and from wherever we see fit.

Unfazed by the threats, unfazed by the maneuvers, we shall remember that there was a time that we were only 12 men and that, comparing that strength we had then with the strength of the [Batista] dictatorship, our strength was so small and insignificant that nobody would have believed it was possible to resist. However, we believed that we were resisting aggression then, just as we believe that we are resisting today. And we believe that we not only know how to resist any aggression but that we will know how to overcome any aggression, and that, once again, we will have no choice to make but the one with which we began our revolutionary struggle: that of freedom or death. Except that, now, freedom means even more than it did then. Freedom means our country. And our choice will be: Homeland or death!

6

NATIONALIZATION OF U.S. COMPANIES

August 6, 1960

Cuba's history had seen the island turned into an economic colony of what is now the United States. The process began even before the colonies that were to become the United States of America had gained their independence from England. Naturally, those trade and financial ties — which were already decisive in the 19th century — became much stronger following the U.S. military intervention in Cuba in 1898 and throughout the first six decades of the so-called Republic.

Large U.S. companies were the main owners of the land, sugar mills, mines, oil refineries, industries of all kinds, chain stores, public services and a large part of the banks and import trade.

Cuba's traditional sugar quota on the U.S. market — that is, the part of U.S. sugar imports that Cuba provided every year — was the island's main source of income.

The first measures that the U.S. Government took to force Cuba to its knees following the 1959 triumph of the revolution — diplomatic pressure, conspiracies, acts of sabotage, pirate attacks, armed uprisings, subversive radio broadcasts and the organization of a mercenary invasion — failed. In 1960 it quickly started escalating economic actions that were aimed at paralyzing and crushing the country's productive life.

As part of the steps Cuba took to meet that challenge, it signed a trade agreement with the Soviet Union in February 1960, during a visit that

Soviet Deputy Prime Minister Anastas Mikoyan made to Havana. Under that agreement, Cuba would receive oil, wheat, steel and some equipment in exchange for sugar and other Cuban products. The Soviet Union promised to buy 5 million tons of sugar in five years and also gave Cuba a 12-year credit of US$100 million at 2.5 percent interest per year.

In June, the United States responded by refusing to refine Soviet crude oil in the Esso, Sinclair and Texaco refineries in Cuba, which also announced that they wouldn't supply any more oil to Cuba. The Revolutionary Government responded to this crisis − which might have meant the end of the revolution if it hadn't been for Soviet solidarity − by taking over those refineries.

The next blow from the United States was the reduction of Cuba's sugar quota. The U.S. Congress authorized President Eisenhower to dispose of that quota by means of Executive Orders, and, on July 6, he resolved to end the U.S. purchase of 700,000 tons of sugar − which Cuba had already produced.

That same day, in Havana, the Revolutionary Government adopted Law 851, whose Article 1 authorized "the President of the Republic and the Prime Minister, acting jointly, to issue resolutions nationalizing, by means of forcible expropriation, the companies and other property owned by U.S. citizens and/or bodies corporate of the United States and/or by companies in which they have an interest or participation, even if the same have been constituted under Cuban law, whenever they deem this advisable for the defense of the nation's interests."

On August 6, 1960, in view of the maneuver that was being planned in the Organization of American States (OAS), with the calling of a meeting of foreign ministers in Costa Rica, the revolution proceeded to nationalize the main U.S. companies in Cuba. Fidel Castro made the announcement of this measure in Cerro Stadium, during the closing session of the First Latin American Congress of Youth.

The Cuban Government also issued Law 980, of October 13, 1960, which nationalized industries and businesses, regardless of the nationality of their owners; Law 981, of the same date, which declared banking to be a public activity; the Urban Reform Law, of October 14, 1960, which gave tenants title to their homes; and Law 1076, of December 5, 1962, which nationalized certain small retail businesses.

*

The Executive Power[1]
Resolution 1

WHEREAS Law 851, of July 6, 1960, which was published in the *Official Gazette* on July 7, authorized the undersigned to jointly order a nationalization by means of forcible expropriation of the assets and/or companies owned by individuals and/or bodies corporate of the United States of America and/or of the companies in which they have interests and/or participation, even if the said companies have been constituted in accord with Cuban laws, when they consider it to be in the defense of the national interest;

WHEREAS the attitude of constant aggression that the Government and legislative power of the United States of America have assumed for political purposes against the fundamental interests of the Cuban economy, as expressed in the amendment to the sugar law passed by Congress, by means of which the President of that country was granted exceptional powers to reduce Cuban sugar's access to the U.S. sugar market as a weapon of political action against Cuba, was contemplated in laying the foundations for that law;

WHEREAS the executive branch of the Government of the United States of America, making use of the said exceptional powers and in a notorious attitude of economic and political aggression against our country, has proceeded to reduce Cuban sugar's participation in the U.S. market, with the unquestionable purpose of attacking Cuba and the development of its revolutionary process;

WHEREAS that act constitutes a reiteration of the Government of the United States of America's continued conduct aimed at keeping our people from exercising their sovereignty and integral development, thus corresponding to the slippery interests of the U.S. monopolies that have hindered the growth of our economy and the affirmation of our political freedom;

WHEREAS, in view of these facts, the undersigned, aware of their great historic responsibilities and in the legitimate defense of the nation's sovereignty, are forced to anticipate measures needed to counteract the damage caused by the attacks to which our nation has been subjected;

WHEREAS, in accord with our Constitution and code of laws, in the exercise of our sovereignty and as an internal legislative measure, the undersigned understand that it is advisable, in view of

---

[1] Olga Miranda Bravo, *Cuba-USA, nacionalizaciones y bloqueo* (Cuba-USA, Nationalizations and Blockade) (Havana: Editorial de Ciencias Sociales, 1996), 108-13.

the consummation of the aggressive measures referred to in the previous whereases, to make use of the powers conferred on them by Law 851, of July 6, 1960 — that is, to proceed to the forcible expropriation for the Cuban Government of the assets and/or companies owned by individuals who are citizens of the United States of America — as a decision justified by the nation's need to be compensated for the damage caused in its economy and to affirm the consolidation of the country's economic independence;

WHEREAS the Cuban Electric Company (Compañía de Electricidad) and the Cuban Telephone Company have been typical examples of the extortionist, exploiting monopolies that have drained and thwarted the nation's economy and the people's interest for many years;

WHEREAS the sugar companies seized the best land in our country under the Platt Amendment, that clause which threatens and curtails our national economy and facilitated the country's invasion by the imperialist capital of insatiable, unscrupulous foreign owners, who have recovered the value of their investments many times over;

WHEREAS the oil companies have continuously defrauded the nation's economy by demanding to be paid monopoly prices — which, for many years, meant outlays of enormous amounts of hard currency — and, in their eagerness to perpetuate their privileges, treated the laws of the nation disrespectfully and devised a criminal plan of boycotting our homeland, forcing the Revolutionary Government to control them; and

WHEREAS it is the duty of the peoples of Latin America to strive to recover their national wealth, removing them from the domain of foreign interests and monopolies that impede their progress, promote political interference and infringe on the sovereignty of the underdeveloped peoples of the Americas,

THEREFORE, in exercise of the powers invested in us, in accord with the provisions of Law 851, of July 6, 1960,

WE RESOLVE
FIRST: to nationalize, by means of forcible expropriation, and award to the Cuban Government, in fee simple, all of the assets and/or companies located in Cuban national territory and the rights and actions that arise from the exploitation of those assets and/or companies, which are owned by individuals who are citizens of the United States of America or operators of companies in which citizens of that country have a prevailing interest, which are listed below:

1. Cuban Electric Company (Compañía Cubana de Electricidad);
2. Cuban Telephone Company;
3. Esso Standard Oil, S.A., Cuba Division;
4. Texas Co. West Indies (Ltd.);
5. Sinclair Cuba Oil Co., S.A.;
6. Cunagua Sugar Mill, Inc. (Central Cunagua, S.A.);
7. Atlantic Gulf Sugar Company, Inc. (Compañía Azucarera Atlántica del Golfo, S.A.);
8. Altagracia Sugar Mill Company, Inc. (Compañía Central Altagracia, S.A.);
9. Miranda Sugar Estates;
10. Cuban Company, Inc. (Compañía Cubana, S.A.);
11. Cuban American Sugar Mills;
12. Cuban Trading Company;
13. New Tuinicú Sugar Co., Inc.;
14. Francisco Sugar Company;
15. Céspedes Sugar Company (Compañía Azucarera Céspedes);
16. Manatí Sugar Company;
17. Punta Alegre Sugar Sales Company;
18. Baraguá Industrial Corporation of New York;
19. Florida Industrial Corporation of New York;
20. Macareño Industrial Corporation of New York;
21. General Sugar Estates;
22. Vertientes Camagüey Sugar Company of Cuba (Compañía Azucarera Vertientes Camagüey de Cuba);
23. Guantánamo Sugar Company;
24. United Fruit Sugar Company;
25. Soledad Sugar Company, Inc. (Compañía Azucarera Soledad, S.A.); and
26. Ermita Sugar Mill, Inc. (Central Ermita, S.A.);

SECOND: as a result, to declare the Cuban Government subrogated in the place and degree of the bodies corporate listed in the preceding paragraph in terms of the assets, rights and actions mentioned and in terms of the assets and liabilities of which the capital of the said companies consists;

THIRD: to declare that these forcible expropriations are being made from causes of the public need and utility and of the national interest as set forth in the whereases of this resolution;

FOURTH: in accord with the provisions of Article 3 of Law 851, of July 6, 1960, to appoint the National Institute of the Agrarian Reform as the agency which will be in charge — through the

Department of Industrialization, the General Administration of Sugar Mills and the Cuban Oil Institute (Instituto Cubano del Petróleo), with all of the powers inherent to the function entrusted to them — of administering the assets and/or companies expropriated under the provisions of this resolution;

FIFTH: to have the agencies mentioned in the preceding paragraph select and appoint the officials who will, on their behalf, assume the full administration of the said assets and/or companies, without limitations of any kind and, after they have assumed those powers, inform the undersigned so they may proceed to naming experts who will assess the assets appropriated, in order to determine the amount of the compensation to be paid in accord with Law 851, of July 6, 1960;

SIXTH: to authorize the administrators who are appointed to go ahead with the immediate preventive intervention of the bodies corporate, companies, and subsidiary and other assets linked to or connected with those covered by this resolution and, once the said interventions have been carried out, to inform the undersigned; and

SEVENTH: to authorize the designated agencies to send out notifications stating that ownership of the companies, assets, rights and actions referred to in this resolution has been transferred to the Cuban Government and to issue writs to the registrars of deeds and to the provincial registrars of companies and businesses, so they may make the necessary inscriptions of ownership by the Cuban Government.

Havana, August 6, 1960
Osvaldo Dorticós Torrado, President
Fidel Castro Ruz, Prime Minister

7

FIRST DECLARATION OF HAVANA

September 2, 1960

The Seventh Consultative Meeting of Foreign Ministers of the Organization of American States was inaugurated in the National Theater in San José, Costa Rica, on August 22, 1960. That meeting had been formally called in response to a request from the Peruvian Government "to consider the requirements of hemispheric solidarity and the defense of the regional system and American democratic principles, in view of threats that may harm that system."

In fact, the U.S. Government was pulling the strings behind the scenes, once again using the OAS as a cover to isolate and attack governments that displeased it, as had already occurred in 1954 with the CIA and United Fruit Company's conspiracy to overthrow the administration of Jacobo Arbenz in Guatemala.[1]

The pretext that was used — and would continue to be used for many years — was that Cuba constituted a threat to the so-called inter-American system, because of its links with the Soviet Union.

Fidel Castro had already declared, "I should state here that the upcoming OAS meeting is nothing but a U.S. maneuver against Cuba and

---

[1] In 1954, a conspiracy and military invasion organized by the CIA and the United Fruit Company overthrew the progressive administration of Jacobo Arbenz in Guatemala, beginning a stage of repression and bloody regimes that took the lives of over 150,000 people.

that U.S. imperialism proposes to use the OAS meeting to isolate Cuba."[2]

One of the most shameful chapters in that history was the United States' sharing out among several Latin American governments the sugar quota it had taken away from Cuba and its use of those extra quotas, credits and other advantages as bribes to obtain votes for its maneuvers against Cuba in the OAS.

As in other memorable diplomatic battles, Raúl Roa, known as Cuba's Foreign Minister of Dignity,[3] represented the Cuban Revolution in San José.

On August 28, after intensive debates in which the courage of Uruguay, Bolivia and Mexico kept U.S. Secretary of State Christian Herter from obtaining a direct denunciation of the Cuban Government, the OAS meeting approved the Declaration of San José.

At the end of the meeting, the Cuban Foreign Minister asked for the floor and said, "Gentlemen, the delegation that I have the honor to head has decided to withdraw from this consultative meeting of American foreign ministers. The main reason for our doing so is that, in spite of all the statements and postulations that have been made that Cuba might seek protection and support against the attacks of another American government, the denunciations presented by my delegation have not been supported here. My people and all the peoples of Latin America go with me."[4]

On the afternoon of Friday, September 2, more than a million people who had gathered in Havana's José Martí Revolution Square listened attentively to a document read by Fidel Castro and then raised their hands to vote for what, from then on, would be known as the First Declaration of Havana.

The First Declaration of Havana

The people of Cuba, Free Territory of America, acting with the inalienable powers that flow from an effective exercise of their sovereignty through direct, public and universal suffrage, have

[2] Fidel Castro, *El Pensamiento de Fidel Castro* (The Thought of Fidel Castro) (Havana: Editora Política, 1983), vol. I, book 1, 105.

[3] Raúl Roa García (1907-82), outstanding Cuban intellectual, politician and diplomat. Imprisoned for opposing the Machado tyranny, he later fought against the Batista dictatorship. After the triumph of the revolution, he served as Cuba's ambassador to the OAS and then as Minister of Foreign Relations. He was also Vice-President and President ad interim of the National Assembly of People's Power.

[4] Nicanor León Cotayo, *El bloqueo a Cuba* (The Blockade of Cuba) (Havana: Editorial de Ciencias Sociales, 1983), 129.

formed themselves in National General Assembly close to the monument and memory of José Martí.

The National General Assembly of the People of Cuba, as its own act and as an expression of the sense of the people of Our America:

FIRST: Condemns in its entirety the so-called "Declaration of San José, Costa Rica," a document that, under dictation from the imperialism of North America, offends the sovereignty and dignity of other peoples of the Continent and the right of each nation to self-determination.

SECOND: The National General Assembly of the People of Cuba strongly condemns U.S. imperialism for its gross and criminal domination, lasting for more than a century, of all the peoples of Latin America, who more than once have seen the soil of Mexico, Nicaragua, Haiti, Santo Domingo and Cuba invaded; who have lost to a greedy imperialism such wide and rich lands as Texas, such vital strategic zones as the Panama Canal, and even, as in the case of Puerto Rico, entire countries converted into territories of occupation; who have suffered the insults of the Marines toward our wives and daughters and toward the most cherished memorials of the history of our lands, among them the figure of José Martí.

That domination, built upon superior military power, upon unfair treaties and upon the shameful collaboration of traitorous governments, has for more than a hundred years made of Our America — the America that Bolívar, Hidalgo, Juárez, San Martín, O'Higgins, Tiradentes, Sucre and Martí wished to see free — a zone of exploitation, a backyard in the financial and political empire of the United States, a reserve supply of votes in international organizations where we of the Latin American countries have always been regarded as beasts of burden to a "rough and brutal North that despises us."

The National General Assembly of the People of Cuba declares that Latin American governments betray the ideals of independence, destroy the sovereignty of their peoples and obstruct a true solidarity among our countries by accepting this demonstrated and continued domination. For such reasons this Assembly in the name of the Cuban people, with the same spirit of liberation that moved the immortal Fathers of our countries, rejects it, thereby fulfilling the hope and the will of the Latin American peoples.

THIRD: The National General Assembly of the People of Cuba rejects as well the attempt to perpetuate the Monroe Doctrine, until now utilized "to extend the domination in America" of greedy imperialists, as José Martí foresaw, and to inject more easily "the poison of loans, of canals and railroads," also denounced by José Martí long ago. Therefore, in defiance of that false Pan-Americanism that is merely prostration of spineless governments before Washington and rule over the interest of our peoples by the monopolies of the United States, the Assembly of the People of Cuba proclaims the liberating Latin Americanism of Martí and Benito Juárez. Furthermore, while extending the hand of friendship to the people of the United States — a people that includes persecuted intellectuals, Negroes threatened with lynching, and workers subjected to the control of gangsters — the Assembly reaffirms its will to march "with the whole world and not just a part of it."

FOURTH: The National General Assembly of the People of Cuba declares that the spontaneous offer of the Soviet Union to help Cuba if our country is attacked by imperialist military forces cannot be considered an act of intervention, but rather an open act of solidarity. Such support, offered to Cuba in the face of an imminent attack by the Pentagon, honors the government of the Soviet Union as much as cowardly and criminal aggressions against Cuba dishonor the government of the United States. Therefore, the General Assembly of the People declares before America and the world that it accepts with gratitude the help of rockets from the Soviet Union should our territory be invaded by military forces of the United States.

FIFTH: The National General Assembly of the People of Cuba denies absolutely that there has existed on the part of the Soviet Union and the People's Republic of China any aim "to make use of the economic, political and social situation in Cuba... in order to break continental unity and to endanger hemispheric unity." From the first to the last volley, from the first to the last of the 20,000 martyrs who fell in the struggle to overthrow tyranny and win power for the revolution, from the first to the last revolutionary law, from the first to the last act of the revolution, the people of Cuba have moved of their own free will. Therefore, no grounds exist for blaming either the Soviet Union or the People's Republic of China for the existence of a revolution that is the just response of Cuba to crimes and injuries perpetrated by imperialism in America.

On the contrary, the National General Assembly of the People of Cuba believes that the peace and security of the hemisphere and of the world are endangered by the policy of the government of the United States — which forces the governments of Latin America to imitate it. This U.S. policy seeks to isolate the Soviet Union and the People's Republic of China, of engaging in aggressive and provocative acts, and of systematically excluding the People's Republic of China from the United Nations, despite the fact that it represents nearly all the 600 million inhabitants of China.

Therefore, the National General Assembly of the People of Cuba confirms its policy of friendship with all the peoples of the world and reaffirms its intention of establishing diplomatic relations with, among others, the socialist countries of the world. From this moment the Assembly expresses its free and sovereign will to establish relations with the People's Republic of China, therefore rescinding relations with the puppet regime maintained in Formosa by the Seventh Fleet of the United States.

SIXTH: The National General Assembly of the People of Cuba — confident that it is expressing the general opinion of the people of Latin America — affirms that democracy is not compatible with financial oligarchy; with discrimination against the Negro; with disturbances by the Ku Klux Klan, nor with the persecution that drove scientists like Oppenheimer from their posts, deprived the world for years of the marvelous voice of Paul Robeson, held prisoner in his own country, and sent the Rosenbergs to their death against the protests of a shocked world, including the appeals of many governments and of Pope Pius XII.

The National General Assembly of the People of Cuba expresses the Cuban conviction that democracy does not consist solely of elections that are nearly always managed by rich landowners and professional politicians in order to produce fictitious results, but rather in the right of citizens to determine their own destiny, as this Assembly of the people is now doing. Furthermore, democracy will come to exist in Latin America only when people are really free to make choices, when the poor are not reduced — by hunger, social discrimination, illiteracy and the judicial system — to sinister desperation.

Therefore, The National General Assembly of the People of Cuba:

Condemns the backward and inhuman latifundium system of large, poorly cultivated holdings of land, a source of misery for the rural population; condemns the starvation wages and the heartless exploitation of human labor by illegitimate and privileged interests; condemns the illiteracy, the absence of teachers, schools, doctors and hospitals, and the lack of care for the aged that prevail in the countries of America; condemns discrimination against the Negro and the Indian; condemns the inequality and exploitation of women; condemns military and political oligarchies that keep our peoples wretched, hinder the full exercise of their sovereignty and their progress toward democracy; condemns the concession of the natural resources of our countries to foreign monopolies as a give-away that disregards the interest of the people; condemns governments that render homage to Washington while they ignore the sentiments of their own people; condemns the systematic deception of the people by the press and other media serving the interests of political oligarchies and the imperialist oppressor; condemns the monopoly of news by agencies that are the instruments of Washington and of U.S. trusts; condemns repressive laws that deter workers, peasants, students and intellectuals, who together form a majority in every country from joining together to seek patriotic and social goals; condemns the monopolies and imperialist enterprises that plunder our resources, exploit our workers and peasants, bleed our economies and keep them backward while subjecting politics in Latin America for their own designs and interests.

Finally, the National General Assembly of the People of Cuba condemns:

The exploitation of man by man and the exploitation of underdeveloped countries by imperialist finance capital.

In consequence, the National General Assembly of the People of Cuba proclaims before America:

The right of peasants to the land; the right of the workers to the fruit of their labor; the right of children to receive education; the right of the sick to receive medical and hospital care; the right of the young to work, the right of students to receive free instruction, practical and scientific; the right of Negroes and Indians to "a full measure of human dignity"; the right of women to civic, social and political equality; the right of the aged to a secure old age; the right of intellectuals, artists and scientists to fight through their work for a better world; the rights of states to nationalize imperialist monopolies as a means of recovering national wealth and resources; the right of countries to engage freely in trade with all other countries of the world; the right of nations to full sovereignty; the right of the people to convert their fortresses into schools and to arm their workers, peasants, students, intellectuals, Negroes, Indians, women, the young, the old, all the oppressed and exploited; that they may better defend, with their own hands, their rights and their future.

SEVENTH: The National General Assembly of the People of Cuba affirms:

The duty of workers, peasants, students, intellectuals, Negroes, Indians, youth, women, the aged, to fight for their economic, political and social rights; the duty of oppressed and exploited nations to fight for their liberation; the duty of every people to make common cause with all other oppressed, exploited, colonized and afflicted peoples, wherever they are located, regardless of distance or geographical separation. All peoples of the world are brothers!

EIGHTH: The National General Assembly of the People of Cuba affirms its faith that Latin America, united and victorious will soon be free of the bonds that now make its economies rich spoils for U.S. imperialism; that keeps its true voice from being heard at conferences, where cowed ministers form a sordid chorus to the despotic masters. The Assembly affirms, therefore, its decision to work for this common Latin American destiny, which will allow our countries to build a true solidarity, founded in the free decision of each and the common goals of all. In this fight for a liberated Latin America there now arises with invincible power — against the obedient voice of those who hold office as usurpers — the genuine voice of the people, a voice that breaks forth from the depths of coal and tin mines, from factories, and sugar mills, from feudal lands where *rotos, cholos, gauchos, jíbaros,* the heirs of Zapata and Sandino, take up the arms of liberty; a voice heard in poets and novelists, in students, in women and in children, in the old and helpless.

To this voice of our brothers the Assembly of the People of Cuba responds: We are ready! Cuba will not fail. Cuba is here today to proclaim before Latin America and the world its historic and unchangeable resolution: Homeland or death!

NINTH: The National General Assembly of the People of Cuba resolves that this declaration shall be known as the "Declaration of Havana."

Havana, Cuba, Free Territory of America, September 2, 1960

8

ASSASSINATION PLOTS AGAINST FIDEL CASTRO

September 9, 1960

This is a symbolic date — one of many, most of which are unknown — which marked a course that has lasted nearly 40 years in which the CIA, some U.S. political figures and the counterrevolutionary terrorist groups in the United States have held stubbornly to their purpose of assassinating Fidel Castro and other leaders of the revolution. Never before in the history of any country had there been such a record.

On September 9, 1960, CIA agent Robert Maheu — following instructions from high-ranking CIA chiefs Richard Bissell, Colonel King and Colonel Sheffield Edwards — met in the Brown Derby in Beverley Hills, California, with John Rosselli, a Mafia figure linked to Las Vegas gambling. Maheu told Rosselli that senior figures in the U.S. Government needed to get rid of Fidel Castro and asked him to recruit the right people for the job. Rosselli hesitated at first but then agreed, saying that he had to help his government. As a condition, he asked for a meeting with one of its official representatives. Four days later, senior CIA official Jim O'Connell met with Rosselli in the Plaza Hotel in New York and offered him the guarantees he wanted.

Fidel Castro was scheduled to arrive in New York a few days later, on September 18, to attend the UN General Assembly.

The CIA operatives then met in the Waldorf-Astoria Hotel to draw up a plan. It called for recruiting the head of the New York police who were responsible for Fidel Castro's security and getting him to sneak a pack of cigars into the Cuban leader's room. When Fidel opened the pack, it would explode in his face. The police officer angrily refused to go along with the plan, saying that his job was to protect Fidel Castro, not kill him.

In the following years, the Mafia, the CIA and the counter-revolutionary organizations run by the CIA both inside and outside Cuba drew up and tried to implement — with varying degrees of success — scores of plans for assassinating Fidel Castro.

Some of them came close to achieving their purpose. One such near miss occurred in 1971, during Fidel's trip to Chile, when a terrorist pretending to be a journalist managed to get in front of Fidel with a gun hidden in a TV camera. He didn't use it, however, because he didn't think he could escape.

After the political scandal of Watergate and the statements made in court by Mafia boss John Rosselli, the U.S. Congress decided to investigate the assassination plans that had been drawn up in the United States in the 1960s. Though fragmentary and incomplete, that investigation brought out some amazing things that had been kept from the public. In 1975, a committee of the U.S. Senate headed by Senator Church issued a special report on alleged assassination conspiracies against the leaders of other countries.

Concrete proof about at least eight plots to assassinate Fidel Castro between 1960 and 1965

(Excerpt from "Alleged Assassination Plots Involving Foreign Leaders", Church Commission report, November 1975)

We have found concrete evidence of at least eight plots involving the CIA to assassinate Fidel Castro from 1960 to 1965. Although some of the assassination plots did not advance beyond the stage of planning and preparation, one plot, involving the use of under-world figures, reportedly twice progressed to the point of sending poison pills to Cuba and dispatching teams to commit the deed. Another plot involved furnishing weapons and other assassination devices to a Cuban dissident. The proposed assassination devices ran the gamut from high-powered rifles to poison pills, poison pens, deadly bacterial powders, and other devices which strain the imagination...

From March through August 1960, during the last year of the Eisenhower Administration, the CIA considered plans to undermine Castro's charismatic appeal by sabotaging his speeches.

According to the 1967 Report of the CIA's Inspector General, an official in the Technical Services Division (TSD) recalled discussing a scheme to spray Castro's broadcasting studio with a chemical that produced effects similar to LSD, but the scheme was rejected because the chemical was unreliable. During this period, TSD impregnated a box of cigars with a chemical that produced temporary disorientation, hoping to induce Castro to smoke one of the cigars before delivering a speech. The Inspector General also reported a plan to destroy Castro's image as "The Beard" by dusting his shoes with thallium salts, a strong depilatory that would cause his beard to fall out. The depilatory was to be administered during a trip outside Cuba, when it was anticipated Castro would leave his shoes outside the door of his hotel room to be shined. TSD procured the chemical and tested it on animals, but apparently abandoned the scheme because Castro cancelled his trip...

Poison Cigars
A notation in the records of the Operations Division, CIA's Office of Medical Services, indicates that on August 16, 1960, an official was given a box of Castro's favorite cigars with instructions to treat them with lethal poison. The cigars were contaminated with a botulinum toxin so potent that a person would die after putting one in his mouth. The official reported that the cigars were ready on October 7, 1960; TSD notes indicate that they were delivered to an unidentified person on February 13, 1961.

Poison is Prepared And Delivered to Cuba
The Inspector General's Report described conversations among Bissell, Edwards, and the Chief of the Technical Services Division (TSD), concerning the most effective method of poisoning Castro. There is some evidence that Giancana or Rosselli originated the idea of depositing a poison pill in Castro's drink to give the "asset" a chance to escape.

Edwards rejected the first batch of pills prepared by TSD because they would not dissolve in water.

A second batch, containing botulinum toxin, "did the job expected of them" when tested on monkeys. The Support Chief received the pills from TSD, probably in February 1961, with assurances that they were lethal, and then gave them to Rosselli. The record clearly establishes that the pills were given to a Cuban for delivery to the island some time prior to the Bay of Pigs invasion mid-April 1961.

The Support Chief recalled that Colonel J. C. King, head of the

Western Hemisphere Division, gave him $50,000 in Bissell's office to pay the Cuban if he successfully assassinated Castro.

Joseph Shimon, a friend of Rosselli and Giancana who testified that he was present when the passage occurred, testified that he had accompanied Maheu to Miami and that he, Giancana, Rosselli, and Maheu shared a suite in the Fountainebleau Hotel. During a conversation, Maheu stated that he had a "contract" to assassinate Castro, and had been provided with a "liquid" by the CIA to accomplish the task. Shimon testified that Maheu had said the liquid was to be put in Castro's food, that Castro would become ill and die after two or three days, and that an autopsy would not reveal what had killed him.

Shimon testified that a few days later, he received a phone call from Maheu, who said: "...did you see the paper? Castro's ill. He's going to be sick two or three days. Wow, we got him."

The Operation Is Reactivated

In early April 1962, Harvey, who testified that he was acting on "explicit orders" from [CIA director Richard] Helms, requested Edwards to put him in touch with Rosselli.

Harvey, the Support Chief and Rosselli met for a second time in New York on April 8-9, 1962. A notation made during this time in the files of the Technical Services Division indicates that four poison pills were given to the Support Chief on April 18, 1962. The pills were passed to Harvey, who arrived in Miami on April 21, and found Rosselli already in touch with the same Cuban who had been involved in the pre-Bay of Pigs pill passage. He gave the pills to Rosselli, explaining that "these would work anywhere and at any time with anything." Rosselli testified that he told Harvey that the Cubans intended to use the pills to assassinate Che Guevara as well as Fidel and Raúl Castro. According to Rosselli's testimony, Harvey approved of the targets, stating "everything is all right, what they want to do."

The Cuban requested arms and equipment as a *quid pro quo* for carrying out the assassination operation.

Rosselli kept Harvey informed of the operation's progress. Sometime in May 1962, he reported that the pills and guns had arrived in Cuba.

Plans in Early 1963

Two plans to assassinate Castro were explored by Task Force W, the CIA section then concerned with covert Cuban operations, in early

1963. Desmond Fitzgerald (now deceased), Chief of the Task Force, asked his assistant to determine whether an exotic seashell, rigged to explode, could be deposited in an area where Castro commonly went skin diving.

A second plan involved having James Donovan (who was negotiating with Castro for the release of prisoners taken during the Bay of Pigs operation) present Castro with a contaminated diving suit.

The Technical Services Division bought a diving suit, dusted it inside with a fungus that would produce a chronic skin disease (Madura foot), and contaminated the breathing apparatus with tubercule bacillus.

The Poison Pen Device

Another device offered to AM/LASH was a ball-point pen rigged with a hypodermic needle. The needle was designed to be so fine that the victim would not notice its insertion.

According to the Inspector General's Report, when Case Officer 2 was interviewed in 1967, he stated that AM/LASH had requested the Agency to "devise some technical means of doing the job that would not automatically cause him to lose his own life in the try."

Fitzgerald's assistant told the Committee that the pen was intended to show "bona fides" and "the orders were to do something to get rid of Castro... and we thought this other method might work whereas a rifle wouldn't."

Helms confirmed that the pen was manufactured "to take care of a request from him that he have some device for getting rid of Castro, for killing him, murdering him, whatever the case may be."

A CIA document dated January 3, 1965 states that B-1, in a lengthy interview with a case officer, said that he and AM/LASH had reached a firm agreement on the following points: B-1 is to provide AM/LASH with a silencer for the FAL; if this is impossible, B-1 is to cache in a designated location a rifle with a scope and silencer plus several bombs, concealed either in a suitcase, a lamp or some other concealment device that he would be able to carry, and place next to Fidel Castro.

9

FIDEL AT THE UNITED NATIONS

September 26, 1960

Fidel Castro and the other members of the Cuban delegation arrived in New York on September 18, 1960, to take part in the 15th session of the General Assembly of the United Nations. They arrived in the midst of a climate of hysteria and hostility on the part of U.S. authorities along with support from members of minority groups and U.S.-based Cubans who supported the revolution.

As part of the protest against him, the management of the Shelburne Hotel, where the Cuban delegation was staying, presented unacceptable and offensive financial demands that led the Cuban leader to leave that hotel.

The head of the Cuban Revolution then threatened to put up a tent on the grounds of UN headquarters, by the East River, or in New York's Central Park. It wasn't necessary, however. Prominent African Americans in New York expressed their solidarity, and Fidel Castro was welcomed in the Theresa Hotel, at 125th Street and 7th Avenue, in Harlem. Enthusiastic crowds acclaimed him night and day throughout his stay.

Fidel and U.S. black Muslim leader Malcolm X had a history-making meeting in the hotel.[1]

There, too, Fidel met with Soviet Premier Nikita Khrushchev, Egyptian President Gamal Abdel Nasser and Indian Prime Minister Jawaharlal Nehru.

---

[1] Rosemari Mealy, *Fidel & Malcolm X, Memories of a Meeting* (Melbourne: Ocean Press, 1993), 41-61.

On September 26, Fidel Castro addressed the UN General Assembly. He spoke for an hour and a half, describing the roots of the historic conflict between Cuba and the United States; denouncing the OAS for punishing Cuba, the victim of attacks, rather than the attacking power; and explaining that, even at that moment, the U.S. Government was organizing still more subversive activities against Cuba.

Sure enough, the process of recruiting and training the mercenaries who would form Brigade 2506 was under way. This Brigade was to be the invading force at the Bay of Pigs in April 1961.

Two days later, on September 28, Prime Minister Fidel Castro returned to Havana. On arriving at the airport, he drove straight to the former Presidential Palace, where a huge crowd filled the street, and addressed the people. During his remarks, counterrevolutionaries set off bombs nearby. Fidel then announced, to great applause, that a new organization would be created to establish revolutionary vigilance throughout Cuba: the Committees for the Defense of the Revolution (CDRs).

The case of Cuba is the case of all developing countries

(Excerpt of speech by Fidel Castro to United Nations on September 26, 1960)

When the revolution was successful in Cuba, what did it uncover? What did it find? What marvels lay spread out before the eyes of the victorious revolutionaries of Cuba? First of all, the revolution found that 600,000 Cubans, able and ready to work, were unemployed — as many, proportionally, as were unemployed in the United States at the time of the Great Depression that shook this country, and which almost produced a catastrophe in the United States. This is what we met with — permanent unemployment in my country. Three million out of a population of somewhat over six million had no electric light and none of the advantages and comforts of electricity. Three and a half million out of a total population of more than six million lived in huts, in slums, without the slightest sanitary facilities.

In the cities, rents took almost one-third of family incomes. Electricity rates and rents were among the highest in the world. Some 37.5 percent of our population were illiterate; 70 percent of the rural children lacked teachers; 2 percent of our population suffered from tuberculosis, that is to say, 100,000 persons, out of a total population of a little over six million, were suffering from the ravages of tuberculosis. Ninety-five percent of the children in rural areas were suffering from parasites. Infant mortality was astronomical. The standard of living was the opposite. On the other hand, 85 percent of the small farmers were paying rent on their land to the extent of almost 30 percent of their gross income, whilst 1.5 percent of the total landowners controlled 46 percent of the total area of the country. Of course, the proportion of hospital beds to the number of inhabitants of the country was ludicrous when compared to countries that have even half-way decent medical services.

Public services, electricity and telephone services, all belonged to U.S. monopolies. A major portion of the banking business, of the importing business and the oil refineries, a greater part of the sugar production, the lion's share of the arable land of Cuba and the most important industries in all fields in Cuba belonged to U.S. companies. The balance of payments in the last 10 years, from 1950 to 1960, has been favorable for the United States vis-à-vis Cuba to the extent of $1 billion.

This is without taking into account the hundreds of millions of dollars that were extracted from the treasury of the country by the corrupt officials of the dictatorship and were later deposited in U.S. or European banks.

One billion dollars in 10 years. The poor and underdeveloped country in the Caribbean, with 600,000 unemployed, was contributing to the economic development of the most highly industrialized country in the world!

This was the situation that confronted us. Yet it should not surprise many of the countries represented in this Assembly, because, when all is said and done, what we have said about Cuba is, one may say, an X-ray that could be superimposed and applied to many of the countries represented here in the Assembly.

What alternative was there for the Revolutionary Government? To betray the people? As far as the president of the United States is concerned, what we have done is treason to our people, but it surely would not have been so if, instead of the Revolutionary Government being true to its people, it had rather been true to the monopolies that were exploiting Cuba. At least let note be taken here of the marvels that were laid out before our eyes as we won our revolution. They were no more and no less than the usual marvels of imperialism, which are in themselves no more and no less than the marvels of the free world as far as we, the colonies, are concerned.

We surely cannot be blamed if there were 600,000 unemployed in Cuba and 37.5 percent of the population were illiterate, if 2 percent of the population suffered from tuberculosis and 95 percent suffered from parasites. Until that moment none of us had any say in the destiny of our country. Until that moment when the revolution was victorious, the voices listened to in our country were those of the monopolies. Did anyone tell them nay? Did anyone hinder them? No one. The monopolies went about their nefarious business, and there we found the fruit of the monopolies.

What was the state of the reserves of the nation? When the dictator Batista came to power there were $500 million in the national treasury. It was a goodly amount, and it would have been well to have invested it in the development, industrial or otherwise, of the country. When the revolution was victorious, we found in our reserves some $70 million.

Did they ever show any concern for the economic and industrial development of our country? No, never. That is why we were astonished, and we are still amazed and stunned when we hear it said here that extraordinary concern is shown by the U.S. Government for the fate of the countries of Latin America, of Africa and of Asia. We cannot overcome our amazement, because after 50 years we had to deal with the results...

Cuba was not the first victim of aggression. Cuba was not the first country in danger of aggression. In this hemisphere everybody knows that the government of the United States has always imposed its law, the law of the mightiest; in accordance with this law it has destroyed the Puerto Rican nationality and has kept its dominion over that island; that law, in accordance with which it took over the Panama Canal and holds the Panama Canal.

This was nothing new. Our country should have been defended. But our country was not defended. Why? And let us here dig into the depths of this matter and let us not merely study the forms. If we stick to the dead letter, then we are guaranteed; if we stick to reality, we have no guarantee whatsoever, because reality imposes itself over and above the law set forth in international codes, and that reality is that a small country attacked by a powerful country was not defended and could not be defended.

But what happened in Costa Rica? Lo and behold, by an ingenious production a miracle happened in Costa Rica. What resulted from Costa Rica was not a condemnation of the United States.

I do wish to avoid any misunderstanding about our feelings for the government of the United States. We regard the government of the United States and the people of the United States as two completely different entitles. The government of the United States was not condemned in Costa Rica for the 60 over flights by pirate aircraft. The government of the United States was not condemned for the economic and other aggression of which we had been the victim. No, the Soviet Union was condemned. That was really bizarre. We had not been attacked by the Soviet Union. We had not been the victims of aggression by the Soviet Union. No Soviet aircraft had flown over our territory. Yet in Costa Rica there was a finding against the Soviet Union for interference. The Soviet Union only said that, figuratively speaking, if there was military aggression against our country the Soviet Union could support the victim with rockets.

Since when is support for a weak country, support conditioned on an attack by a powerful country, regarded as interference?

In law there is something called an impossible condition. If a country considers that it is incapable of committing a certain crime, well then, it is enough for it to say that there is no possibility that the Soviet Union will support Cuba, because there is no possibility that they will attack the little country. The principle was established that the intervention of the Soviet Union had to be condemned. About the bombing of Cuba nothing was said. Of the aggression against Cuba? Nothing...

Those are the circumstances in which the revolutionary process in Cuba has taken place. How did we find the country? Why have the difficulties arisen? And yet the Cuban Revolution is changing things. What was yesterday a hopeless land, a land of misery, a land of illiterates, is gradually becoming one of the most enlightened, advanced and developed lands of this continent...

Still, the case of Cuba is not an isolated case. It would be an error to think of it only as the case of Cuba. The case of Cuba is the case of all underdeveloped peoples. It is, as it were, the case of the Congo; it is like the case of Egypt, of Algeria, of West Irian; it is like that of Panama, which wishes to have its canal; it is like that of Puerto Rico, whose national spirit they are destroying; like that of Honduras, a portion of whose territory has been taken away. In short, although we have not made reference specifically to other countries, the case of Cuba is the case of all the underdeveloped colonial countries.

The problems that we have been describing in relation to Cuba apply perfectly well to all of Latin America. The control of Latin American economic resources is exercised by the monopolies, which, when they do not directly own the mines and take charge of the working of them — as in the case of copper in Chile, Peru and Mexico and in the case of zinc in Peru and Mexico, as well as in the case of oil in Venezuela — they are the owners of the public utility companies, which is the case with the electricity services in Argentina, Brazil, Chile, Peru, Ecuador and Colombia, or of the telephone services, which is the case in Chile, Brazil, Peru, Venezuela, Paraguay and Bolivia. Or, they commercially exploit our products, as is the case with coffee in Brazil, Colombia, El Salvador, Costa Rica and Guatemala, or with the exploitation, marketing and transportation of bananas by the United Fruit Company in Guatemala, Costa Rica and Honduras, or with cotton in Mexico and Brazil. That economic control is exercised by U.S. monopolies of the most important industries of the country, industries that are dependent completely on the monopolies.

Woe betide them on the day when they, too, shall wish to carry out agrarian reform. They will be asked for immediate, efficient and just payment. And if, in spite of everything, they carry out agrarian reform, the representative of a sister nation who comes to the United Nations will be confined to Manhattan; they will not rent hotel space to him; insults will be poured upon him and he may even, possibly, be mistreated, in fact, by the police themselves.

The problem of Cuba is only an example of what Latin America is. How long must Latin America wait for its development? According to the point of view of the monopolies it will have to wait *ad calendas Graecas*. Who is going to industrialize Latin America? The monopolies? Certainly not.

There is a report of the United Nations on economic matters that explains how even private capital, instead of going to the countries that need it most, for the setting up of basic industries in order to contribute to the development of those countries, is probably being channeled to the more industrialized countries, because there, according to their findings, private capital finds greater security. Naturally the economic secretariat of the United Nations has had to recognize the fact that there is no possible chance of development through investment of private capital — that is, through the monopolies.

The development of Latin America will have to be achieved through public investment planned and granted unconditionally without any political strings attached because, naturally, we all like to be representatives of free countries. None of us likes to represent a country that does not feel itself to be in full possession of its freedom. None of us wants the independence of their country to be subjected to any interest other than that of the country itself. Therefore the assistance must be without any political strings attached.

That help has been denied to us does not matter. We did not ask for it. However, in the interest of and for the benefit of the Latin American peoples we do feel duty bound, out of solidarity, to stress the fact that the assistance must be given without any political conditions whatsoever. Public investment for economic development, not for social development, is the latest thing that has been invented to hide the true need for economic development of the countries.

The problems of Latin America are like the problems of the rest of the world: Africa and Asia. The world is divided up among the monopolies; those same monopolies that we see in Latin America are also seen in the Middle East. There the oil is in the hands of monopolistic companies that are controlled by the financial interests of the United States, the United Kingdom, the Netherlands, France, in Iran, in Iraq, in Saudi Arabia, in Kuwait, in Qatar and, finally, in all corners of the world...

Has there ever been a lack of pretexts for the colonialists or imperialists when they wanted to invade a country? They have never lacked pretexts; somehow they have always managed to pull out of the hat the pretext that they wanted. Which are the colonialist countries? Which are the imperialist countries? There are not four or five countries but four or five groups of monopolies which possess the world's wealth.

If a person from outer space were to come to this Assembly, someone who had read neither the *Communist Manifesto* of Karl Marx nor the cables of the UP or the AP or the other publications of a monopolistic character, and if he were to ask how the world was divided and if he saw on a map of the world that its riches were divided among the monopolies of four or five countries, he would say: "The world has been badly divided up, the world has been exploited." Here in this Assembly, where there is a majority of the underdeveloped countries, he would say that the great majority of the people you represent are being exploited, that they have been exploited for a long time; the forms of exploitation may have varied, but they are still being exploited. That would be the verdict.

In the statement made by Premier Khrushchev there is a statement that attracted our attention because of the value that it holds, and that was when he said that the Soviet Union did not have colonies and that the Soviet Union has no investments in any country. How great would our world be today, our world that today is threatened with catastrophe, if all the representatives of all countries could make the same statement: Our country has no colonies and no investments in any foreign country.

But why labor the matter any further? This is the essence of the matter; including the essence of peace and war, the essence of the arms race or of disarmament. Wars, since the beginning of humanity, have emerged for one reason, and one reason alone — the desire of some to despoil others of what the others possess. Do away with the philosophy of plunder, and you will have done away forever with the philosophy of war. Do away with the colonies, wipe out the exploitation of countries by monopolies, and then humanity will have achieved a true period of progress...

10

PROCLAMATION OF THE SOCIALIST CHARACTER OF THE CUBAN REVOLUTION

April 16, 1961

While preparations for the U.S.-supported invasion brigade were being made in Guatemala under the direct command of the CIA, the situation in Cuba became very tense. During the last few months of 1960 and the first months of 1961, the Cuban people were organized and active. Battalions of workers' and farmers' militias waged intensive campaigns in the Escambray Mountains to root out the bands of armed counter-revolutionaries supplied by airlifts from the United States. Counter-revolutionary organizations appeared in Cuban cities, creating a difficult situation for the recently formed units of State Security.

On November 18, 1960, CIA Director Allen Dulles and Deputy Director Richard Bissell informed U.S. President-elect John F. Kennedy of the plans for invading Cuba.

On December 16, President Eisenhower ordered the elimination of Cuba's sugar quota for the January-April 1961 period.

On December 31, 1960, considering that Kennedy's inauguration would constitute a particularly dangerous time in terms of a possible military attack on Cuba, the leaders of the revolution declared a general mobilization of the armed forces, the militias and the people as a whole. Hundreds of thousands of men and women took up defensive positions along Cuba's coasts.

On January 3, 1961, the U.S. Government broke off diplomatic relations with Cuba.

On January 5, at the beginning of the year in which the national Literacy Campaign was waged, bands of counterrevolutionaries in the mountains of Sancti Spíritus Province kidnapped and murdered Conrado Benítez, an 18-year-old volunteer teacher.

During the same period, saboteurs using incendiary materials supplied by the CIA gutted several large department stores in Havana.

John F. Kennedy was sworn in as president in Washington on January 20, 1961. The day before, out-going President Dwight D. Eisenhower informed Kennedy that the mercenary brigade was being trained and, according to the notes that Clark Clifford took during the meeting, told him, "It was the policy of this government to help these forces to the utmost. At the present time, we are helping train anti-Castro forces in Guatemala. It was [Eisenhower's] recommendation that this effort be continued and accelerated."[1]

During those months of hard struggle, the Cuban people's political awareness advanced with tremendous speed. Their patriotic feelings and class interests grew very strong. The solidarity they received from the Soviet Union and other socialist countries during that difficult period contrasted sharply to the aggression of the U.S. Government.

Moreover, in practice, with the great nationalizations that were carried out in the latter half of 1960, a broad sector of the state economy had been formed, based on ownership by all the people, and was being administered on a socialist basis, even though this hadn't been publicly announced.

On April 13, 1961, Havana's El Encanto Department Store was burned to the ground in an act of sabotage. Sales clerk Fe del Valle died in the flames.

On April 15, B-29 planes provided by the CIA took off from bases in Puerto Cabezas, Nicaragua, to unleash the prelude to the mercenary invasion that took place at the Bay of Pigs a few days later. Their task was to destroy the few, obsolete fighter planes that the revolution had, while they were still on the ground, to guarantee that the invaders would control the air. The planes, painted with insignias of the Cuban Air Force, attacked the airports at Ciudad Libertad, San Antonio de los Baños and Santiago de Cuba. One of the attacking pilots flew to Miami and issued statements there aimed at making people believe that the attack was part of an uprising in Cuba.

Seven Cuban combatants were killed that day while repulsing the

---

[1] Arthur M. Schlesinger, Jr, *Robert Kennedy and His Times* (Boston: Houghton Mifflin Company, 1978), 463.

attack. On April 16, in his funeral oration for those fighters, Fidel Castro told the armed militia who filled the area at 23rd and 12th Streets, at the entrance to Colón Cemetery, "That's what they can't forgive us for — the fact that we're still here, right under their noses, and that we have carried out a socialist revolution so close to the United States."

We are defending this revolution with the men and women of our nation...

(Excerpts from the speech of Fidel Castro at the burial of the victims of the bombing raid on Havana, April 16, 1961)[2]

Yesterday, as everybody knows, three groups of bombers, coming from outside the country, entered our national territory at 6 o'clock in the morning and attacked three different points of our national territory. In each of these places, our men defended themselves heroically; in each of these places the valuable blood of our defenders was shed; in each of these places there were thousands and, where there were not thousands, hundreds and hundreds, of witnesses to what happened there. Moreover, this was something we expected; it was something that was awaited every day; it was the logical culmination of the burning of the sugarcane fields, of the hundreds of violations of our air space, of the pirate air raids, of the pirate attacks on our refineries from vessels that enter our waters before the sun is up. It was the consequence of what everyone knows; it was the consequence of the plans to attack us that were being hatched by the United States in complicity with its lackey governments in Central America; it was the consequence of the air bases that everyone knows about, and everyone knows only too well, because even the U.S. newspapers and news agencies have published this news, and even their own news agencies and newspapers are tired of talking about the mercenary armies that are being organized, about the air fields that they have made ready, about the planes that the U.S. Government has given to them, about the Yankee instructors, about the air bases they have established in Guatemalan territory...

Imperialism plans the crime, organizes the crime, arms the criminals, trains the criminals, pays the criminals and the criminals come here and kill seven children of our workers and then calmly go

---

[2] Fidel Castro, *El pensamiento de Fidel Castro*, tomo 1 (Havana: Editora Politica, 1983), 446–7.

back and land in the United States. Even when the whole world knows about their deeds, they then say it was Cuban pilots who did it and they prepare their truculent and fantastic tale, spread it all around the world, publish it in all the newspapers, propagate it from all the radio and television stations of the Miami reactionaries throughout the world, and then come the archbishops to bless and sanctify the lie. Thus the whole throng of mercenaries, exploiters and phonies from all around the world comes together in crime...

This is because what these imperialists can't forgive is that we are here, and what these imperialists can't forgive is the dignity, the firmness, the courage, the ideological integrity, the spirit of sacrifice and the revolutionary spirit of the Cuban people.

This is what they can't forgive, the fact that we are here right under their very noses, and that we have brought about a socialist revolution right under the nose of the United States!

And we are defending this socialist revolution with these guns! And we are defending this socialist revolution with the same courage that our anti-aircraft artillery yesterday showed in riddling the attacking planes with bullets!...

We are not defending this revolution with mercenaries; we are defending this revolution with the men and women of our people.

Who has the arms? Perhaps it is the mercenary who has the arms? [*shouts of "No!"*] Perhaps it is the millionaire who has the arms? Perhaps the mercenary and the millionaire are one and the same thing. Perhaps the little boys of rich daddies have the arms? [*shouts of "No!"*] Perhaps the overseers have the arms? [*shouts of "No!"*] Who has the arms? What kind of hands are those that bear the arms? Are they the hands of playboys? [*shouts of "No!"*] Are they the hands of the rich? Are they the hands of the exploiters? [*shouts of "No!"*] What hands are those that bear these arms? Are they not workers' hands? [*shouts of "Yes!"*] Are they not peasants' hands? [*shouts of "Yes!"*] Are they not hands that are hardened by work? [*shouts of "Yes!"*] Are they not the hands that create? [*shouts of "Yes!"*] Are they not the humble hands of our people? And who are the majority of our people? Millionaires or workers? Exploiters or exploited? The privileged or the humble? Do the privileged have arms? Do the humble have arms? [*shouts of "Yes!"*] Are the privileged a minority? Are the humble a majority? [*shouts of "Yes!"*] Is a revolution where the humble bear arms democratic? [*shouts of "Yes!"*]

Comrades, workers and peasants: this is the socialist and democratic revolution of the humble, by the humble and for the humble. And for this revolution of the humble, by the humble, for the humble, we are ready to give our lives.

Workers and peasants, humble men and women of our country: do you swear to defend this revolution of the humble, by the humble, for the humble, to the last drop of your blood? (*cries of "Yes!"*)

Comrades workers and peasants of our country, yesterday's attack was a prelude to mercenary aggression. Yesterday's attack, which cost seven heroic lives, aimed to destroy our planes on the ground, but was a failure. They only destroyed two planes while most of the enemy planes were damaged or shot down. Here, before the tomb of our fallen comrades, here, next to the remains of these heroic young people, children of workers, children of the humble, we reaffirm our resolve that, just as they exposed themselves to the bullets, just as they gave their lives, we too, all of us, proud of our revolution, proud of defending this revolution of the humble, by the humble and for the humble, we shall not hesitate, whenever the mercenaries come, no matter who is against us, to defend it to our last drop of blood.

Long live the working class! Long live the peasants! Long live the humble! Long live the martyrs of our country! May the martyrs of our country live forever! Long live the socialist revolution! Long live a free Cuba!

Homeland or death!

We will win!

11

BAY OF PIGS

April 17-19, 1961

While Fidel Castro was giving the funeral oration for the combatants killed in the air attack and proclaiming the socialist nature of the Cuban Revolution, the fleet with the invading brigade was advancing through the Caribbean escorted by U.S. Navy warships. The mercenaries had been taken from their camps in Retalhuleu, Guatemala, to Puerto Cabezas, Nicaragua, where the obese and histrionic Luis Somoza — son of Anastasio Somoza, the dictator — saw them off and asked them to bring back "at least a hair from Castro's beard."

The leaders of the revolution had declared a general mobilization in the face of imminent attack, but they didn't know where the enemy's main thrust would be.

At 1:30 on the morning of April 17, the landing forces' vanguard began to take positions at Larga and Girón Beaches, in the southern part of the Zapata Peninsula. There was a clash with the tiny detachments of militia who were on guard, and the first shots were exchanged.

By dawn, the members of the revolutionary high command had come to the conclusion that Girón — the Bay of Pigs — was the focal point of the enemy actions and had begun to send the men and materiel required to push the attackers back into the sea.

The place that the Pentagon and CIA had chosen, after months of studying various possibilities, was extremely hard to get to. It was a coastal area where the revolution had built some tourist facilities and an airport, but only three narrow roads crossed the thick underbrush and marshy swampland that separated it from the rest of the country.

The U.S. plan was to establish a beachhead; consolidate it under cover of the air control that the invaders hoped to have; dig in along the three roads; and then bring in the members of the new "government," composed of leaders of the so-called Cuban Revolutionary Council (Consejo Revolucionario Cubano), whom the CIA had kept at an unused airport in Opa-Locka, Florida, since April 16, awaiting events. Once that "government" had been promptly recognized, the initiative would pass to the OAS, which was to promote some kind of collective action to legalize the entry of U.S. ships, planes and troops into the conflict — which would subject the population on the island to a war of destruction and annihilation if the Revolutionary Government hadn't already collapsed under the attack.

However, everything turned out differently. On April 17, in spite of the momentary advantage that the invaders had seized, the Revolutionary Air Force — which had managed to preserve a few, old planes — hit the enemy and its ships hard. On April 18, forces of the Rebel Army, Revolutionary National Police and militias, supported by artillery and tanks, advanced along the roads and dislodged the mercenaries from important positions. On April 19, after around 65 hours of incessant fighting, the revolutionary forces took Girón Beach, the last point held by Brigade 2506, by assault.

More than 200 of the invaders were killed in the fighting, and 1,197 were taken prisoner. The Cubans' losses were 156 dead and around 800 wounded.[1]

The Bay of Pigs was not only a military victory. It also constituted a strategic defeat for the plans of the U.S. Government and the counter-revolutionaries it sponsored. It is revealing that the members of the invading brigade who were taken prisoner included over 100 large landowners, 35 industrialists, 194 members of Batista's army, 67 urban landlords, 112 merchants, 89 high-ranking company officials, over 415 members of the middle class and 112 men who were classified as lumpen elements because of their criminal and social records.

Commenting on the victory, Fidel Castro said, "Death holds no terrors for self-respecting men and women. What frightens them and the people as a whole is the idea of a yoke, the idea of seeing themselves once more ruled and oppressed by men of that ilk who pay so little attention to and have so little respect for the people… The comrades who died fighting at Larga and Girón Beaches, San Blas and Yaguaramas — all those places — deserve a beautiful monument. A great monument must be raised here on the Zapata Peninsula to those who were killed, and their names must be inscribed on that monument, which will bear witness to this part of history, telling the

---

[1] Ministry of the Revolutionary Armed Forces, *Peligros y principios: La crisis de octubre desde Cuba* (Dangers and Principles: the October Missile Crisis from Cuba) (Havana: Editora Verde Olivo, 1992), 56.

world that U.S. imperialism was dealt its first great defeat in the Americas that day."[2]

*

Battle Documents[3]
Communiqué 1
April 17, 1961
To the People of Cuba:

Invading troops are attacking various points of national territory in southern Las Villas Province by sea and by air, supported by warships and planes.

The soldiers of the Rebel Army and Revolutionary National Militias have already engaged in combat with the enemy at all landing points.

They are fighting in the defense of our homeland against an attack by mercenaries organized by the imperialist government of the United States.

Our troops are already advancing against the enemy, confident of victory.

The people are already being mobilized, carrying out our watchwords of defending our homeland and maintaining production.

Forward, Cubans! We will reply without quarter to the barbarians who scorn us and who want to force us back into slavery.

They are coming to take away the land that the revolution turned over to the farmers and cooperatives — we are fighting to defend the farmers' and cooperatives' land. They are coming to take away the people's factories, sugar mills and mines — we are fighting to defend our factories, sugar mills and mines. They are coming to take away our children's and farm girls' schools, schools that the revolution has opened for them in all parts of the country — we will defend the children's and farm girls' schools. They are coming to strip from black men and women the dignity that the revolution has returned to them — we will fight to maintain that supreme human dignity for all the people. They are coming to take away the workers' new jobs — we will fight for a free Cuba with a job for every working man and woman. They are coming to destroy our

---

[2] Fidel Castro, *El pensamiento de Fidel*, 186.

[3] Quintín Pino Machado, *La batalla de Playa Girón. Razones de una victoria* (The Battle of the Bay of Pigs: Reasons for a Victory) (Havana: Editorial de Ciencias Sociales, 1983), 94-5, 114, 158-9 and 177.

homeland — we will defend our homeland.

Forward, Cubans; everyone to their post of combat and of work.

Forward, Cubans; the revolution is invincible, and all our enemies will fail in their attempts to crush it and the heroic people who are defending it.

Now, when Cubans are already sacrificing themselves in combat, let us shout with more fervor and determination than ever before:

Long live free Cuba! Homeland or death! We will win!

Fidel Castro Ruz
Commander in Chief and Prime Minister of the Revolutionary Government

Call to the Peoples of the Americas and the Rest of the World
April 18, 1961

U.S. imperialism has launched its advertised and cowardly attack on Cuba.

Its mercenaries and soldiers of fortune have landed in our country.

The revolutionary people of Cuba are fighting them courageously and heroically and are sure to crush them.

However, we call on the peoples of the Americas and the rest of the world for solidarity.

We especially ask our Latin American brothers to make the indisputable force of their action felt by the U.S. imperialists. Let the world know that the people of Latin America — the workers, students, intellectuals and farmers — are with Cuba; with its democratic, patriotic, redeeming people's revolution; and with its Revolutionary Government.

Let us step up the struggle against U.S. imperialism, the main enemy of all humankind.

All Cuba is on the alert and has adopted the watchword of "Homeland or death."

Our battle is yours.

Cuba will win.

Osvaldo Dorticós, President of the Republic
Fidel Castro Ruz, Prime Minister

Communiqué 2
April 18, 1961

The Revolutionary Government announces to the people that the

Armed Forces of the revolution continue fighting heroically against the enemy forces in the southwestern part of Las Villas Province, where the mercenaries landed with imperialist support. In the next few hours, the people will be given details of the successes won by the Rebel Army, the Revolutionary Air Force and the Revolutionary National Militias in the defense of our homeland's sovereignty and the achievements of the revolution.

Fidel Castro Ruz
Commander in Chief and Prime Minister of the Revolutionary Government

Communiqué 3
April 19, 1961
U.S. participation in the attack that is being made on Cuba was dramatically proved this morning when our anti-aircraft batteries shot down a U.S. military plane that was bombing the civilian population and our infantry forces near the Australia Sugar Mill.

The aggressor U.S. pilot, whose body is being held by the revolutionary forces, was Leo Francis Berliss. Several documents were also seized: his pilot's license, number 08323-IM, whose expiration date was December 24, 1962; his Social Security card, number 014-07-6921; and his motor vehicle registration card, which gives his address as 100 Nassau Street, Boston, Mass. The U.S. pilot's registered address was 48 Beacon Street, Boston. He was 5 feet 6 inches tall.

Documents about the mission of an aggressive flight over our homeland were also found in the U.S. pilot's clothing.

This is one of the four enemy military planes that were shot down this morning, making a total of nine planes shot down since the mercenary attack — whose complete liquidation is only a matter of hours away — began on the Zapata Peninsula.

General Staff of the Revolutionary Armed Forces

Communiqué 4
April 19, 1961
Forces of the Rebel Army and Revolutionary National Militias have taken by assault the last positions that the invading mercenary forces had occupied in Cuban territory.

Girón Beach, which was the last point held by the mercenaries, fell at 5:30 in the afternoon.

The revolution has emerged victorious, though at a high cost in lives of the revolutionary combatants who confronted the invaders and attacked them ceaselessly, giving them no respite, thus destroying in less than 72 hours the army which the imperialist government of the United States had spent many months organizing.

The enemy has been dealt a crushing defeat. Some of the mercenaries tried to reembark so as to get away, using diverse vessels that the Rebel Air Force sank. The other mercenaries, after suffering many losses in dead and wounded, scattered in a swampy region from which none of them can escape.

Many U.S.-made weapons were captured, including several heavy Sherman tanks. A complete inventory of the war materiel that was seized has yet to be made.

In the coming hours, the Revolutionary Government will offer the people complete information about everything that has happened.

Fidel Castro Ruz
Commander in Chief of the Revolutionary Armed Forces

12

ADDRESS TO INTELLECTUALS

June 30, 1961

It is an extremely surprising, marvelous fact that, in such a busy year as 1961 — when echoes of the defeated mercenary invasion were still to be heard, when the U.S. rulers were making angry threats every day, when more than 300,000 Cubans were in armed units fighting the bands of counterrevolutionaries in several provinces and protecting Cuban economic targets and its coasts, and when the U.S. blockade was beginning to have a stronger effect on food supplies and daily life — the leaders of the Cuban Revolution were able to put so much energy into and pay so much attention to the campaign against illiteracy, education in general and culture.

That year, in spite of all obstacles, the key bases were laid for the cultural revolution within the Cuban Revolution.

The meetings of writers, artists, critics and others that were held in the Ceremonial Hall of Havana's José Martí National Library were some of the most important events in that process. Fidel Castro took part in them and made the closing address, now known as the "Address to Intellectuals," which summed up the revolution's policy on culture.

To some extent, it was only natural that the proclamation of socialism would lead to many questions among Cuba's intellectuals, who were essentially progressive and patriotic, although with different ideological nuances that expressed a wide range of aesthetic trends and came from different social backgrounds.

The Cuban intellectuals were in favor of the revolution, and many of them supported it militantly, but they also felt apprehensive about the artistic experiences of "socialist realism" and bureaucratic "guidance" of the work of artists in the Soviet Union and other countries.

During the meetings in the National Library, the Cuban Revolution courageously reaffirmed its own path and decisively distanced itself from the errors that had been made elsewhere in the name of socialism in the spheres of art and literature.

The definitions reached after this fruitful collective dialog were so profound that nothing really major has had to be added to those reflections over four decades. During this time, a few mistakes were made and a few attempts were essayed to impose imitative, bureaucratic populist criteria, but they were the work of mediocre officials with imitative minds – never the expression of any policy upheld by the leaders of the revolution.

The "Address to Intellectuals" constituted an important step toward the free development of artistic creation, helped to create a climate of communication and trust between the island's political leaders and intellectuals, and laid the basis for the tremendous variety and richness that Cuba's national culture has today.

*

One of the goals and one of the basic resolves of the revolution is to develop art and culture

(Excerpts of speech made by Fidel Castro on June 30, 1961 in the José Martí National Library)[1]

We have been the agents of this revolution, the socioeconomic revolution that is occurring in Cuba. And in its turn, this socioeconomic revolution must inevitably produce a cultural revolution in our country...

Essentially, unless we are mistaken, the basic problem that has been floating around here was the problem of freedom in artistic creation. Again, when different writers have visited our country, especially political writers, they have touched on this question more than once. There is no doubt that this matter has been discussed in all countries that have had far-reaching revolutions like our own...

One of the characteristics of the revolution has been, then, to confront many problems and in a hurry. And we are like the revolution, by which I mean we have improvised quite a lot. Thus it cannot be said that this revolution has had the period of gestation that other revolutions have had, nor have the leaders of our revolution had the intellectual maturity that leaders of other revolutions have had...

There are certain fears in the air and some of our comrades have

---

[1] In *Política cultural de la revolución cubana. Documentos* (Cultural Policy of the Cuban Revolution: Documents), (Havana: Editorial de Ciencias Sociales, 1977), 5–47.

expressed these fears. Listening to them, we sometimes had the impression that we were dreaming a little. We had the impression that we didn't yet have our feet firmly on the ground. If there is any concern or any fear that restrains us today, it is with respect to the revolution itself. Or is it that we believe that we have already won all the revolutionary battles? Is it that we believe that the revolution holds no dangers? What should be the first concern of every citizen? Concern that the revolution is going to go too far, that the revolution is going to asphyxiate art, that the revolution is going to asphyxiate the creative genius of our citizens, or shouldn't the concern of each and every one of us be the revolution itself? The real or imaginary dangers that might threaten the creative spirit, or the dangers that might threaten the revolution itself?...

We believe that the revolution still has many battles to fight, and we believe that our first thought and our first concern should be: what shall we do to ensure that the revolution is victorious? Because this is what comes first: first of all comes the revolution itself, and later, and only then, can we concern ourselves with the other questions. This does not mean that the other questions should not concern us, but in our soul, given the nature of our soul at least, our basic concern must be the revolution.

The problem that has been under discussion here, and the one we are going to deal with, is the matter of the freedom of writers and artists to express themselves.

The fear that is causing some anxiety is whether the revolution is going to suffocate this freedom, is whether the revolution is going to suffocate the creative spirit of writers and artists.

Here, formal freedom has been under discussion. Everybody was in agreement that formal freedom should be respected. I think there is no doubt about this matter.

The question becomes subtler and really becomes the essential point of the discussion when we are dealing with freedom of content. This is the subtlest point because it is the one that is exposed to the greatest number of interpretations. The most polemical point of this question is: should there or should there not be freedom of content in artistic expression? It seems that some of our comrades are discussing the issue from this point of view. Perhaps it is for fear of this that they prefer to have prohibitions, regulations, limitations, rules, authorities to decide the matter.

Permit me to assure you in the first place that the revolution defends freedom, that the revolution has brought the country a great number of freedoms, that, in essence, the revolution cannot be the enemy of these freedoms and if anybody is concerned that the revolution is going to suffocate his or her creative spirit, this concern is unnecessary, and there is no reason for this concern to exist…

Nobody has ever imagined that all men and women or all writers or all artists have to be revolutionaries, just as nobody could ever imagine that all men and women or all revolutionaries have to be artists, just as any honest person does not have to be a revolutionary just because they are honest. Being a revolutionary also means having a certain attitude toward life, being a revolutionary means having an attitude toward existing reality and there are people who resign themselves to this reality, there are people who adapt to the reality and there are people who cannot resign themselves nor adapt to this reality and who try to change it; this is why they are revolutionaries. But there can also be people who adapt to the realities and who are honest individuals but their spirit is not a revolutionary spirit and their attitude toward the reality is not a revolutionary attitude. And naturally there can also be artists, and good artists, who do not have a revolutionary attitude toward life and it is precisely for this group of artists and intellectuals for whom the revolution in itself constitutes a fact they had not foreseen, a new fact, a fact that can even have a profound effect on their spirits. It is precisely for this group of artists and intellectuals that the revolution can constitute a problem…

Here the issue has been raised, and rightly so, of the cases of many writers and artists who weren't revolutionaries, but who were nonetheless honest writers and artists and who also wanted to support the revolution; moreover, the revolution was interested in having their help; they wanted to work for the revolution and, in turn, it was in the revolution's interests to have the benefit of their knowledge and efforts.

It is easier to appreciate this when particular cases are analyzed, though amongst these particular cases there are many that are not easy to analyze. For example, here a Catholic writer has spoken. He has raised the issue of what was troubling him and he has spoken very clearly. He asked if he could make an interpretation, from his idealist point of view, of a specific problem or if he could write a work defending such a point of view. He asked totally openly if, within a revolutionary regime, he could express himself in a way that was in accordance with these sentiments. He raised the matter in a way that can be seen as symbolic.

What concerned him was to find out if he could write in accordance with these sentiments or in accordance with this ideology that was not precisely the ideology of the revolution because, although he was in agreement with the revolution in economic and social questions, his philosophical position differed from that of the revolution.

And it is worth bearing this case very much in mind because it is a case that is representative of the kind of writers and artists who show that they are favorably disposed toward the revolution and who want to know what degree of freedom they have within the revolutionary conditions in order to express themselves in accordance with their own sentiments.

This is the group that represents a problem for the revolution, just as the revolution represents a problem for them, and it is the duty of the revolution to be concerned about such cases. It is the duty of the revolution to be concerned about the situation of these artists and these writers because the revolution must aspire to having, not only all the revolutionaries marching in its ranks, but also all the revolutionary artists and intellectuals.

It is possible that the men and women who have a truly revolutionary attitude toward reality do not constitute the greater part of the population, but revolutionaries are the vanguard of the people and revolutionaries must aspire to having all the people marching with them. The revolution cannot renounce having all honest men and women, be they artists and intellectuals or not, marching in its ranks. The revolution must aspire to having all its doubters become revolutionaries. The revolution must try to win the greater part of the people to its ideas, must never renounce being able to count on the majority of the people, being able to count not just on the revolutionaries but also on all honest citizens who, while they may not be revolutionaries, or in other words, while they may not have a revolutionary attitude toward life, are with the revolution.

The revolution should only renounce those who are incorrigibly reactionary, who are incorrigibly counterrevolutionary. And the revolution must have a policy for this part of our people; the revolution must have an attitude concerning this group of intellectuals and writers. The revolution must understand this reality and must therefore act in such a way that this whole sector of artists and intellectuals who are not genuinely revolutionaries will find, within the revolution, a domain where they can work and create, and that their creative spirit, even though they may not be revolutionary writers or artists, will have the opportunity and freedom to express itself, within the revolution.

This means: within the revolution, everything; against the revolution, nothing.

Against the revolution nothing, because the revolution also has its rights and the first right of the revolution is the right to exist, and nobody comes before the right of the revolution to be and to exist. Inasmuch as the revolution represents the interests of the people, inasmuch as the revolution means the interests of the entire nation, nobody can properly claim any right that goes against it.

I believe this is perfectly clear. What are the rights of writers and artists, whether they be revolutionary or non-revolutionary? Within the revolution, everything; against the revolution, there is no right.

And there is no law that is an exception to this for the artists and intellectuals. This is a general principle for all our citizens. It is a basic principle of the revolution. The counterrevolutionaries, by which I mean enemies of the revolution, can have no right that goes against the revolution because the revolution also has rights: the right to exist, the right to develop, the right to win, and who could doubt this right of a people who have said "Homeland or death!" or, in other words, revolution or death?...

The revolution does not aim to asphyxiate art or culture when one of the fundamental goals or intentions of the revolution is to develop art and culture, precisely so that art and culture come to be a real heritage of the people. Just as we have wanted a better life in the material domain for our people, we also want a better life for them in all the spiritual domains, and we want a better life in the cultural domain...

It is time now for you to contribute, in an organized manner, and with all of your enthusiasm, to the tasks that are required by the revolution and to constitute a broad-based organism of all the writers and artists. I don't know whether the matters you have raised here will be discussed in the Congress,[2] but we do know that the Congress is going to meet and that the work it is to do, like that which the Association of Writers and Artists should do, would be a good matter to discuss in our coming meetings. We think that we should meet again; at least we would not like to deprive ourselves of the pleasure and the usefulness of these meetings that, for us too, have represented an occasion for attending to all of these problems. What do I mean by that? That we have to keep talking about these problems. This is to say there is going to be something that has to be

---

[2] This refers to the congress that was established by the *Unión de Escritores y Artistas de Cuba* (UNEAC), Union of Writers and Artists of Cuba.

the occasion for making everyone feel better, and that is knowing the interest the government has in these problems while, at the same time, knowing that the opportunity will arise in the future for discussing all the issues in broadly constituted assemblies. It seems that this should be a cause for satisfaction amongst writers and artists and, this way, we too will continue receiving information and acquiring better knowledge...

Does this mean that, here, we are going to tell people what they have to write? No. Let each one write what they like and if what they write is of no use, that's their problem. If what they paint is of no use, that's their problem. We don't prevent anybody from writing about whatever matter they choose. On the contrary: let each and every one express themselves in the way they think opportune, and let them freely express the idea they want to express. We shall always value their creation through the prism, through the revolutionary perspective. This is also the right of the Revolutionary Government and is as respectable as the right of any person to express what he or she wants to express...

It has been our lot to live through a great historic event... And you, writers and artists, have had the privilege of being eyewitnesses to this revolution; when a revolution is such an important event in human history, it is really worth experiencing a revolution, even if only as a witness...

You have the opportunity to be more than spectators, to be actors in this revolution, and to write about it, to express yourselves about it. And the coming generations, what will they ask of you? You can create magnificent artistic works from the technical point of view but if they say to someone from the next generation, or someone in a hundred years' time, that a writer or an intellectual of this time, lived at the time of the revolution but outside it, without expressing the revolution, without being part of the revolution, it will be difficult for them to understand why, in the coming years, there will be so many, many, people who will want to paint the revolution, will want to write about the revolution and will want to express themselves about the revolution, and they'll be collecting all the data and information to discover what it was like, what happened, how we experienced it...

What should be feared is not this supposed authoritarian judge, this executioner of culture, this product of the imagination that we have been discussing here. Fear other more terrible judges, fear the judges of posterity, fear the future generations who will be, after all, those who will pronounce the last word!

13

NATIONAL LITERACY CAMPAIGN

December 22, 1961

"Next year, we're going to do battle with illiteracy. Next year, we must teach everyone in our country how to read and write." With these words, on August 29, 1960, Fidel Castro had announced that 1961 would be the Year of Education and that the task would have to be carried out by means of a mobilization of all the people. "We'll mobilize all the students and everybody else who knows how to read and write, so they can teach those who don't know how," he said.

The eradication of illiteracy was a political, social and humanitarian pledge — and also a basic prerequisite for using the productive forces on the island.

The most recent census had estimated the illiteracy rate in Cuba at around 37 percent of the population of school age and over, and that figure may well have been conservative. In addition, there were many people who, even though they had received a few years of elementary school and knew how to write their names, had, from lack of practice, become functionally illiterate.

In some parts of the most backward areas in the countryside — especially in the mountains — more than 90 percent of the people did not know how to read and write.

A literacy campaign had been in progress ever since the triumph of the revolution, in the Rebel Army and militias. Members of the detachments of *volunteer teachers[1] and other teachers gave it a tremendous boost.*

What was new about the 1961 Literacy Campaign was that it brought all Cubans into an organized mass effort that extended to all parts of the country. The Conrado Benítez Literacy Brigades, composed of 100,000 young students, were the shock force in that effort. These brigades had been named for a young black teacher who had been murdered by a band of counterrevolutionaries in the mountains in central Cuba.

Members of the "Patria o Muerte" Brigades, mobilized by the labor unions, joined in that work, mainly in and around the cities.

The National Literacy Campaign couldn't be stopped. It continued during the Bay of Pigs attack in April 1961, even when the mercenaries captured several young literacy teachers who had been teaching fishermen and their families. It continued in the mountains and other rural regions while militia and army units were searching for and capturing the bands of counterrevolutionaries in the area, and it was stepped up, with even more energy, when, on November 26, the bodies of Manuel Ascunce Domenech, a young literacy teacher, and Pedro Lantigua, the farmer he was teaching, were found — murdered — in the Escambray Mountains.

On December 22, 1961, the members of the Literacy Army marched victoriously through Havana's José Martí Revolution Square wearing their uniforms and knapsacks and carrying their lanterns. It was a day of triumph and joy. A red flag declaring Cuba to be free of illiteracy was raised. The young people shouted, "Fidel, give us another task!" to which he answered, "Study."

There are practically no illiterates in Cuba

(Report presented by Dr. Armando Hart Dávalos, Minister of Education, at the mass meeting held in Revolution Square, Havana, on December 22, 1961, when Cuba was declared free of illiteracy)[2]

I am going to inform the people about a resolution issued by the Revolutionary Government and about a report on the Literacy Campaign.

The Revolutionary Government has decided to institute a Heroes of the Revolution National Order in homage to our people's sons and daughters who have carried out acts of exceptional heroism while doing their duty for their homeland and for the revolution.

---

[1] During 1960 and 1961, in view of the shortage of teachers who were willing to go to the mountains and other isolated parts of the countryside, the revolution trained three contingents of volunteer teachers at Minas de Frío and in nearby camps in the Sierra Maestra Mountains.

[2] In the personal files of Dr. Armando Hart Dávalos.

Manuel Ascunce Domenech; literacy brigade member Conrado Benítez; and Delfín Sen Cedré, a member of the "Patria o Muerte" Workers' Brigade, heroic victims of imperialism and of the counterrevolution, were killed while carrying out the great task of teaching reading and writing. Therefore, the Revolutionary Government has decided to confer the Heroes of the Revolution National Order on these combatants posthumously.

Comrade Osvaldo Dorticós, President of the Republic, will now remove the flag covering the case that contains the medals and present them to the relatives of Manuel Ascunce Domenech and Delfín Sen Cedré.

Thus, all those who lost their lives in the Literacy Campaign are honored.

Let us observe a minute of silence in honor of all those who have lost their lives in the National Literacy Campaign.

(There is a minute of silence.)

Glory to those who died!

Now, I am going to report to the people of Cuba on the state of the great National Literacy Campaign and read the final report by the National Literacy Commission, which met yesterday to analyze the development and culmination of that campaign.

The National Literacy Commission — on which all of the mass and other revolutionary organizations, the six Provincial Literacy Commissions and the Ministry of Education of the Revolutionary Government are represented — meeting on December 21 in its 10th National Meeting to evaluate the final results of the great Literacy Campaign, jubilantly informs the people of Cuba as follows:

First: At this time of reporting on the final results of the great Literacy Campaign, it is fitting to acknowledge, first of all, the preparatory work that was done by the revolution throughout the insurrectional struggle waged by the Rebel Army and through the efforts made in 1959 and 1960. In those initial efforts, the revolution managed to teach around 100,000 adults how to read and write.

Second: The literacy census that was taken in the Year of Education as a result of the direct mobilization of the people's forces in all urban and rural areas in the country showed that there were 979,207 illiterate adults.

Third: During the Year of Education, 707,000 illiterates were taught how to read and write.

Since, according to reports of the Central Planning Board (JCP), the population of Cuba was 6,933,253 in 1961, and keeping in mind that, for various reasons, 272,000 illiterates weren't taught how to read and write, the illiteracy rate in Cuba has been reduced to 3.9 percent of the total population. This makes Cuba one of the countries with the lowest illiteracy rates in the world, along with the Soviet Union, Czechoslovakia, Switzerland, France, England and Japan.

Fourth: That 3.9 percent of the population that is still illiterate includes 25,000 Haitians living in the agricultural parts of Oriente and Camagüey Provinces, who weren't taught how to read and write in the campaign because they don't know Spanish; those with physical or mental impairments; and those whose advanced age or bad health made it impossible to teach them. Thus, there are practically no illiterates in Cuba.

Fifth: Moreover, the illiteracy rate will never increase but will, instead, decrease, since the people's Revolutionary Government has taken the measures needed to combat illiteracy among the productive forces by providing elementary schooling, planning a follow-up campaign and Workers' Improvement Courses, and promoting the adult education plan that is being implemented by the people's forces.

Sixth: This tremendous revolutionary achievement was carried out by a powerful literacy force consisting of 121,000 people's literacy teachers, 100,000 members of the Conrado Benítez Brigades, 15,000 members of the "Patria o Muerte" Brigades and 35,000 teachers, making a total of 271,000 literacy teachers. Together with the leaders, political cadres and administrative workers in the campaign, this makes an impressive total of over 300,000 workers in the National Literacy Campaign — 300,000 Cubans who dedicated themselves to keeping the promise that Comrade Fidel Castro, our leader, made at the United Nations.

Seventh: The Literacy Campaign has been successful because the momentum of the revolution has developed and guided it. The close coordination and unity of the mass and other revolutionary organizations has been a key factor in this triumph. The people's support and the boost given it by all working sectors has made it possible to achieve this victory.

Eighth: This report is the result of a strict control, of rigorous censuses, for which the National Literacy Commission and the Ministry of Education of the Revolutionary Government take responsibility. The data which serve as the basis for this information, the work methods employed for obtaining them and the grass-roots agencies — provincial and municipal — which supplied them place themselves at the disposal of the Revolutionary Government, the National Leadership of the Integrated Revolutionary Organizations

(ORI) and any international educational agency that may need them to carry out similar work. It is an extremely valuable experience of what the people can do when they take revolutionary power and decide to apply all their energy to achieving a great goal.

Homeland or death!

We have won!

14

SECOND DECLARATION OF HAVANA

February 4, 1962

Following the U.S. Government's and CIA's disaster with the Bay of Pigs invasion, throughout 1961 U.S. strategists discussed ways and means for reorganizing counterrevolutionary activities aimed at the Cuban Revolution. Meanwhile, the Kennedy Administration continued to apply pressure internationally through the Organization of American States (OAS), trying to isolate Cuba – especially in the Americas.

With few exceptions – such as Mexico and the Joao Goulart Administration in Brazil – most of the Latin American regimes joined in those maneuvers in exchange for parts of Cuba's former sugar quota and funds from the so-called Alliance for Progress.

In December 1961, the 8th Consultative Meeting of Foreign Ministers of the OAS was held in the San Rafael Hotel in Punta del Este, Uruguay.

The United States, which was the real promoter of the meeting, worked feverishly to achieve its goal: Cuba's expulsion from the OAS and a collective breaking of diplomatic relations as part of a new plan to overthrow the revolution (a plan that also included economic measures – the tightening of the blockade – and military alternatives).

On January 3, 1962, the State Department issued another of its "White Papers," in which it accused Cuba of being a "Soviet satellite." On January 7, 1962, Secretary of State Dean Rusk declared that the OAS meeting should confront the threat of "Castroism" in Latin America and impose sanctions on Cuba. On January 19, nearly on the eve of the Punta del Este meeting, the U.S. Government circulated a proposal that the OAS member countries adopt "automatic sanctions" against Cuba if the Cuban Government didn't break its ties with the "communist countries" within 60 days.

During a television appearance at that time, Fidel Castro stated, "Cuba is going to wage a battle for all America at Punta del Este, because this battle turns on a key principle: the peoples' right to self-determination and sovereignty... What do the imperialists seek there? The right to intervene in any country in Latin America. Wherever the people begin to rebel, wherever the people begin to demonstrate a lack of conformity with imperialist exploitation, they want to have the right to intervene, even with their armed forces."[1]

Osvaldo Dorticós Torrado, President of Cuba, headed the Cuban delegation to the Punta del Este meeting. He was accompanied by Raúl Roa García, the Cuban Foreign Minister.

In his address, Dorticós said, "I would like to ask the foreign ministers who accuse us — and especially the Secretary of State of the United States — one question here: Is it or isn't it true, in your opinion, that the U.S. Government and the U.S. intelligence services, under Allan Dulles, promoted, financed, directed and supported the bombing of Havana and Santiago de Cuba and the invasion of our country at the Bay of Pigs?...

"Why didn't you get upset then? Why didn't the Organization of American States take action? Why didn't you gentlemen who are accusing Cuba — I'm referring only to those of Cuba's accusers who are present today — confront the United States? Is it that, within the rigorous, strict norms of the Organization of American States, the United States has a special dispensation to act with impunity when it invades another country? If so, what good is the Organization of American States?"[2]

On January 30, 1962, following intensive lobbying in which the U.S. representatives dangled money and promises of all kinds in front of the other delegates, a resolution excluding the Cuban Government from participation in the inter-American system was passed (14 votes in favor, 1 opposed and 6 abstentions).

It stated the following:

"1. The adherence by any member of the Organization of American States to Marxism-Leninism is incompatible with the inter-American system, and the alignment of such a government with the Communist bloc destroys hemispheric unity and solidarity.

---

[1] Nicanor León Cotayo, *El bloqueo a Cuba*, 211-12.
[2] Ibid, 221.

"2. The present Government of Cuba, which has officially identified itself as a Marxist-Leninist government, is incompatible with the aims and principles of the inter-American system.

"3. This incompatibility excludes the present Government of Cuba from participating in the inter-American system.

"4. The Council of the Organization of American States and the bodies and agencies of the inter-American system will speedily adopt the measures required to implement this Resolution."[3]

A few days later, on February 13, 1962, the OAS Council excluded Cuba from that organization.

Some days earlier, on February 4, Havana was the scene of one of the largest and most emotion-packed mass meetings in the history of the country. Over a million Cubans filled José Martí Revolution Square to overflowing and, after Fidel Castro read a very different document — the Second Declaration of Havana — they approved it by raising their hands high.

✻

This great mass of humanity has said "enough!" and has begun to march

On May 18, 1895, on the eve of his death from a Spanish bullet through the heart, José Martí, apostle of our independence, said in an unfinished letter to his friend Manuel Mercado:

> Now I am able to write... I am in danger each day of giving my life for my country and for my obligation... of preventing in time — through Cuba's independence — the United States from extending its control over the Antilles and consequently falling with that much more force upon our countries of America. Whatever I have done up to now, and whatever I shall do, has been with that aim...
>
> I have lived inside the monster and know its entrails; and my sling is the sling of David.

In 1895, Martí already pointed out the danger hovering over America and called imperialism by its name: imperialism. He pointed out to the people of Latin America that more than anyone, they had a stake in ensuring that Cuba did not succumb to the greed

---

[3] Ibid, 239.

of the Yankee, so scornful of the peoples of Latin America. And with his own blood, shed for Cuba and America, he wrote the words that posthumously, in homage to his memory, the people of Cuba place at the head of this declaration.

Sixty-seven years have passed. Puerto Rico was converted into a colony and is still a colony saturated with military bases. Cuba also fell into the clutches of imperialism. Their troops occupied our territory. The Platt Amendment was imposed on our first constitution, as a humiliating clause that sanctioned the odious right of foreign intervention. Our riches passed into their hands, our history was falsified, our government and our politics were entirely molded in the interests of the overseers; the nation was subjected to 60 years of political, economic and cultural suffocation.

But Cuba arose. Cuba was able to redeem itself from the bastard guardianship. Cuba broke the chains that tied its fortunes to those of the imperial oppressor, redeemed its riches, reclaimed its culture, and unfurled its banner of Free Territory and People of America.

Now the United States will never again be able to use Cuba's strength against America, but conversely, dominating the majority of the other Latin American states, the United States is attempting to use the strength of America against Cuba.

What is the history of Cuba but the history of Latin America? And what is the history of Latin America but the history of Asia, Africa and Oceania? And what is the history of all these peoples but the history of the most pitiless and cruel exploitation by imperialism throughout the world?

The movement of the dependent and colonial peoples is a phenomenon of universal character that agitates the world and marks the final crisis of imperialism.

Cuba and Latin America are part of the world. Our problems form part of the problems engendered by the general crisis of imperialism and the struggle of the subjugated peoples; the clash between the world that is being born and the world that is dying. The odious and brutal campaign unleashed against our nation expresses the desperate as well as futile effort that the imperialists are making to prevent the liberation of the peoples. Cuba hurts the imperialists in a special way. What is it that is hidden behind the Yankees' hate of the Cuban Revolution? What is it that rationally explains the conspiracy, uniting for the same aggressive purpose the most powerful and rich imperialist power in the contemporary world and the oligarchies of an entire continent, which together are supposed to represent a population of 350 million human beings, against a small country of only seven million inhabitants, economically underdeveloped, without financial or military means to threaten the security or economy of any other country? What unites them and stirs them up is fear. What explains it is fear. Not fear of the Cuban Revolution but fear of the Latin American revolution. Not fear of the workers, peasants, intellectuals, students and progressive layers of the middle strata which by revolutionary means have taken power in Cuba; but fear that the workers, peasants, students, intellectuals and progressive sectors of the middle strata will, by revolutionary means, take power in the oppressed and hungry countries exploited by the Yankee monopolies and reactionary oligarchies of America; fear that the plundered people of the continent will seize the arms from their oppressors and, like Cuba, declare themselves free people of America.

By crushing the Cuban Revolution they hope to dispel the fear that torments them, the specter of the revolution that threatens them. By liquidating the Cuban Revolution, they hope to liquidate the revolutionary spirit of the people. They imagine in their delirium that Cuba is an exporter of revolutions. In their sleepless, merchants' and usurers' minds there is the idea that revolutions can be bought, sold, rented, loaned, exported and imported like some piece of merchandise.

But the development of history, the ascending march of humanity does not hold back, nor can it be held back. The forces that impel the people, who are the real makers of history, determined by the material conditions of their existence and the aspirations for higher goals of well-being and liberty which emerge when the progress of man in the fields of science, technology and culture make it possible, are superior to the will and the terror unleashed by the ruling oligarchies.

The subjective conditions of each country, that is to say, the conscious factor, organization, leadership, can accelerate or retard the revolution, according to its greater or lesser degree of development, but sooner or later, in each historical epoch, when the objective conditions mature, consciousness is acquired, the organization is formed, the leadership emerges and the revolution takes place.

Whether this takes place peacefully or in painful labor does not depend on the revolutionists, it depends on the reactionary forces of the old society, who resist the birth of the new society engendered by the contradictions carried in the womb of the old society. The revolution is in history like the doctor who assists at the birth of a new life. It does not needlessly use the tools of force, but will use them without hesitation whenever necessary to help the birth, a birth that brings to the enslaved and exploited masses the hope of a new and better life.

In many countries of Latin America the revolution is today inevitable. That fact is not determined by anyone's will. It is determined by the horrifying conditions of exploitation in which American man lives, the development of the revolutionary consciousness of the masses, the world crisis of imperialism and the universal movement of struggle of the subjugated peoples.

What is the attitude of Yankee imperialism before the objective reality and the historically inexorable Latin American revolution? To prepare to wage a colonial war against the peoples of Latin America; to create an apparatus of force, the political pretexts and the pseudo-legal instruments subscribed to by the reactionary oligarchies to repress with blood and fire the struggle of the Latin American peoples.

This policy of gradual strangulation of the sovereignty of the Latin American nations and of a free hand to intervene in their internal affairs culminated in the recent meeting of foreign ministers at Punta del Este. Yankee imperialism gathered the ministers together to wrest from them — through political pressure and unprecedented economic blackmail in collusion with a group of the most discredited rulers of this continent — the renunciation of the national sovereignty of our peoples and the consecration of the Yankees' odious right of intervention in the internal affairs of Latin America; the submission of the peoples entirely to the will of the United States of America, against which all our great men fought, from Bolívar to Sandino.

At Punta del Este a great ideological battle unfolded between the Cuban Revolution and Yankee imperialism. Who did they represent there, for whom did each speak? Cuba represented the people; the United States represented the monopolies. Cuba spoke for America's exploited masses; the United States for the exploiting, oligarchic and imperialist interests; Cuba for sovereignty; the United States for intervention; Cuba for the nationalization of foreign enterprises; the United States for new investments by foreign capital. Cuba for culture; the United States for ignorance. Cuba for agrarian reform; the United States for great landed estates. Cuba for the industrialization of America; the United States for underdevelopment. Cuba for creative work; the United States for the sabotage and counterrevolutionary terror practiced by its agents — the destruction of sugarcane fields and factories, the bombing by their pirate planes of a peaceful people's labor. Cuba for the murdered literacy teachers; the United States for the assassins. Cuba for bread; the United States for hunger. Cuba for equality; the United States for privilege and discrimination. Cuba for truth; the United States for lies. Cuba for liberation; the United States for oppression. Cuba for the bright future of humanity; the United States for the past without hope. Cuba for the heroes who fell at the Bay of Pigs to save the country from foreign domination; the United States for the mercenaries and traitors who serve the foreigner against their country. Cuba for peace among peoples, the United States for aggression and war. Cuba for socialism; the United States for capitalism.

What Alliance for Progress can serve as encouragement to those 107 million men and women of our America, the backbone of labor in the cities and fields, whose dark skin — black, mestizo, mulatto, Indian — inspires scorn in the new colonialists? How are they — who with bitter impotence have seen how in Panama there is one wage scale for Yankees and another for Panamanians, who are regarded as an inferior race — going to put any trust in the supposed Alliance?

What Cuba can give to the people, and has already given, is its example. And what does the Cuban Revolution teach? That revolution is possible, that the people can make it, that in the contemporary world there are no forces capable of halting the liberation movement of the peoples.

No nation in Latin America is weak — because each forms part of a family of 200 million brothers, who suffer the same miseries, who harbor the same sentiments, who have the same enemy; who dream about the same better future and who count upon the solidarity of all honest men and women throughout the world.

Great as the epic of Latin American independence was, heroic as that struggle was, today's generation of Latin Americans is called upon to engage in an epic that is even greater and more decisive for humanity. That struggle was for liberation from Spanish colonial power, from a decadent Spain invaded by the armies of Napoleon. Today the call for struggle is for liberation from the most powerful world imperialist center, from the strongest force of world imperialism and to render humanity a greater service than that rendered by our predecessors.

But this struggle, to a greater extent than the earlier struggle, will be waged by the masses, will be carried out by the people; the people are going to play a much more important role now than they did then, the leaders are less important and will be less important in this struggle than in the one before.

This epic before us is going to be written by the hungry Indian masses, the peasants without land, the exploited workers. It is going to be written by the progressive masses, the honest and brilliant intellectuals, who so greatly abound in our suffering Latin American countries. Struggles of masses and ideas. An epic that will be carried forward by our people, despised and maltreated by imperialism. Our people, unreckoned with until today, who are now beginning to shake off their slumber. Imperialism considered us a weak and submissive flock, and now it begins to be terrified of that flock; a gigantic flock of 200 million Latin Americans in whom Yankee monopoly capitalism now sees its gravediggers.

This toiling humanity, these inhumanly exploited, these paupers, controlled by the system of whip and overseer, have not been reckoned with or have been little reckoned with. From the dawn of independence their fate has been the same: Indians, gauchos, mestizos, zambos, quadroons, whites without property or income, all this human mass that formed the ranks of the "nation," which never reaped any benefits, which fell by the millions, which was cut into bits, which won independence from the mother country for the bourgeoisie, which was shut out from its share of the rewards, which continued to occupy the lowest rung on the ladder of social benefits, continued to die of hunger, curable diseases and neglect, because for them there were never enough life-giving goods — ordinary bread, a hospital bed, the medicine that cures, the hand that aids.

But now from one end of the continent to the other they are signaling with clarity that the hour has come — the hour of their redemption. Now this anonymous mass, this America of color, somber, taciturn America, which all over the continent sings with the same sadness and disillusionment, now this mass is beginning to enter conclusively into its own history, is beginning to write that history with its own blood, is beginning to suffer and die for it.

Now in the fields and mountains of America, on its slopes and prairies and in its jungles, in the wilderness or in the traffic of its cities, this world is beginning to erupt. Anxious hands are stretched forth, ready to die for what is theirs, to win those rights that were laughed at by one and all for 500 years. Yes, now history will have to take the poor of America into account, the exploited and spurned of Latin America, who have decided to begin writing history for themselves for all time. Already they can be seen on the roads, on foot, day after day, in an endless march of hundreds of kilometers to the governmental "eminences," there to obtain their rights.

Already they can be seen armed with stones, sticks, machetes, in one direction and another, each day, occupying lands, sinking hooks into the land that belongs to them and defending it with their lives. They can be seen carrying signs, slogans, flags, letting them flap in the mountain or prairie winds. And the wave of anger, of demands for justice, of claims for rights, which is beginning to sweep the lands of Latin America, will not stop. That wave will swell with every passing day. For that wave is composed of the greatest number, the majorities in every respect, those whose labor amasses the wealth and turns the wheels of history. Now they are awakening from the long, brutalizing sleep to which they had been subjected.

For this great mass of humanity has said, "enough!" and has begun to march. And their giant march will not be halted until they conquer true independence for which they have vainly died more than once. Today, however, those who die will die like the Cubans at the Bay of Pigs. They will die for their own, true and never-to-be-surrendered independence.

Homeland or death!

We will win!

THE PEOPLE OF CUBA
Havana, Cuba
Free Territory of America
February 4, 1962

15

BLOCKADE

February 7, 1962

As soon as it had pushed through the resolution on Cuba's expulsion from the Organization of American States (OAS) — without even waiting for the OAS Council to begin to implement it — the Kennedy Administration took a new step in the program that had been drawn up after the Bay of Pigs. On February 3, 1962, President John F. Kennedy signed Executive Order 3447, which established a total blockade on all trade between the United States and Cuba as of 12:01 a.m. on February 7 of that year.

Economically, this would be the culmination of an escalation of measures imposed by the U.S. Government and U.S. companies since 1959 to cause Cuba difficulties and paralyze its functioning. Those measures included the August 1959 cancellation of credit that had been granted to improve the electric power network; the U.S. refineries' refusal, in June 1960, to process Soviet crude oil; the first reduction of Cuba's sugar quota, which President Eisenhower ordered in July 1960; and subsequent Presidential orders that eliminated Cuba's sugar quota altogether while closing off exports to Cuba and stopping U.S. purchases of other Cuban products, such as fruit and nickel concentrate.

Legally, it was necessary to construct a very complex legislative scaffolding in order to justify, within U.S. laws, what was, manifestly, an illegal action: the imposition of wartime measures against a tiny neighboring nation in times of peace.

As outstanding jurists have emphasized, there is no norm of international law that justifies a "peaceful blockade," because, ever since the

London Naval Conference of 1909, it has been recognized that a blockade is an act of war and that it may be used only between belligerents.[1]

Therefore, the United States resorted to the inexact term "embargo" — when, in fact, it doesn't consist, as that term suggests, of retaining a debtor's property until they have fulfilled the obligations they contracted in a legitimate way or of simply canceling the trade between two countries. Rather, over the last four decades, the United States has harassed and done its utmost to disrupt Cuba's normal trade and financial activities with other countries. That policy of blockade, according to still incomplete figures, has cost Cuba more than US$60 billion during this period.

Nor was Kennedy's Executive Order of February 3, 1962, the imposition of the U.S. blockade of Cuba, the end of the legal attack. In later years, new orders were incorporated to tighten the blockade. Some measures were eased during the Carter Administration, but they were tightened again when the "new right" in the United States held sway in government and became particularly acute with the 1992 Torricelli Act and 1996 Helms-Burton Act, following the collapse of the Soviet Union.

Presidential executive order no. 3447 of the United States of America, February 3, 1962

Embargo on all trade with Cuba

WHEREAS the Eighth Meeting of Consultation of Ministers of Foreign Affairs, Serving as Organ of Consultation in Application of the Inter-American Treaty of Reciprocal Assistance, in its Final Act resolved that the present Government of Cuba is incompatible with the principles and objectives of the Inter-American system; and, in the light of the subversive offensive of Sino-Soviet Communism with which the Government of Cuba is publicly aligned, urged the member states to take those steps that they may consider appropriate for their individual and collective self-defense;

WHEREAS the Congress of the United States, in section 620(a) of the Foreign Assistance Act of 1961 (75 Stat. 445), as amended, has authorized the President to establish and maintain an embargo upon all trade between the United States and Cuba; and

---

[1] Dr. Olga Miranda Bravo, *Cuba/USA: nacionalizaciones y bloqueo* (Cuba/USA: Nationalizations and Blockade) (Havana: Editorial de Ciencias Sociales, 1996), 40-6.

WHEREAS the United States, in accordance with its international obligations, is prepared to take all necessary actions to promote national and hemispheric security by isolating the present Government of Cuba and thereby reducing the threat posed by its alignment with the communist powers:

NOW, THEREFORE, I, JOHN F. KENNEDY, President of the United States of America, acting under the authority of section 620(a) of the Foreign Assistance Act of 1961 (75 Stat.445), as amended, do

1. Hereby proclaim an embargo upon trade between the United States and Cuba in accordance with paragraphs 2 and 3 of this proclamation.
2. Hereby prohibit, effective 12.01 A.M. Eastern Standard Time, February 7, 1962, the importation into the United States of all goods of Cuban origin and all goods exported from or through Cuba; and I hereby authorize and direct the Secretary of the Treasury to carry out such prohibition, to make such exceptions thereto, by license or otherwise, as he determines to be consistent with the effective operation of the embargo hereby proclaimed, and to promulgate such rules and regulations as may be necessary to perform such functions.
3. AND FURTHER, I do hereby direct the Secretary of Commerce, under the provisions of the Export Control Act of 1949, as amended (50 U.S.C. App. 2021-2032) to continue to carry out the prohibition of all exports from the United States to Cuba, and I hereby authorize him, under that Act, to continue, make, modify, or revoke exceptions from such prohibition.

(Signed by President John F. Kennedy with the seal of the United States of America, in Washington, on February 3 in the year of Our Lord nineteen sixty-two).

16

RATION CARDS

March 12, 1962

It may not be easy for Cubans today to remember this date. On March 12, 1962, as a result of the total blockade ordered by the U.S. Government, the Revolutionary Government passed Law 1015, which established a ration system throughout the country.

The Agrarian Reform and the increase in job opportunities that followed the triumph of the revolution meant that millions of people became consumers, and the illusion of abundance that capitalist display cases had offered quickly disappeared.

Months before, a shortage of food and industrial products had hit hard. It was only logical. In Cuba's underdeveloped, dependent economic structure, its imports from foreign markets — especially from the United States — served as an umbilical cord supplying the daily needs of the people, industry, transportation and public services. Cuba was notorious for not having any wholesale warehouses, drawing its supplies directly from ports and other cities in the southern part of the United States.

Because of the historical deformation of its plantation economy, Cuba could not meet many of its food needs. One study showed that, in the years just before the triumph of the revolution, Cuba had to import 60 percent of the grain, 37 percent of the vegetables, 41 percent of the cereals, 84 percent of the fat, 69 percent of the canned meat, 80 percent of the canned fruit and

83 percent of the cookies and candy that were consumed in the country.[1]

It is obvious that, in order to be able to purchase those products, Cuba had to export sugar and, to a lesser extent, nickel and tobacco products. When the United States closed its doors to a market that it had been molding for almost 200 years – from before the 13 colonies declared their independence from England – Cuba could not immediately redirect its foreign trade and compensate for this harsh blow.

However, the solidarity of the Soviet Union and other socialist countries helped to provide basic foodstuffs and enabled the people to survive.

Rationing was the necessary response to the state of undeclared war to which Cuba was subjected, in conditions in which the nation's defense was swallowing up enormous resources and human energy. In particular, it was the expression of a political principle: to share whatever food there was, whether much or little, among everybody, so nobody would be left out; not to allow the law of money and of supply and demand to be imposed, but to ensure justice; and not to allow intolerable inequalities to arise in the heart of society between those with smaller incomes and those with larger ones.

Thus, rationing was linked to the idea of the people's unity and national consensus as bases for holding out in the long term against the U.S. policies of blockade, permanent hostility and the undermining of the revolution.

In later years, with the consolidation of a state of relative peace and the gradual reestablishment of the economy, new market formulas appeared; supplies of products and durable goods were enlarged and diversified; and rationing was turned into a kind of social guarantee for all families, a vital minimum strongly subsidized by the government. This allowed them to acquire a supply of staples at constant, low prices, thus bolstering the real income of working people.

Some economists, both in and outside Cuba, have debated whether the continuation of the system of rationing for nearly four decades has or has not been a factor that has worked against increasing productivity and economic efficiency, because of the egalitarianism it obviously embodies.

The answer to this problem cannot be technocratic. To answer it, you must place yourself in Cuba's specific conditions – a poor country subjected to a blockade imposed by the strongest power in the world, which uses its level of wealth as a permanent element of ideological penetration and confusion. In those conditions, Cuba must provide its citizens with the certainty of solidarity and the most equitable possible distribution of those goods that are available.

It has been an unwritten truth since 1962 that, as long as the blockade and threats from abroad continue, ration cards may be an effective tool with

---

[1] Oscar Pino-Santos, *El imperialismo norteamericano en la economía de Cuba* (U.S. Imperialism in Cuba's Economy) (Havana: Editorial de Ciencias Sociales, 1973), 101-2.

which to confront adverse situations. This was confirmed in the 1990s at the time of the economic crisis, the application of the Torricelli and Helms-Burton Acts and Cuba's "special period in times of peace."

Setting up a system of rationing
(Law 1015, March 12, 1962)[2]

Whereas: The development of our revolutionary process has, through urban employment, the reduction of rents for housing, the elimination of payments for schooling and other analogous measures, meant a considerable increase in the urban population's buying power;

Whereas: by turning the former tenant farmers and squatters — who, as small farmers, used to be exploited by large landowners, companies and middlemen — into landowners and by increasing employment in the countryside; whilst the Agrarian Reform has given farmers and former agricultural workers — now turned into the members of cooperatives and state farms — a buying power that immediately raised the level of consumption of agricultural products in the rural areas and created a demand for manufactured articles in those areas that is many times the demand that existed in January 1959;

Whereas: the increase in agricultural and industrial production never achieved before is, however, limited by the brutal economic wall that U.S. imperialism has raised against our national economy by means of the blockade on sales of raw materials, spare parts, fertilizers, pesticides and other things, which has forced our agriculture and industry to make abrupt changes in the organization of their productive resources and therefore prevents the agrarian and industrial production of certain articles from meeting the growing demand at this time;

Whereas: counterrevolutionaries and other individuals who are hostile to the well-being of society have taken advantage of this situation of the relative scarcity of certain articles to engage in speculation, promote campaigns urging people to hoard, and arouse uncertainty among consumers concerning articles whose supplies are large enough to meet present consumption needs; and

Whereas: it is the duty of the Revolutionary Government to

---

[2] *Leyes del Gobierno Revolucionario de Cuba* (Laws of the Revolutionary Government of Cuba) (Havana: Editorial Nacional de Cuba, 1963), XLII, March-May 1962, 5-9.

confront this abnormal situation by organizing a form of distribution that is equitable and which gives all parts of the citizenry equal access to the articles of standard consumption, thus eliminating the distribution defects that have arisen as a result of the situation described above,

Therefore: making use of the powers conferred on it, the Council of Ministers resolves to issue the following:

Law 1015
Better Distribution of Supplies

Article 1. In order to achieve better distribution of the supplies of articles of standard consumption, a National Board for the Distribution of Supplies is created.

Article 2. The National Board for the Distribution of Supplies will be composed of a representative of the National Institute of Agrarian Reform (INRA), a representative of the Ministry of Industry, a representative of the Ministry of Domestic Trade, a representative of the Ministry of Labor, a representative of the Executive Committee of the Central Organization of Cuban Trade Unions (CTC), a representative of the Committees for the Defense of the Revolution (CDRs) and a representative of the Federation of Cuban Women (FMC).

Article 3. The National Board for the Distribution of Supplies is empowered to

a. prepare, after consultation with the Council of Ministers, a list of consumer articles that, for justified reasons, should be rationed, either locally or nationally;

b. prepare, after consultation with the Council of Ministers, a system of rationing that should be adopted with regard to each article and the quantities of each that should be distributed to the population;

c. prepare, after consultation with the Council of Ministers, the relative corrections that should be made concerning supplies of products that are rationed to private and government-run industry and to the businesses in the private and government-run networks of restaurants and cafeterias;

d. organize, after consultation with the Council of Ministers, a system of rationing and its implementation and decide on which governmental and people's agencies should take part in implementing and overseeing the rationing system; and

e. propose to the Council of Ministers as many measures as it deems necessary to ensure the smooth functioning of rationing.

Article 4. Any legal provisions and/or regulations that go counter to the implementation of what is set forth in this Law are annulled. This Law will go into effect upon its publication in the Official Gazette of the Republic.

Therefore: I order that this Law be implemented and carried out in full.

Dr. Fidel Castro Ruz
Prime Minister of the Revolutionary Government

17

OPERATION MONGOOSE: THE DIRTY WAR

March 14, 1962

This is one of many dates marking the general plan that the Kennedy Administration adopted in spring 1961 in response to the U.S. resentment and desire for revenge following the crushing defeat of the Bay of Pigs invasion.

On April 22, 1961, the President of the United States assigned General Maxwell Taylor the task of investigating the causes of the disaster the United States had suffered at the Bay of Pigs.

The Taylor report, issued on June 13, brought out the mistakes made by the CIA, which became the scapegoat for the failure and whose main officials were removed in the following months. The work of covert action was redefined. Special Group 5412 was reconstituted with power over CIA missions, and General Maxwell Taylor was named as its head.

General Taylor had recommended to Kennedy that new guidelines be drawn up for political, military, economic and propaganda actions against Fidel Castro.

In late 1961, the U.S. President put General Edward Lansdale in charge of drawing up a secret plan of operations aimed at "helping Cuba" topple the communist regime. That program was given the code name Operation Mongoose. In subsequent months, it was reworked, refocused and readjusted. Its general philosophy consisted of promoting destabilizing activities inside Cuba — such as acts of sabotage, the creation and support of bands of armed counterrevolutionaries, assassination attempts and propaganda actions. At the same time, the economic blockade would reduce the capacities of Cuba's economy, thus promoting discontent among the people, splitting the revolutionary leadership and finally bringing about an internal uprising by the Cuban people − or by a section of them − which would serve as a pretext for direct military intervention by the U.S. armed forces.

A special enlarged group reporting directly to President Kennedy was created to direct the plan. Attorney General Robert Kennedy played a key role in this group.

On January 19, 1962, in a new meeting of the group, Robert Kennedy declared that the solution of the Cuban problem was a priority issue for the U.S. Government. He urged the participants to devote all of their time, money, efforts and human resources into implementing the program and emphasized that special attention should be given to espionage, with a view to acts of sabotage and the future use of U.S. military forces.[1]

To support that project, the U.S. Government created Task Force W and built an enormous CIA station in southern Florida.

On March 14, 1962, General Maxwell Taylor, head of the Special Group (Augmented), issued a series of guidelines for Operation Mongoose, which explicitly stated that, in the effort to overthrow the Cuban Government, the United States would make maximum use of the native resources, both internal and external, although it recognized that final success would require decisive military intervention by the United States. Moreover, the said native resources would be used, as they developed, to prepare and justify that intervention and, from then on, to support and facilitate it.[2]

Two days later, on March 16, in the presence of the special enlarged group, President Kennedy personally approved those guidelines.

From January through August 1962, there were 5,780 acts of sabotage, terrorism and subversion; 716 of them damaged important economic and social targets. In the Escambray Mountains alone, the number of bands of armed counterrevolutionaries increased from 42 in March to 79 in September. The number of counterrevolutionary groups illegally sent into the country increased, as did the burning of cane fields, plans for assassination attempts, espionage and enemy reconnaissance flights.[3]

On July 25, in a memorandum to President Kennedy, General Lansdale proposed four alternatives for action:

---

[1] *Peligros y principios. La Crisis de Octubre desde Cuba* (Dangers and Principles: The October Missile Crisis from Cuba) (Havana: Editorial Verde Olivo, 1992), 65.

[2] Fabián Escalante Font, *The Secret War: CIA Covert Operations Against Cuba, 1959-62* (Melbourne: Ocean Press, 1995).

[3] *Peligros y principios*, 66.

1. *To cancel operational plans, treat Cuba as a member of the Communist bloc and protect the hemisphere from it.*

2. *To bring all possible kinds of pressure to bear — diplomatic, economic, psychological, etc. — so as to overthrow Castro's Communist regime without the overt use of the U.S. Army.*

3. *To have the United States pledge to help the Cubans to overthrow Castro's Communist regime by means of step-by-step phases, including the use of U.S. military forces if required at the last minute.*

4. *To use an act of provocation and overthrow Castro's Communist regime by means of U.S. military force.*[4]

In fact, at that time, the U.S. Government and Armed Forces were already developing the various alternatives for direct military action against Cuba.

The failure of the various facets of Operation Mongoose — which, in one of General Lansdale's original versions, had predicted that the Revolutionary Government would be overthrown in eight months — led those in charge to opt for even more energetic measures. On August 20, 1962, General Maxwell Taylor reported to President Kennedy that the Special Group (Augmented) saw no possibility of Fidel Castro's government being deposed by means of internal subversion and that the group favored putting a more aggressive Mongoose program into effect.

Knowledge of these antecedents is required in order to understand what took place later on, in October 1962, when a crisis broke out that pushed the world to the brink of nuclear war.

✳

No time, money, effort or manpower is to be spared

(Excerpts from the U.S. Senate Committee that investigated Operation Mongoose as part of its report on "Alleged Assassination Plots Involving Foreign Leaders", 1975)

In November 1962 the proposal for a major new covert action program to overthrow Castro was developed. The President's Assistant, Richard Goodwin, and General Edward Lansdale, who was experienced in counterinsurgency operations, played major staff roles in creating this program, which was named Operation MONGOOSE. Goodwin and Lansdale worked closely with Robert Kennedy, who took an active interest in this preparatory stage, and Goodwin advised the President that Robert Kennedy "would be the most effective commander" of the proposed operation. In a memorandum to Robert Kennedy outlining the MONGOOSE

---

[4] Ibid, 66-7.

proposal, Lansdale stated that a "picture of the situation has emerged clearly enough to indicate what needs to be done and to support your sense of urgency concerning Cuba."

At the end of the month, President Kennedy issued a memorandum recording his decision to begin the MONGOOSE project to "use our available assets [deleted] to help Cuba over-throw the Communist regime."

The establishment of Operation MONGOOSE resulted in important organizational changes.

A new control group, the Special Group (Augmented) (SGA), was created to oversee Operation MONGOOSE. The SGA comprised the regular Special Group members (ie, McGeorge Bundy, Alexis Johnson of the Department of State, Roswell Gilpatric of the Department of Defense, John McCone [of the CIA], and General Lyman Lemnitzer of the Joint Chiefs) augmented by Attorney General Robert Kennedy and General Maxwell Taylor. Although Secretary of State Rusk and Secretary of Defense McNamara were not formal members of the Special Group or the Special Group (Augmented), they sometimes attended meetings.

In late 1961 or early 1962, William Harvey was put in charge of the CIA's Task Force W, the CIA unit for MONGOOSE operations. Task Force W operated under guidance form the Special Group (Augmented) and employed a total of approximately 400 people at CIA headquarters and its Miami Station. McCone and Harvey were the principal CIA participants in Operation MONGOOSE. Although Helms attended only 7 of the 40 MONGOOSE meetings, he was significantly involved, and he testified that he "was as interested" in MONGOOSE as were Harvey and McCone.

Lansdale's concept for Operation MONGOOSE envisioned a first step involving the development of leadership elements "a very necessary political basis" among the Cubans opposed to Castro. At the same time, he sought to develop "means to infiltrate Cuba successfully" and to organize "cells and activities inside Cuba [deleted] who could work secretly and safely." Lansdale's plan was designed so as not to "arouse premature actions, not to bring great reprisals on the people there and abort any eventual success."

On January 19, 1962, a meeting of principal MONGOOSE participants was held in Attorney General Kennedy's office. Notes taken at the meeting by George McManus, Helms' Executive Assistant, contain the following passages:

"Conclusion Overthrow of Castro is Possible

"[deleted] a solution to the Cuban problem today carried top priority in U.S. Government. No time, money — or manpower is to be spared."

"Yesterday [deleted] the President had indicated to him that the final chapter had not been written — it's got to be done and will be done."

McManus attributed the words "the top priority in the U.S. Government — no time, money, effort or manpower is to be spared" to the Attorney General [Robert Kennedy].

On January 18, 1962, Lansdale assigned 32 planning tasks to the agencies participating in MONGOOSE... The 32 tasks comprised a variety of activities, ranging from intelligence collection to planning for "use of U.S. military force to support the Cuban popular movement" and developing an operational schedule for sabotage actions inside Cuba. In focusing on intelligence collection, propaganda, and various sabotage actions, Lansdale's tasks were consistent with the underlying strategy of MONGOOSE to build gradually toward an internal revolt of the Cuban people...

The SGA approved Lansdale's 32 tasks for planning purposes on January 30, 1962. On February 20, Lansdale detailed a six-phase schedule for MONGOOSE, designed to culminate in October 1962 with an "open revolt and overthrow of the Communist regime." As one of the operations for this "Resistance" phase, Lansdale listed "attacks on the cadre of the regime, including key leaders." Lansdale's plan stated:

> "This should be a 'Special Target' operation [deleted]. Gangster elements might provide the best recruitment potential for actions against police — G2 (intelligence) officials."...

The Kennedy Administration pressed the MONGOOSE operation with vigorous language. Although the collection of intelligence information was the central objective of MONGOOSE until August 1962, sabotage and paramilitary actions were also conducted, including a major sabotage operation aimed at a large Cuban copper mine. Lansdale described the sabotage acts as involving "blowing up bridges to stop communications and blowing up certain production plants." During the Missile Crisis in the fall of 1962, sabotage was increasingly urged.

On August 20, Taylor told the President that the SGA saw no likelihood that Castro's Government would be overturned by internal means without direct United States military intervention, and that the SGA favored a more aggressive MONGOOSE program. On August 23, McGeorge Bundy issued NSC Memorandum No. 181, which stated that, at the President's directive, "the line of activity projected for Operation MONGOOSE Plan B plus should be developed with all possible speed." On August 30, the SGA instructed the CIA to submit a list of possible sabotage targets and noted that: "The Group, by reacting to this list, could define the limits within which the Agency could operate on its own initiative."

The onset of the Cuban Missile Crisis initially caused a reversion to the stepped-up Course B plan. At an SGA meeting on October 4, 1962, Robert Kennedy stated that the President "is concerned about progress on the MONGOOSE program and feels that more priority should be given to trying to mount sabotage operations." The Attorney General urged that "massive activity" be undertaken within the MONGOOSE framework. In response to the proposal, the SGA decided that "considerably more sabotage" should be undertaken, and that "all efforts should be made to develop new and imaginative approaches with the possibility of getting rid of the Castro regime." However, on October 30, 1962, the Special Group (Augmented) ordered a halt to all sabotage operations...

Helms testified that the "intense" pressure exerted by the Kennedy Administration to overthrow Castro had led him to perceive that the CIA was acting within the scope of its authority in attempting Castro's assassination, even though assassination was never directly ordered. He said:

"I believe it was the policy at the time to get rid of Castro and if killing him was one of the things that was to be done in this connection, that was within what was expected. I remember vividly (the pressure to overthrow Castro) was very intense."

Helms stated that this pressure intensified during the period of Operation MONGOOSE and continued through much of 1963. As the pressure increased, "obviously the extent of the means that one thought were available [deleted] increased too."

Helms recalled that during the MONGOOSE period, "it was made abundantly clear [deleted] to everybody involved in the operation that the desire was to get rid of the Castro regime and to get rid of Castro [deleted] the point was that no limitations were put on this injunction."

18

THE DENUNCIATION OF SECTARIANISM

March 26, 1962

The main revolutionary forces that opposed the Batista dictatorship — first of all, the July 26 Movement (Movimiento 26 de Julio) and the Rebel Army (Ejército Rebelde), and, with them, the March 13 Revolutionary Directorate (Directorio Revolucionario 13 de Marzo) and the People's Socialist Party (Partido Socialista Popular) — were separate entities at the time of the revolution on January 1, 1959, though they cooperated and had dialogs with one another.

In the new stage that was ushered in, it was necessary to unite all the people in the long struggle to defend, consolidate and advance the revolution. As the political objectives of complete national liberation, anti-imperialism and socialism became more clearly defined, unity became even more necessary.

Right from the beginning, under Fidel Castro's leadership, the revolution had to take a stand against various forms of exclusion and sectarianism, such as those that some of the guerrillas and combatants in the underground struggle in the cities; some of the veterans of the Rebel Army and members of the workers', farmers' and student militias; and some of the old communists who had belonged to the old Marxist-Leninist party for between 15 and 20 years expressed for the members of other organizations.

At the highest level of the revolutionary leadership and among the main leaders of the various organizations, however, a sense of historic responsibility, generosity and the larger view prevailed.

The popular and prestigious Blas Roca Calderío, General Secretary of the People's Socialist Party since 1934, set an outstanding example. He turned over the flags of his organization to the head of the revolution, placed his party under Fidel's leadership and expressed his decision to join the ranks of the new, unified organization of all Cuban Revolutionaries.

In 1960, an integrated political leadership began to function in practice, meeting informally as a consultative body to analyze important decisions.

In 1961, the process of fusion at the base and of the creation of the first leadership structures were initiated. April 16 of that year, the date on which the socialist character of the revolution was proclaimed, was taken as a milestone marking the appearance of a new party.

Serious mistakes were made, however, when the nuclei of the Integrated Revolutionary Organizations (Organizaciones Revolucionarias Integradas, ORI), embryo of the nascent political vanguard, were created.

Since the People's Socialist Party had the most organizational experience, Aníbal Escalante was appointed Organizing Secretary of the ORI. He began to use his key position to promote a sectarian policy in line with his craving for personal power. Claiming that he should direct the party and decide on everything it did, Aníbal Escalante tried to turn himself into a kingpin, in charge of appointing the main cadres in the country.

He appointed yes-men to important posts (passing over men and women of great merit who had fought for the revolution but didn't belong to the PSP or who didn't subordinate themselves to him) and placed the main focus on controlling the party apparatus and State Security. At the grass-roots level, the party cells created as a result of these twisted concepts were weak, functioned apart from and behind the backs of the workers, and often confused their role with that of administrative work.

The phenomenon came to a head on March 13, 1962, during the traditional ceremony held on the anniversary of the attack on the Presidential Palace. Fidel Castro presided at the ceremony. The person who was reading the political testament of José Antonio Echeverría[1] left out his invocation of God's blessing on the action in which he gave his life. A student leader, pressured by the prevailing atmosphere, had crossed it out. On addressing the people a few minutes later, Fidel Castro criticized that

---

[1] José Antonio Echeverría Bianchi (1932-57), President of the Federation of University Students (FEU) and founder of the Revolutionary Directorate (DR). In 1956, with Fidel Castro, he signed the "Letter from Mexico." He organized the March 13, 1957, attack on the Presidential Palace and headed the group that seized Radio Reloj, where he went on the air to announce the expected execution of Batista. Minutes later, on his way back to the University of Havana, he was killed in a clash with Batista's police.

omission as an example of the deviations that had been taking place.

On March 26, in an address to the public, Fidel Castro analyzed the mistakes made by Aníbal Escalante and the others responsible for the sectarian policy that had been applied and explained the decision of the national leadership of ORI, which he headed, to rectify the process of the construction of the future United Party of the Socialist Revolution of Cuba (*Partido Unido de la Revolución Socialista de Cuba, PURSC*) by involving the masses.

Meeting in assemblies, the workers would elect exemplary workers, from among whom the members of specially appointed commissions would select those who had the required merits and wanted to be members of the vanguard political organization.

Those definitions about a party closely linked to the workers and the rest of the people — which would reflect the feelings of the masses and act in response to them; report back to the people for what it did; and, above all, be guided by the principles of merit and capacity; a party that would be united politically and ideologically and would have an extensive democratic, disciplined and creative inner life — became the standards guiding the party heading the Cuban Revolution.

As Fidel Castro put it, "In the crucible of a revolutionary process, this party was formed from unity and ideas, unity and doctrine. We will always have to watch over these two things — unity and doctrine — because they are the main pillars of the party and ensure that merit, revolutionary virtues, modesty and selflessness prevail within it. We must ensure that it always maintains close ties with the masses, from whom it must never be separated, because it exists for the masses, and it is the masses who give it its prestige, authority and strength. Never above the masses; always with the masses and in the hearts of the people."[2]

The Communist Party of Cuba, with around 800,000 members at the time of the 40th anniversary of the triumph of the revolution, is the fruit of that policy.

*

The best of the country's workers must be in the Communist Party

(Excerpts of a speech by Fidel Castro on March 26, 1962)

It was logical that the revolution should concern itself with the problem of organizing its political apparatus, its revolutionary

---

[2] Fidel Castro and Raúl Castro, *Selección de discursos acerca del Partido. Fidel Castro, Raúl Castro* (Selected Speeches about the Party. Fidel Castro and Raúl Castro) (Havana: Editorial de Ciencias Sociales, 1975), 121. Excerpts from Fidel Castro's address in the June 1974 Evaluation Assembly of the Party in City of Havana Province.

apparatus. And there began that whole process, which we have explained here on more than one occasion, through which the different forces that had participated in the process, that represented the masses, the forces of ideas, the forces of public opinion, began to be integrated; it was those forces that represented experience, represented a wealth of values that the revolution had to integrate into a single organization...

So, has that whole process of the integration of the revolutionary forces been free of errors? No, it has not been free of errors. Could these errors have been avoided? It cannot be determined precisely up to what point these errors could have been avoided. My personal opinion is that those errors could not have been avoided...

One of the fundamental problems produced in the struggle against reactionary ideas, against conservative ideas, against the deserters, against those who wavered, against those with negative attitudes, was sectarianism. It may be said that this was the fundamental error produced by the struggle of an ideological nature that was being waged.

That type of error was produced by the conditions in which the revolutionary process developed, and by the serious and fundamental struggle that revolutionary ideas had to wage against conservative elements and against reactionary ideas.

What tendency was manifesting itself? An opposite tendency began to manifest itself. The tendency to mistrust everybody, the tendency to mistrust everyone who could not claim a long record of revolutionary militancy, who had not been an old Marxist militant. It is logical that in certain phases of this process — when a serious struggle of ideas was underway, when there was confusion, when there were many who wavered, if a *compañero* was to be named to a post of high trust, if it was a post in which an especially important job was to be done, a post requiring persons who were firm in their ideas, that is to say, persons unaffected by doubt, who did not waver — it was correct to select a *compañero* about whom, because of their record of militancy, there existed not the least doubt regarding the steadfastness of his ideas, a *compañero* who entertained no doubts as to the course of the revolution...

But the revolution continued its forward march. The revolution became a powerful ideological movement. Revolutionary ideas slowly won the masses over. The Cuban people, in great numbers, began to accept revolutionary ideas, to uphold revolutionary ideas. That ardor, that rebelliousness, that sense of indignant protest against tyranny, against abuse, against injustice, was slowly converted into the firm revolutionary consciousness of our people...

If that was a self-evident truth, could we then apply methods that were applicable to other conditions? Could we convert that system, which the struggle in a specific phase required, could we convert that into a system? Could we turn that policy into a system? Could we turn those methods for the selection of *compañeros* for various administrative posts into a system? We could not turn those methods into a system!

It is unquestionable, and dialectics teaches us, that what at a given moment is a correct method, later on may be incorrect. Anything else is dogmatism, mechanism. It is a desire to apply measures that were determined by our special needs at a given moment to another situation in which the needs are different, in which other circumstances prevail. And we turned certain methods into a system and we fell into a frightful sectarianism.

What sectarianism? Well, the sectarianism of believing that the only revolutionaries, that the only *compañeros* who could hold positions of trust, that the only ones who could hold a post on a people's farm, on a cooperative, in the government, anywhere, had to be old Marxist militants. We fell into that error partly unconsciously, or at least it seemed that all those problems brought about by sectarianism were problems which were the product of unconscious forces, that they came about with a fatal inevitability, that it was a virus, that it was an evil that had become lodged in the minds of many people, and that it was difficult to combat...

Others worked at tasks related to the formation of the party; and the party was taking shape, rather the ORI was taking shape, the ORI was being integrated. But, were we really forming a true Marxist party? Were we really constructing a true vanguard of the working class? Were we really integrating the revolutionary forces?

We were not integrating the revolutionary forces. We were not organizing a party. We were organizing or creating or making a straitjacket, a yoke, *compañeros*. We were not furthering a free association of revolutionaries, rather we were forming an army of tamed and submissive revolutionaries...

The *compañero* who was authorized — it is not known whether he was invested with the authority or whether he assumed it of his own accord, or whether it was because he had slowly begun to assume leadership on that front, and as a result found himself in charge of the ask of organizing, or of working as the Secretary in Charge of Organization of the ORI. The one who enjoyed everyone's confidence, who acted with the prestige given him by the revolution, who, while speaking with the authority of the revolution because he spoke in its name and in the name of the other *compañeros* of the revolution, the one who despite this fell, who regrettably — most regrettably — fell into the errors we have been enumerating, was comrade Aníbal Escalante...

We reached the conclusion — we were all convinced — that comrade Aníbal Escalante, abusing the faith placed in him, in his post as Secretary in Charge of Organization, followed a non-Marxist policy, followed a policy that departed from Leninist norms regarding the organization of a workers' vanguard party, and that he tried to organize an apparatus to pursue personal ends.

We believe that comrade Aníbal Escalante has had a lot to do with the conversion of sectarianism into a system, with the conversion of sectarianism into a virus, into a veritable sickness during this process.

Comrade Aníbal Escalante is the one responsible for having promoted the sectarian spirit to its highest possible level, of having, promoted that sectarian spirit for personal reasons, with the purpose of establishing an organization that he controlled. He is the one responsibility for introducing, in addition, a series of methods within the organization that were leading to the creation, not of a party — as we were saying — but rather of a tyranny, a straitjacket.

We believe that Aníbal Escalante's actions in these matters were not the product of oversight nor were they unconscious, but rather that they were deliberate and conscious. He simply allowed himself to be blinded by personal ambition. And as a result of this, he created a series of problems, in a word, he created veritable chaos in the nation.

Why? It's very simple. The idea of organizing the United Party of the Socialist Revolution, the idea of organizing a vanguard, a vanguard party, a workers' party, meets with the greatest acceptance among the masses. Marxism has the full support of the masses. Marxism-Leninism is the ideology of the Cuban people...

In such a situation, when all the people accept this principle, it was very easy to convert that apparatus, already accepted by the people, into an instrument for the pursuit of one's personal ambitions. The prestige of the ORI was immense. Any order, any directive coming from the ORI was obeyed by all. But the ORI was not the ORI.

Comrade Aníbal Escalante had schemed to make himself the ORI. How? By the use of a very simple contrivance. Working from his post as Secretary in Charge of Organization he would give instructions to all revolutionary cells and to the whole apparatus as if these instructions had come from the National Directorate. And he began to encourage them in the habit of receiving instructions from there, from the offices of the Secretary in Charge of Organization of the ORI, instructions that were obeyed by all as if they had come from the National Directorate. But at the same time, he took advantage of the opportunity to establish a system of controls that would be completely under his command...

On the other hand, on the level of the Secretary in Charge of Organization, it already was impossible for a minister to change an official or to change an administrator without having to call the office of the ORI, because of habits which this *compañero* — by deceiving government officials, by making them think that he was acting under instructions from the National Directorate — tried to establish, and succeeded in establishing to a large degree...

What is the function of the party? To orient. It orients on all levels, it does not govern on all levels. It fosters the revolutionary consciousness of the masses. It is the link with the masses. It educates the masses in the ideas of socialism and communism. It encourages the masses to work, to strong endeavor, to defend the revolution. It spreads the ideas of the revolution. It supervises, controls, guards, informs. It discusses what has to be discussed. But it does not have authority to appoint and to remove officials...

The nucleus has other tasks. Its tasks are different from those of state administration. The party directs; it directs through the party as a whole, and it directs through the governmental apparatus.

Today an official must have authority. A minister must have authority, an administrator must have authority. They must be able to discuss whatever is necessary with the Technical Advisory Council. They must be able to discuss with the masses of workers; with the nucleus. Administrators must decide, the responsibility must be theirs.

The party, through its National Directorate, endows the administrative personnel with authority. But in order to demand an accounting from them, it must endow them with true authority. If it is the nucleus that decides, if it decides at the provincial level, or at the level of the work center, or at the local level, how then can we make the minister responsible for these decisions? They cannot be made responsible because they have no power.

The minister has the power to appoint, to remove, to appoint within the norms established by the rules and the laws of the nation.

But at the same time he is charged with responsibility, he or she is responsible to the political administration of the revolution for their actions, for their work. In a word, ministers must give an accounting of their stewardship. Now, to give an accounting one must have powers...

Was this power real? No, it was not a real power; it was a power in form only; it was a fictitious power. There was no real power in the hands of that *compañero*. Fortunately, there was no real power! The real power did not rest there. The real power of the revolution cannot simply be usurped in that fashion. It cannot be circumvented in that way, *compañeros*. That is a ridiculous and idiotic attempt at circumvention!...

It was important to discuss this problem because it was vital to the revolution, basic for the revolution, simply because it was imperative to correct those errors, that incorrect and absurd policy, forced here into the midst of a revolutionary process filled with glory and greatness. The conditions that made possible such a state of affairs had to be rooted out and the conditions that permitted the organization and the functioning of a true workers' vanguard party had to be created...

I believe sincerely and firmly in the principles of collective leadership, but no one forced me to do so; rather it came from a deep and personal conviction, a conviction with which I have known how to comply. I believe what I said on December 2: I believe in collective leadership; I believe that history is written by the masses, I believe that when the best opinions, the opinions of the most competent individuals, the most capable individuals, are discussed collectively, that they are cleansed of their vices, of their errors, of their weaknesses, of their faults. I also believe that neither the history of countries, nor the lives of nations, should be dependent on individuals, on human beings, on personalities. I state that which I firmly believe...

How did this affect the masses? Well, clearly this discouraged the masses. Did this turn the masses against the revolution? No, the masses did not turn against the revolution, the masses are with the revolution and they will always be with the revolution, in spite of its errors. But this cooled the enthusiasm of the masses; this cooled the fervor of the masses.

How did this affect the political organization of the revolution? Very simply, *compañeros*. We were not creating an organization; I already said that we were preparing a yoke, a straitjacket. I'm going to go a little further: we were creating a mere shell of an organization. How? The masses had not been integrated. We speak here of the Integrated Revolutionary Organizations. It was an organization composed of the militants of the Popular Socialist Party [Partido Socialista Popular].

The rest of the organizations, the Student Directorate, the July 26 Movement, what were they? Were they organizations that had an old organized membership? No. They were organizations that had great mass support; they had an overwhelming mass support. That is what July 26 was; that is what the other organizations were. They enjoyed great prestige, great popularity. These people were not organized into an organization.

If we are going to form an organization, an integration, and we do not integrate the masses, we will not be integrating anything, we will be falling into a sectarianism just like we did.

Then how were the nuclei [units of the Integrated Revolutionary Organization] formed? I'm going to tell you how. In every province the general secretary of the PSP was made general secretary of the ORI, in all the nuclei, the general secretary of he PSP was made general secretary of the ORI; in every municipality, the general secretary of the PSP was made general secretary of the ORI; in every nucleus, the general secretary − the member of the PSP − was made general secretary of the nucleus. Is that what you would call integration? Aníbal Escalante is responsible for that policy…

So when the socialist revolution is in power, that sectarianism fosters anticommunism anew. What Marxist-Leninist mind could think of employing the methods employed when Marxism-Leninism was not in power, when it was completely surrounded and isolated? To isolate oneself from the masses when one is in power − that is madness. It is another matter to be isolated by the ruling classes, by the exploiters, when the *latifundistas* and the imperialists are in power; but to be divorced from the masses when the workers, the *campesinos*, when the working class is in power, is a crime. Then sectarianism becomes counterrevolutionary because it weakens and harms the revolution…

The best workers in the country should be members of that party. Who are they? They are the model workers, the model laborers, who are in abundant supply.

In other words, the first requirement for belonging to the nucleus is to be a model worker. One cannot be a builder of socialism, or a builder of communism, if one is not an outstanding worker. No vagrant, no idler, has any right to be a member of a revolutionary nucleus.

Very well now, that is not enough. Our experience during the course of this meeting has provided us with many interesting examples. One has to be an exemplary worker, but in addition one must accept the socialist revolution; one must accept the ideology of the revolution; one must want, of course, to belong to that revolutionary nucleus; one must accept the responsibilities that go with membership in the revolutionary nucleus. But, in addition, it is necessary to have led a clean life...

After all, the masses are not going to elect the nucleus; the party is not an elected party. It is a "selection," which is organized through the principle of democratic centralism. Now, the opinion of the masses must be taken into consideration. It is of the utmost importance that those who belong to that revolutionary nucleus have the complete support of the masses, that they enjoy great prestige with the masses...

How could we keep the masses out? How could we divorce ourselves from the masses? There are many model workers among the old revolutionaries who are recognized as such by the masses. There are others who are not model workers. There is no reason why there should be disagreement with this, because being a communist does not endow one with a hereditary title or with a title of nobility. To be a communist means that one has a certain attitude towards life, and that attitude has to be the same from the first day until the moment of death. When that attitude is abandoned, even though one has been a communist, it ceases to be a communist attitude toward life, toward the revolution, toward one's class, toward the people. If this is so, let us then not convert that into a hereditary title!...

What is the revolution? It is a great trunk that has its roots. Those roots, coming from different directions, were united in the trunk. The trunk begins to grow. The roots are important, but what begins to grow is the trunk of a great tree. All of us together made the trunk. The growing of the trunk is all that remains for us to foster and together we will continue to make it grow.

The day will come, *compañeros* — think well upon this, because this is basic, think well upon this — when what we have done in the past will be less important, when what each of us has done on his or her own account will be less important than what we done together. Le us take this idea with us. Within 10 years, within 20 years, we will have the common history of having done this together, and then no one will be talking about what each one did on their own — in the Popular Socialist Party, in the July 26 Movement, in the Revolutionary Directorate, in the other group. Then those things will be like the roots that come from afar, which now remain in the distance. The important thing is what we are already doing as a trunk, in which we are all united. And we have said this...

Rest assured, *compañeros,* that by doing this our revolution will be invincible. Rest assured, *compañeros,* that by doing this there will be no force in the world that will be able to defeat our revolution; and I repeat here what I said once when we arrived at the capital of the republic: "We have overcome our own obstacles. No enemies but ourselves, but our own errors, remain. Only our own errors will be able to destroy this revolution!" I repeat it today, but I add that there will be no error that we will not oppose, and therefore there will be no error that will be able to destroy the revolution! There will be no errors that will not be overcome, and that is why our revolution will be invincible.

19

OCTOBER MISSILE CRISIS

October 22, 1962

The Missile Crisis of October 1962 was one of the most serious events in the Cold War period and brought the world to the brink of nuclear conflagration. Its causes can be found, first of all, in the U.S. Government's plans — explicitly approved by the president — to carry out a series of actions against Cuba, including direct intervention by U.S. armed forces.

As historian Arthur Schlesinger, Jr., acknowledged, "Certainly Castro had the best grounds for feeling under siege. Even if double agents had not told him the CIA was trying to kill him, the Mongoose campaign left little doubt that the American government was trying to overthrow him. It would hardly have been unreasonable for him to request Soviet protection. But did he request Soviet missiles? The best evidence is that he did not. Castro's aim was to deter American aggression by convincing Washington that an attack on Cuba would be the same as an attack on the Soviet Union. This did not require nuclear weapons."[1]

In fact, after the Bay of Pigs, Cuba was rushing through preparations for meeting a large-scale attack by the United States. Two agreements had been signed with the Soviet Government on supplies of conventional weapons for Cuba's Army, Air Force and Navy. The Revolutionary Armed Forces were reorganized into the three units with the kinds of armed forces it now has and provided with more and better weapons.

On the other side of the Straits of Florida, the U.S. Armed Forces also prepared, attaining an impressive level of soldiers and weaponry, and the

---

[1] Schlesinger, Jr. *Robert Kennedy*, 524-5.

details of various contingency plans for an attack on Cuba were refined.

It was in those conditions, in May 1962, that it occurred to Soviet Premier Nikita S. Khrushchev that nuclear missiles might be installed in Cuba. The military hierarchy of the Soviet Union supported the idea. A Soviet delegation including Marshal Sergei Biriuzov, head of the Strategic Missile Forces, went to Cuba on May 29 and presented the proposal to the leadership of the revolution. The main argument was that the United States would only halt its plans if it knew that an attack on the island would mean a confrontation not only with conventional weapons but also with Soviet nuclear power.

Without denying his solidarity with Cuba, Khrushchev also acted in this episode with his typical shrewdness, seeking advantages for the Soviet Union in the world balance of power.

In spite of the Soviet Union's emphatic declarations that strategic response parity with the United States and the NATO bloc had already been reached, it was still at a great disadvantage. If 42 medium- and intermediate-range missiles with nuclear warheads were installed in Cuba, its situation would improve dramatically.

Fidel Castro and the other Cuban leaders didn't like the idea but finally agreed that the missiles be sent, since it was a step that would strengthen socialism and constitute a gesture of solidarity with the Soviet Union, which was running great risks to defend Cuba's physical integrity.

The Cubans' main reservations concerned not the dangers that the action implied but the political price Cuba might have to pay – how the other Latin American countries and the rest of the world would view the action. Under the agreement with the Soviets, it meant bringing in 48,000 Soviet soldiers with full technical support who were directly subordinate to the government of the Soviet Union. In effect, this turned Cuba into a military base of the Soviet Union.

For Cuba, it was clear that it wasn't absolutely necessary to have those missiles for the defense of the country and the revolution. The same results could have been attained with a public announcement of a military pact in which the Soviet Union proclaimed that a direct military attack on Cuba would be equivalent to an attack on the Soviet Union.

However, in spite of repeated urging by Cuba, the Soviets made the serious mistake of keeping the agreement secret. Later on, this gave the Kennedy Administration a great advantage when its spy planes showed the installation of missiles, for this enabled the United States to seize the military initiative. It took advantage of the political and psychological circumstances of being able to present the world with its reaction as a legitimate act against lies and deceit.

The Soviet missile group was sent to Cuba in the summer of 1962. The medium-range missiles were installed and made operational, although the *nuclear warheads were never attached, but remained in storage. The intermediate-range missiles were still on the high seas when the crisis broke out and were returned to the Soviet Union.*

On October 14, a U.S. spy plane took photographs of a missile emplacement near San Cristóbal, Pinar del Río Province. During the next few days, although it wasn't aware of this, Cuba was in extreme danger while the U.S. Government examined its various military options. On October 20, the U.S. National Security Council decided to declare a naval blockade (which it called a "quarantine") of Cuba and to take other — political, diplomatic and military — measures.

On October 22, Kennedy announced this decision publicly in a message to the nation. On the afternoon of that same day, Fidel Castro decreed a combat alert for the Revolutionary Armed Forces and the Cuban people. A total of 400,000 men and women took up arms in a calm and orderly way.

Those were the "brilliant yet sad" days to which Che Guevara referred. Tension reached a peak starting on October 26, when a massive air attack by the United States seemed imminent. The Cuban and Soviet troops' morale was very high. They had received orders to open fire on the U.S. planes that made barnstorming flights over Cuban territory. Cuban batteries opened fire on October 27, and, that same day, an anti-aircraft missile fired from a Soviet emplacement shot down a U-2 spy plane over northern Oriente Province.

However, in the diplomatic negotiations between the Soviet Union and the United States, in which Cuba didn't participate, the Soviet leadership made more mistakes — in addition to those committed in the process of drawing up the agreement of military cooperation and mutual defense. The worst was the October 28 accord, in which Khrushchev — without consulting or even informing the Cuban Government — accepted Kennedy's "compromise" of not attacking or invading the island if the construction of the installations was halted and the missiles were dismantled and returned to the Soviet Union.

Cuba was far from happy with this, since much more could have been achieved with a firm negotiating position that would have forced the United States to discuss matters directly with Cuba and provide effective guarantees regarding its future. This was one of the roots of the differences that cooled Soviet-Cuban relations during the following years.

The Cuban Revolution's response to this fait accompli was expressed in the Five Points of Dignity, which Fidel Castro announced on television on October 28, the same day as the U.S.-Soviet accord. That night, in Santiago de Cuba, Raúl Castro emphasized, "We will never negotiate our rights and sovereignty. We will fight for them."

*

The Five Points of Dignity

FIRST. The economic blockade and all of the other measures that the United States is taking all over the world to bring trade and economic pressure to bear against Cuba must cease.

SECOND. All subversive activities, airlifts and landings of arms and explosives by air and by sea, the organization of mercenary invasions, the sending of spies into our country illegally and acts of sabotage — whether carried out from U.S. territory or from that of accessory countries — must cease.

THIRD. The pirate attacks that are carried out from bases in the United States and Puerto Rico must cease.

FOURTH. All violations of Cuba's airspace and territorial waters by U.S. planes and warships must cease.

FIFTH. U.S. troops must be withdrawn from the Guantánamo Naval Base, and that part of Cuban territory occupied by the United States must be returned.

Fidel Castro Ruz
Prime Minister of the Revolutionary Government[2]

Now, I'm prouder than ever before of being a son of this nation

(Excerpts from Fidel Castro's address explaining aspects of the October Missile Crisis, November 1, 1962)[3]

We don't constitute an obstacle to a peaceful solution, a truly peaceful solution. We are neither a warlike nor an aggressive nation. Ours is a peaceful nation, but being peaceful doesn't mean allowing ourselves to be trampled upon. If anyone should try it, we will fight as much as need be to defend ourselves. The facts bear this out.

We will never constitute an obstacle to a truly peaceful solution. The prerequisites for a truly peaceful solution are the five-point guarantees set forth by the Government of Cuba.

We want the United States to start giving proof, not promises, of its good faith. Deeds, not words! It would be convincing if the United States were to return the territory it occupies at the Guantánamo Naval Base. That would be much more convincing than any words or promises by the United States.

And if the United States doesn't agree to the guarantees that Cuba wants? Then there won't be any truly peaceful solution, and

---

[2] *Obra revolucionaria*, No. 32, November 2, 1962.
[3] Ibid.

we will have to keep on living with this tension that we have endured so far. We want peaceful solutions, but they must also be honorable. We are entitled to peace, a truly peaceful solution, and, sooner or later, we will get it, because we have won that right with our people's spirit, resistance and honor...

They don't let us work in peace. More than weapons, we want to use work tools. We want to create, not kill and destroy. Our people aren't allowed to create and are constantly forced to mobilize, to place themselves on a war footing, to defend themselves, to be ready for anything. They are forced to do this; it isn't that we want that policy. It's a policy that the aggressors impose on our country. What our country wants is to work, to develop its resources, to develop its people and to carry out its peaceful work.

We won't accept just any old formula. We *will* accept any formula for peace that is truly honorable. I think that, with such a formula, we wouldn't be the only ones to benefit: everybody would — the Americas, the rest of the world, the United States. That is, even those responsible for this situation would benefit from a solution of honorable peace for our country...

In the course of this crisis, while this crisis was developing, some discrepancies arose between the Soviet and Cuban governments, but I want to tell all Cubans one thing: this isn't the place for discussing those problems, because discussing them here could help our enemies, who could benefit from such differences. We must discuss such things with the Soviets at the government and party levels; we have to sit down with them and discuss whatever is needed, using reason and principles; because, above all, we are Marxist-Leninists; we are friends of the Soviet Union. There will be no breaches between the Soviet Union and Cuba.

I would like to say something else, too: we have confidence in the Soviet Union's policy of principles, and we have confidence in the leadership of the Soviet Union — that is, in the government and in the party of the Soviet Union.

If my fellow countrymen ask me for my opinion now, what can I tell them, what advice should I give them? In the midst of confusing situations, of things that haven't been understood or aren't understood clearly, what should we do? I would say that we must have confidence and realize that these international problems are extremely complex and delicate and that our people, who have shown great maturity, extraordinary maturity, should demonstrate that maturity now...

And, above all, there are some things that need saying now,

when some people may be annoyed because of misunderstandings or discrepancies. It is good to remember, above all, what the Soviet Union has done for us in every one of the difficult moments we have had, what it has done to offset the economic attacks of the United States, suppression of our sugar quota and ending of oil shipments to our country. Every time the United States has attacked us — *every* time — the Soviet Union has extended its hand to us in friendship. We are grateful, and we should say so here, loud and clear...

The principal weapons used by our armed forces were sent to us by the Soviet Union, which hasn't demanded payment for them.

A few months ago, the Soviet Union decided to cancel all of our country's debt for weapons.

Some of these matters, of a military nature, must be treated with great care. However, I can tell you one thing: Cuba didn't own the strategic weapons that were used for its defense. This isn't the case of the tanks and a whole series of other weapons that do belong to us, but we didn't own the strategic weapons.

The agreements covering their being sent to our country to strengthen our defenses in the face of threats of attack stated that those strategic weapons, which are very complex and require highly specialized personnel, would remain under the direction of Soviet personnel and would continue to belong to the Soviet Union. Therefore, when the Soviet Government decided to withdraw those weapons, which belonged to it, we respected that decision. I'm explaining this so you will understand about their withdrawal...

Don't think that the withdrawal of the strategic weapons will leave us unarmed. It doesn't mean that we will be unarmed.

We have impressive — very powerful — means of defense, extraordinary resources with which to defend ourselves. The strategic weapons are leaving, but all the other weapons will stay in our country. They are extremely powerful means of defense, with which we can handle any situation that may arise. Don't misunderstand this.

Little by little, the confusion will disappear.

There is one thing that I would like to emphasize today, an appreciation that I would like to express, which refers to the people, to the way the people have behaved during the past few days. The people's attitude, in terms of determination, courage and discipline, has been more impressive than even the greatest optimists could ever have imagined...

Such a nation is invincible!

Such a nation, whose people confront such difficult situations so serenely and admirably, is a nation that has the right to get what it desires, which is peace, respect, honor and prestige.

We have long-range moral missiles that cannot and will never be dismantled. They are our most powerful strategic weapons, for both defense and attack.

That is why, here and now, I want to express my admiration for the Cuban people. Based on this experience, all revolutionaries feel doubly obliged to struggle and work tirelessly for our people. In closing, I would like to say, from the bottom of my heart, that, now, I am prouder than ever before of being a son of this nation.

20

HURRICANE FLORA

October 4, 1963

At the end of September 1963, a tropical storm began to form over the Atlantic east of the Lesser Antilles. On October 4, having attained the force of a hurricane and now named Flora (it was the sixth hurricane of the year), it was over the Windward Passage, and heavy rain began to scourge a large part of the mountain areas of what was then Oriente Province.

During the next six days, the hurricane followed one of the most erratic courses recorded in the history of hurricanes in Cuba.

Moving slowly – sometimes nearly standing still – the hurricane moved into the middle of Oriente Province, looped around the Cauto Valley, advanced along the length of that vast plain, emerged near Manzanillo on the southern coast, went into the Gulf of Guacanayabo, turned north again, entered Camagüey Province, turned east, headed back to Oriente Province and finally left Cuba for the Straits of Florida between Gibara and Lucrecia Point.

It wasn't Flora's winds but the heavy rainfall that caused the worst damage. In some places, 29 inches (735 millimeters) of rain fell in 24 hours, and totals of up to 63 inches (1,600 millimeters) were recorded during the hurricane.

An enormous mass of water accumulated in the Sierra Maestra Mountains, at the headwaters of the Cauto and its main tributaries, and in the mountains in the northern part of Oriente Province, which also feed into that watershed. Like an avalanche, this water came crashing down to the plains, overflowing the banks of the rivers and dragging everything *along in its path. Such towns as Cauto el Paso, Cauto Embarcadero and Guamo, along the lower reaches of the Cauto, were the worst hit. Later, the farmers who survived remembered having heard a roar-like deafening thunder in the night, followed by the sound of the water — which, in a matter of minutes, swallowed up houses, people, animals and crops.*

The very mountains were molded by Flora's passage. Landslides buried entire families and changed the courses of the rivers.

The leaders of the Cuban Revolution, headed by Fidel Castro and other important Rebel Army commanders, were in charge of operations to try to save as many lives as possible. Fleets of helicopters from the Revolutionary Armed Forces played a key role in saving people who were isolated — sitting on the roofs of their houses or clinging to the branches of trees that surfaced out of the immense sea of muddy water that had once been the plains of the Cauto, waiting to be rescued. The crews of amphibious vehicles also performed an important role. Riding on one of those combat vehicles, Fidel Castro went into the heart of the flooded area to get a precise idea of just how bad the catastrophe was, direct the work on the spot, and, with his example, inspire those taking part in the rescue operation and the people as a whole.

When the water finally subsided the final toll was around 1,200 dead and damage of hundreds of millions of pesos.

Subjected to a tight blockade and to an undeclared war by the CIA, the country thus had to face one of the worst tragedies in its history — both the number of lives lost and the amount of material damage done. Far from easing the blockade or offering any assistance to the Cuban people, political circles in Washington and Miami greeted the news with rejoicing. Help, as before, came mainly from the Soviet Union and other socialist countries.

Flora wasn't just a terrible blow dealt by nature; it was also a useful experience. It led to the water projects program: the building of dams along the main rivers, in the Cauto Valley and other parts of the country, both to prevent future flooding and to use the water for the benefit of the population as well as agriculture.

A revolution is a force stronger than nature

(Excerpts from Fidel Castro's address on Hurricane Flora's passage through Oriente and Camagüey Provinces, October 22, 1963)[1]

The scenes of the people's pain and suffering can never be forgotten. From the human point of view, they constitute a terrible tragedy. As I have already said, nobody could invent anything worse than what

---

[1] *Revolución*, October 23, 1963.

has happened. Everything that anyone with a lively imagination could invent has happened, and even more serious things, too. Extraordinary things have become daily occurrences for the people there.

I was afraid that there would be enormous numbers of victims, in spite of the evacuation. Large numbers of people were evacuated before and even during the hurricane. Even so, I thought there would be a large number of victims. Why? Because nobody thought that some of the people who were in danger would be at risk.

Naturally, people who live in places where the river has reached before are always evacuated, as are those in places near the sea and in low-lying areas. We had the experience of what happened in Santa Cruz del Sur. Of course, the measures that were taken were mainly aimed at reducing the possible effects of rip tides in all areas close to the sea. The people living in towns in low-lying areas were evacuated, but the worst danger came from floods, which reached levels never seen before. That is, there was a rip tide, but it came from the mountains rather than the sea — a rip tide that came from inland...

We still don't know exactly how many victims there are, because new cases are still being reported. At the time I received those reports — that is, as of October 20 — the party had confirmed a total of 1,126 victims in Oriente Province. Naturally, the total will be larger, because of the people who have disappeared who may be found. Little by little, they are being found — some dead and others alive. There may be hundreds more victims...

I had the opportunity to learn the details of some cases. For example, there was a farm family that had two little houses — the parents in one, and the children in the other. They were separated. The father says he saw that the house where the children were was beginning to crack, so he swam over and made a hole in the roof so the children could get out. Then he saw something in the other house and went back there. When he looked back at the children's house, which contained three of his children, a cousin and some other people — around six or seven in all — he saw that the water was carrying it away...

Then he set out to swim after the house, and his wife started swimming, too. After a mile, they managed to catch up with it. It was caught in some trees. The father got there first, and then the mother. They practically tore their hands to pieces cutting wire. Then he tied the house, which was floating, to the trees there, and they got in the house and held out for three days.

It's certain that, if they hadn't done what they did, the children would have died, because everything would have been too much for them. The current would have kept dragging them off, and they would have grown weak. The parents — especially the father, because the wife was very weak — were able to save the children's lives because they defended and protected them. Just imagine what it must have been like at night, those interminable nights with the rain coming down all the time; cold, hunger and trauma must have made the children very weak. They stayed there for three days, but they saved the children's lives.

Then they went back home — where, they said, they had around 200 animals: chickens and pigs. They lost all of them, all their clothes and the furniture...

When it became possible for helicopters to fly in, even at great risk, they went into action. The helicopters did a tremendous job. They are marvelous things for situations such as this...

Really, everybody made a terrific effort. The regional committees and grass roots committees of our party in the two provinces did an incredible, extraordinary job and inspired everybody else to do great things, too. Everybody did their utmost. Those who could do more, such as the helicopter pilots, did more. The pilots and mechanics, who knew the importance of the humanitarian service they were providing, worked indefatigably. It reminded me of the spirit of the men in the Air Force at the time of the [1961] Bay of Pigs invasion: the pilots' courage; the nonstop efforts of the mechanics, who didn't rest for a minute, carrying and repairing equipment; and the people's attitude...

It can be said that the human solidarity that was achieved there, under those circumstances, reached its highest peak — a most incredible and inconceivable level of human solidarity. If anyone should say that the revolution has done nothing but produce this kind of person — that has been produced in the conditions of the revolution — and developed this feeling of solidarity among human beings, this alone would justify the revolution. What happened there was the opposite of selfishness, of everybody interested only in saving themselves and solving their own problems. There, everybody helped everybody else, as if they were sons and daughters and brothers and sisters. They were in a battle with nature, and their determination, courage, stoicism and calmness — even of those who lost everything — was impressive...

A revolution is a force stronger than nature. Hurricanes and things like that are nothing compared to what a revolution can do. A revolution has forces much greater than those of natural phenomena and cataclysms. A revolution is a social upheaval; it is a powerful people's movement that overflows everything and can sweep away whatever is in its way, including all obstacles. That is a revolution. We know this, and we are calm. Some people don't know this and get frightened. They are frightened just as much by the revolution as by what may happen when they have problems. And then there are the enemies of the revolution, who have illusions. They shut their eyes to reality and never see things as they are…

Here, two upheavals have clashed: the social one, that is the revolution, and the other, that is of nature. The revolution will emerge victorious. There's no doubt about that…

We will do something to compensate those who have suffered losses and to help the families. We will wage a veritable battle with nature; protect our country against such misery and pain; and turn what is now a center of desolation, devastation and death into a center of incalculable wealth for our country. Of course, the whole country will reap the benefits. That is what our response should be, one of honor… In short, what we intend to do is build dams on all the rivers: the Cauto, the Contramaestre, the Mayarí, those in the Guantánamo Valley and all their tributaries. We will build dams on all the rivers, and there won't be any more floods. When there is torrential rain, instead of causing problems, it will be a good thing for the country, because then we will fill all the reservoirs and have plenty of water, so we can irrigate the agricultural areas.

21

SOLIDARITY WITH VIETNAM

December 20, 1963

Major Ernesto Che Guevara gave an address on December 20, 1963, the third anniversary of the founding of the National Liberation Front of South Vietnam.

The Vietnam War had a greater influence on the Cuban people's awareness than any other international event of the past 40 years. The war was a great school in which millions of Cubans could see, day by day, as if in a movie, what would happen to their country if U.S. Armed Forces attacked directly.

During the more than 14 years that passed between December 20, 1960, when the liberation movement began in South Vietnam, and April 30, 1975, when the defeat of the United States and its puppets was completed in Saigon, solidarity with the Vietnamese people's cause was an important part of Cubans' lives.

Vietnam was a relatively small, poor country that stood up with impressive dignity and heroism against a big political and military power, which turned its territory into a proving ground for the most cruel practices — "strategic hamlets," chemical warfare, carpet bombing with B-52s, napalm, torture and the mass murder of women and children. Vietnam was palpable proof that it was possible to oppose and defeat the invaders, and this was an encouraging message for the revolutionaries in Cuba.

Moreover, Cubans were sure that the Vietnamese were fighting for the sake of Cuba, too. There was no doubt about the fact that, by drawing off U.S. military, political and diplomatic efforts for an extended period —

forcing the empire to concentrate most of its resources in distant Indochina — Vietnam was making a generous contribution by giving Cuba the time it needed to grow stronger, to become better organized and to keep the always latent threat of direct U.S. aggression at a distance.

Fidel Castro stated, "We are willing to give even our lives for Vietnam." Vietnam didn't ask for help in the form of fighters, but Cubans helped to build the Ho Chi Minh Trail; Cuban doctors went to alleviate the terrible wounds of the war; and Cuban sailors took their ships loaded with sugar and other products to Vietnam's blockaded and bombed ports.

What Vietnam needed, above all, was solidarity. The unequal struggle in which that nation was engaged was taking place in the difficult circumstances of the split in the international revolutionary and communist movement, which often turned Vietnam into a hostage and victim of the struggles between the main socialist nations. Thus, it was obvious that the liberation struggles of other peoples in Asia, Africa and Latin America could and should be the best response in solidarity with the sacrifices that Vietnam was making for all humanity.

In his famous "Message to the Peoples of the World," issued through Tricontinental *magazine,[1] Ernesto Che Guevara wrote: "This is the painful reality: Vietnam, a nation representing the aspirations and hopes for victory of all the world's disinherited, is tragically alone. This people must endure the pounding of U.S. technology — in the south almost without defenses, in the north with some possibilities of defense — but always alone.*

"The solidarity of the progressive world with the Vietnamese people has something of the bitter irony of the plebeians cheering on the gladiators in the Roman Circus. To wish the victim success is not enough; one must share his or her fate. One must join that victim in death or in victory.

When we analyze the isolation of the Vietnamese we are overcome by anguish at this illogical moment in the history of humanity. U.S. imperialism is guilty of aggression. Its crimes are immense, extending over the whole world. We know this, gentlemen! But also guilty are those who, at the decisive moment, hesitated to make Vietnam an inviolable part of socialist territory — yes, at the risk of a war of global scale, but also compelling the U.S. imperialists to make a decision. And also guilty are those who persist in a war of insults and tripping each other up, begun quite some time ago by the representatives of the two biggest powers in the socialist camp.

---

[1] The First Tricontinental Conference of Solidarity was held in Havana January 13-15, 1966, at Cuba's initiative. It led to the creation of the Organization of Solidarity of the Peoples of Africa, Asia and Latin America (OSPAAAL).

"Let us ask, seeking an honest answer: Is Vietnam isolated or not, as it tries to maintain a dangerous balancing act between the two quarrelling powers?

"And what greatness has been shown by this people! What a stoic and courageous people! And what a lesson for the world their struggle holds...

"What is the role that we, the exploited of the world, must play?

The peoples of three continents are watching and learning a lesson for themselves in Vietnam. Since the imperialists are using the threat of war to blackmail humanity, the correct response is not to fear war. Attack hard and without letup at every point of confrontation — that must be the general tactic of the peoples...

"Latin America, a continent forgotten in the recent political struggles for liberation, is beginning to make itself felt through the Tricontinental in the voice of the vanguard of its peoples: the Cuban Revolution. Latin America will have a much more important task: the creation of the world's second or third Vietnam, or second and third Vietnam...

"How close and bright would the future appear if two, three, many Vietnams flowered on the face of the globe, with their quota of death and their immense tragedies, with their daily heroism, with their repeated blows against imperialism, forcing it to disperse its forces under the lash of the growing hatred of the peoples of the world!

And if we were all capable of uniting in order to give our blows greater strength and certainty, so that the aid of all kinds to the peoples in struggle was even more effective — how great the future would be, and how near!"[2]

The final result will be the victory of South Vietnam and the reunification of the country

(Excerpts of speech by Ernesto Che Guevara at the closing ceremony of the Solidarity with Vietnam Week, December 20, 1963)[3]

Comrades of the South Vietnam Liberation Front, comrade ambassador of the Republic of Vietnam, the Revolutionary Government and the United Party of the Revolution have asked me to hail, in their name, and in the name of the people of Cuba, the liberation struggle of the South Vietnamese people and the third anniversary of the armed struggle for the liberation of your country.

The struggle of the Vietnamese people has been fought for many

[2] Ernesto Che Guevara [David Deutschmann (ed.)], *Che Guevara Reader: Writings on Guerrilla Strategy, Politics & Revolution* (Melbourne: Ocean Press, 1997), 316-28.

[3] Ernesto Che Guevara, *Ernesto Che Guevara: Obras, 1957-1967* (Ernesto Che Guevara: Works, 1957-67) (Havana: Casa de las Américas, 1970), 507-14.

years now because we cannot consider the people of Vietnam in the framework of the artificial division that was established following the Geneva Agreements. Even when the whole of Vietnam was part of the French colonial empire and was known in our geography as Indochina, the people's forces had already begun a long struggle for liberation...

We are unable to say how long this struggle is going to last. These struggles take a long time, and are processes that are sometimes, or almost always, very slow, involving great sacrifices. Nevertheless, the people's forces keep geometrically increasing, and almost as soon as these forces come together to give a small margin to the people's party, the solutions quickly fall into place.

This is what happened in our country of Cuba, and it also happened in North Vietnam, and it happened, too, in the long, long war of national liberation that finally resulted in the establishment of the People's Republic of China.

There comes a point when all the people's forces become so powerful that they can move immediately into a large-scale offensive, transform their guerrilla forces into regular or semi-regular armies and move from simple guerrilla actions to the operational tactics of the military column. At that point they soon destroy the power of the oppressor.

We do not know when we shall be able to hail the definitive liberation of South Vietnam. We will never be able to say when each one of the peoples who are struggling today, their arms in their hands, fighting for their freedom, will attain their liberation. What we do know is that the result will unfailingly be the liberation of the people. And the more energy, the more enthusiasm, the more faith the people put into this, the shorter is the time that the population will have to suffer the violence of the oppressor.

Some months ago, conditions in South Vietnam became such that the United States decided to make changes in the team they had in power. The dictator of the moment did not want to accept this, and yet again the United States provided us with an example of what happens to puppets who, at some point, do not obey orders. From what the news agencies informed us, it seems that the dictator Ngo Dinh Diem and his brother died in what was described then as an "accidental suicide." More or less the same thing happened, in our part of the world, to Trujillo when he also refused to be pushed around in opportunistic deals made by the imperial power when their team no longer serves its purpose.

This indicates, however, that the situation is getting out of control for the forces of oppression in South Vietnam, and our comrades in the National Liberation Front have stated this clearly. There are three roads imperialism can now take. There are signs that the present one, that of using South Vietnamese troops and only a special team of U.S. advisers in the struggle, and for their use in repression and torture, is impossible to maintain. There is the alternative of moving on to a direct invasion of South Vietnam and the massive use of Yankee expeditionary forces...

Today, when with all our enthusiasm we raise the cause of South Vietnam, we are not doing it merely in the interests of proletarian internationalism, and for the love of justice that the revolution has inculcated in all of us. We are also doing it because this front of the struggle is supremely important for the entire future of America.

There in Vietnam, they are training the forces that one day might overcome our guerrillas — the guerrillas we have throughout our American territory. There, they are testing all the new weapons for extermination and the most modern techniques for fighting against the freedom of our peoples. Right now, South Vietnam is the great laboratory of Yankee imperialism where they are preparing all their teams for a future struggle, even more impressive and more significant, if that is possible, than what we have already seen, and this is going to occur in the backyard of their colonial possession, in all of Latin America.

They know that if this struggle today has a victorious finale it will also mean the end of U.S. imperialism.

This is why they are giving it so much attention; and, it goes without saying, there is also the strategic importance of South Vietnam as an operational base for attacking the entire flank of the socialist bloc in Asia. These two strategic characteristics ensure that South Vietnam is classified as one of the serious problems confronting the new Yankee administration and, right now, they are doubtless making a painstaking analysis of what they should do.

Nobody should believe that there is going to be any easy progress toward a real and democratic formula for peace that — without further ado — would permit the Vietnamese people to win their victory, to become unified into one nation, and to move actively, as their brothers in the north have already done, into the construction of socialism over the legacy of backwardness that was left them by colonialism.

The oppressors are thinking about other techniques and in a different strategic direction. What will their decision be? We cannot know it yet, but we do foresee a long struggle and great suffering for the heroic people of South Vietnam — in other words, the same as we foresee for all peoples who are fighting for their freedom.

Nonetheless, the vigorous presence of the liberation forces of Vietnam, their constant successes, their continuous advance toward the most heavily defended zones of the enemy, represent an example that all the peoples of the world are taking in. Our mission here in Cuba is to take this living example, to incarnate it here amongst our people because of the justice it represents and for what it means as an integral part of the whole great fraternal spirit amongst the oppressed peoples of the world; and to transmit this example, by whatever means we can, to the oppressed peoples of America to demonstrate how, in all continents, it is possible to fight for the emancipation of the people. And we wish to show our people in America even more than this, and that is, when the peaceful conditions for this struggle are exhausted, when the reactionary powers deceive the people again and again, not only is it possible to raise the flag of revolution, but also that the flag of revolution must be raised...

They are trying to destroy Cuba today in order to destroy the "bad example," and they are surely thinking that, if they won, they would wipe out everything that this government has done, all our conquests in the social field, along with all the representatives of this government. We all know this very well. This is why our struggle is a fight to the death. The people of South Vietnam also know this.

There is no alternative but victory. Otherwise it is destruction with years and years of imperialist power and with the oppressed countries firmly under their boot.

Therefore, the struggle must be well thought out, must be properly mature but, once it is begun, it must be seen through to the end. Deals cannot be made and neither can there be any compromises.

Making peace that only partly guarantees the stability of a country cannot be done either. Victory must be total. It is with this understanding that our people are still ready to fight. It was with the same understanding that the people of Algeria were prepared to fight for seven years. And, with this conviction, the people of South Vietnam are ready to fight today. Though it may not seem possible, there are also some advantages: they have the support of their brothers and sisters in North Vietnam, nearer to them than anyone else, and they have the example of what a tireless battle of a people for their freedom means. In other words, they have the example of their brothers and sisters who fought for nine years to rid themselves of the yoke of French colonialism. They have the present example of North Vietnam as a contrast with what South Vietnam is now undergoing.

With all of this, their faith must be even deeper, their belief that they will win still greater. Because of all of this, we know — as our comrade delegate has already stated — that, whatever kind of fighting is resorted to by U.S. imperialism, the end result will be victory for South Vietnam and the reunification of the whole country.

To bring to an end this week's festivities held to celebrate the third anniversary of the foundation of the National Liberation Front, we send our greetings to our brothers and sisters, the people of South Vietnam, as our brothers and sisters in struggle, as our exemplary comrades in these difficult moments of the world's history. And, even more than this, they are our colleagues, like soldiers in the vanguard, in the front-line trenches of the fight of the proletarians of the world against imperialism.

For all these reasons, when we come together here to send our greetings to the Vietnamese people, we are greeting our true brothers and sisters, we are opening our arms to men and women, who in a far-away part of the world, are fighting for our security, and who are fighting for the common yearnings that unite the peoples of the three oppressed continents of today: Asia, Africa and Latin America.

22

FORMATION OF COMMUNIST PARTY OF CUBA

October 3, 1965

October 3, 1965, was an important date in the process of unifying the Cuban Revolutionary forces and the people as a whole. On that evening, the secretaries of all the PURSC cells met in the Chaplin Theater (later renamed the Karl Marx Theater) to be consulted about the main agreements adopted by the leadership of the revolution and main cadres of the party in the preceding days.

The first Central Committee of the political organization heading the people and government had been created on October 1. The Political Bureau of the party had also been established on that day, headed by Fidel and Raúl Castro, as First and Second Secretaries, respectively.

It was the result of the process of radical rectification of the sectarian methods that had been employed in building the ORI cells, a process that had begun in March 1962. This involved searching among the workers for the men and women with the greatest merit, both past and present, and selecting from among them those who, because of their vanguard attitude, their ideas and actions, deserved the honor of being members of the new party.

As Fidel Castro later commented, "From then on, we would act as a single organization, under a cohesive leadership. The brilliant ideas of Martí and Lenin on the need for a party to direct the revolution were more palpable than ever before. Its ideology could not be liberal or bourgeois thinking; rather, it had to be that of the revolutionary social class that history itself had placed at the head of the struggle for the liberation of humanity: that of the working class, Marxism-Leninism, which Baliño and Mella had already propounded courageously in 1925.[1]

"This ideology was historically linked with the aspirations of the heroic mambí fighters for Cuba's independence in the 19th century. The only difference was that, now, the nation's enemy was U.S. imperialism, and its social enemy, the modern advocates of slavery: foreign monopolies, large landowners and the bourgeoisie. This ideology linked the national struggle with the world revolutionary movement, which was absolutely necessary for our people's national and social liberation. The building of a Marxist-Leninist party, which now heads the revolution and guarantees its continuity, is one of the greatest feats our people carried out in that historic period."[2]

The leaders who met on October 3 approved the new name — the Communist Party of Cuba — by acclamation. Fidel Castro had proposed this at the first meeting of the Central Committee.

Fidel Castro asked that the party be given "a name that implies the absolute unity of all the people and, at the same time, expresses the final goals of our revolution. This is why I have suggested that it be called the Communist Party of Cuba. The imperialists don't like this, so we will give them a triple dose…"[3]

The moment of greatest emotion in the ceremony came when Fidel Castro referred to "the absence in our Central Committee of one who has all the merits and all the virtues — and in the highest degree — required for belonging to it."

For several months, the international press had been conjecturing about the disappearance from Cuban public life of Major Ernesto Che Guevara, President of the National Bank. Now, Fidel Castro revealed the news that had remained secret when, in a voice charged with emotion, he read the letter Che had written to him on leaving Cuba to do what he believed his duty: to struggle against imperialism in other parts of the world. At the

---

[1] Carlos Baliño, together with José Martí, founded the Cuban Revolutionary Party (Partido Revolucionario Cubano, PRC), in 1892; in 1925, he founded the first Communist Party of Cuba. Julio Antonio Mella (1903-29) was an outstanding student leader and communist who headed the struggle for university reform in 1923. He was also one of the 13 delegates who founded the Communist Party of Cuba. Opposing the Machado dictatorship, he had to go into exile in Mexico, where he continued his revolutionary and internationalist activities. He was assassinated by agents of the Machado dictatorship on January 10, 1929.

[2] *Informe del Comité Central del PCC al Primer Congreso* (Report of the Central Committee of the Communist Party of Cuba to the First Congress) (Havana: Editorial de Ciencias Sociales, 1978), 46-7.

[3] Fidel Castro and Raúl Castro, *Selección de discursos*, 47-8.

time the letter was made public in Havana, the revolutionary of Argentine origin had been at a base in the Congo (Kinshasa) for several months, heading the contingent of Cuban combatants who had gone to that part of Africa to support the liberation movements fighting against Moise Tshombe's pro-imperialist regime.

Thus, the process of political unification and internal strengthening of the revolution was firmly linked to the idea and practice of internationalist solidarity. It would continue to be so in the years to come.

*

There is no sacrifice, there is no combat, no feat that is not represented in the Central Committee

[Excerpts of a speech by Fidel Castro on the presentation of the Central Committee of the Communist Party of Cuba, October 3, 1965]

The whole country received the news of the formation of our Central Committee with joy and enthusiasm.

The names of the comrades who form this Committee and their histories are well known. If all of them are not known by everyone, all of them are known by a considerable and important number of the people. We have tried to choose those who in our judgment represent to the fullest extent the history of the revolution. Those who, in the fight for the revolution, as well as in the fight for the consolidation, defense and development of the revolution, have worked and fought firmly and tirelessly.

There is no heroic period in the history of our revolution that is not represented here. There is no sacrifice, there is no combat, no feat — either military or civilian, heroic or creative — that is not represented. There is no revolutionary or social sector that is not represented. I am not speaking of organizations. When I speak of a sector I speak of the workers, I speak of the youth, I speak of the farmers, I speak of our mass organizations...

The list of comrades of the Revolutionary Armed Forces would be interminable for their history both before and after the triumph — both before and after the triumph! — as outstanding revolutionaries, as tireless workers, as examples of improvement in studies, in cultural development, in cultural and political levels, comrades of extraordinary modesty, in whose hands the defense of the nation has principally rested during these seven dangerous and threat-filled years.

It is not necessary to speak about the best known. That does not mean that they are the only heroes of the nation. No, far from it!

Fortunately our country has innumerable heroes and above all a mass of the new comrades, now being developed, who will some day — without a doubt — demonstrate their sense of responsibility and honor.

If we ask ourselves whether we have left anyone out, of course we have to answer in the affirmative.

It would be impossible to form a Central Committee of 100 revolutionary comrades without leaving out many comrades. What is important is not those who have been left out. They will come later. What is important is those who are there, and what they represent. We know that the party and the people have received the formation of this committee with satisfaction.

This Committee, which met yesterday, reached various agreements:

First, it ratified the measure adopted by the former National Leadership. It ratified the Political Bureau, the Secretariat and the Work Commissions, as well as the comrade elected Secretary of the Organization. The Committee also reached two important agreements which had been submitted by the former National Leadership.

One of these agreements concerns our official organ. Instead of publishing two newspapers of a political nature, we are going to concentrate all human resources, all resources in equipment and paper on establishing a single morning paper of a political nature, in addition to the newspaper *El Mundo*, which is not exactly a political organ. We will concentrate all these resources and establish a new newspaper. It will be called *Granma*, the symbol of our revolutionary concepts and goals.

An even more important agreement is the one which refers to the name of our party.

Our first name was the ORI [Integrated Revolutionary Organizations]. That was during our first stage in the uniting of all revolutionary forces, which had its positive and negative aspects.

Later we became the United Party of the Socialist Revolution [PURS], which constituted an extraordinary step forward in the creation of our political apparatus. These efforts took three years during which time innumerable valuable comrades emerged from the inexhaustible source of the people and the workers to form what we are today.

The name United Party of the Cuban Socialist Revolution tells much, but not everything. The name United Party suggests something that is need of uniting, it still reminds us a little bit of the origin of each one. And since we are of the opinion that we have already reached that level in which all shades and all types of origin distinguishing one revolutionary from another must forever disappear, since we have already arrived at that stage of history in which our revolutionary process has only one type of revolutionary, and since it is necessary for the name of our party to show, not what we were yesterday, but what we will be tomorrow, what name, in your opinion should our party have? (*shouts of "Communist Party!"*) Those comrades here! (*they shout "Communist Party!"*) Cuban Communist Party.

That is the name which, in view of the development of our party, of the revolutionary consciousness of its members and the objectives of our revolution, was adopted by the first Central Committee yesterday...

We are on the road toward a communist society. And if the imperialists don't like it, they can lump it.

From now on, gentlemen of UPI and AP, be it known that when you call us "communists" you are giving us the greatest honor you can give us.

Absent from our Central Committee is someone who possesses in the highest degree all the necessary merits and virtues to be on it but who, nevertheless, is not among those announced as members of our Central Committee.

The enemy has been able to conjure up a thousand conjectures. The enemy has tried to sow confusion, to spread discord and doubt, and we have waited patiently because it was necessary to wait...

In short, the moral spectacle of our adversaries is truly lamentable. Thus the soothsayers, the pundits, the specialists on the Cuba question have been working incessantly to unravel the mystery: Has Ernesto Guevara been purged? Is Ernesto Guevara sick? Does Ernesto Guevara have differences? And things of this sort.

Naturally the people have confidence, the people have faith. But the enemy uses these things, especially abroad, to slander us. Here, they say, is a frightening, terrible communist regime: people disappear without a trace, without a sign, without an explanation. And when the people began to notice his absence, we told them that we would inform them at the appropriate time, that there were reasons for waiting.

We live and work surrounded by the forces of imperialism. The world does not live under normal conditions. As long as the criminal bombs of the Yankee imperialists fall on the people of Vietnam, we cannot say we live under normal conditions. When more than

100,000 Yankee soldiers land there to try to crush the liberation movement; when the soldiers of imperialism land in a republic that has legal rights equal to those of any other republic in the world, to trample its sovereignty, as in the case of the Dominican Republic, the world doesn't live under normal conditions. When surrounding our country, the imperialists are training mercenaries and organizing terrorist attacks in the most shameless manner, as in the case of [the attack by counterrevolutionary Cuban exiles on the Spanish merchant ship] *Sierra Aránzazu*, when the imperialists threaten to intervene in any country in Latin America or in the world, we do not live under normal conditions.

When we fought in the underground against the Batista dictatorship, revolutionaries who did not live under normal conditions had to abide by the rules of the struggle. In the same way — even though a revolutionary government exists in our country — so far as the realities of the world are concerned we do not live under normal conditions, and we have to abide by the rules of that situation.

To explain this I am going to read a letter, handwritten and later typed, from comrade Ernesto Guevara, which is self-explanatory. I was wondering whether I needed to tell of our friendship and comradeship, how it began and under what conditions it began and developed, but that's not necessary. I'm going to confine myself to reading the letter.

It reads as follows: "Havana…" It has no date, because the letter was intended to be read at what we considered the most appropriate moment, but to be strictly precise it was delivered April 1 of this year — exactly six months and two days ago. It reads:

Havana
Fidel,

At this moment I remember many things — when I met you in María Antonia's house, when you proposed I come along, all the tensions involved in the preparations. One day they came by and asked who should be notified in case of death, and the real possibility of that fact struck us all. Later we knew that it was true, that in a revolution one wins or dies (if it is a real one). Many comrades fell along the way to victory.

Today everything has a less dramatic tone, because we are more mature. But the event repeats itself. I feel that I have fulfilled the part of my duty that tied me to the Cuban

Revolution in its territory, and I say goodbye to you, to the comrades, to your people, who now are mine.

I formally resign my positions in the leadership of the party, my post as minister, my rank of commander, and my Cuban citizenship. Nothing legal binds me to Cuba. The only ties are of another nature — those that cannot be broken as can appointments to a post.

Recalling my past life, I believe I have worked with sufficient honesty and dedication to consolidate the revolutionary triumph. My only serious failing was not having had more confidence in you from the first moments in the Sierra Maestra, and not having understood quickly enough your qualities as a leader and a revolutionary.

I have lived magnificent days, and at your side I felt the pride of belonging to our people in the brilliant yet sad days of the Caribbean crisis. Seldom has a statesman been more brilliant than you in those days. I am also proud of having followed you without hesitation, identified with your way of thinking and of seeing and appraising dangers and principles.

Other nations of the world call for my modest efforts. I can do that which is denied you because of your responsibility at the head of Cuba, and the time has come for us to part.

I want it known that I do so with a mixture of joy and sorrow. I leave here the purest of my hopes as a builder and the dearest of my loved ones. And I leave a people who received me as a son. That wounds a part of my spirit. I carry to new battlefronts the faith that you taught me, the revolutionary spirit of my people, the feeling of fulfilling the most sacred of duties: to fight against imperialism wherever it may be. This comforts and heals the deepest wounds.

I state once more that I free Cuba from any responsibility, except that which stems from its example. If my final hour finds me under other skies, my last thought will be of this people and especially of you. I am thankful for your teaching, your example, and I will try to be faithful up to the final consequences of my acts.

I have always been identified with the foreign policy of our revolution, and I continue to be. Wherever I am, I will feel the responsibility of being a Cuban Revolutionary, and I shall behave as such. I am not ashamed that I leave nothing material to my children and my wife; I am happy it is that way. I ask nothing for them, as the state will provide them with enough to live on and have an education.

I would have a lot of things to say to you and to our people, but I feel they are unnecessary. Words cannot express what I would want them to, and I don't think it's worthwhile to keep scribbling pages.

Hasta la victoria siempre! Patria o muerte!

I embrace you with all my revolutionary fervor.

Che

Those who speak of revolutionaries, those who consider revolutionaries as cold people, insensitive people, and unfeeling people will have in this letter the example of all the feeling, all the sensitivity, all the purity that can be held within a revolutionary soul.

23

DEATH OF CHE GUEVARA

October 8, 1967

Ever since mid-September 1967, the international wire services had been carrying disquieting reports stating that the Bolivian Army might be laying a tactical encirclement around the tiny guerrilla group that Ernesto Che Guevara commanded in the mountains in the southeastern part of Bolivia.

Using information obtained from captured prisoners, the Bolivian military regime was already certain that Che and the Cuban combatants were with the Bolivian revolutionaries in the guerrilla group that had begun armed actions in a jungle area near Ñancahuazú on March 23 of that year.

U.S. advisers and CIA agents had been sent to La Paz and to the zone of operations to help capture him, dead or alive.

Diverse factors had combined at that time to place Che in an especially difficult situation; moreover, the beginning of every struggle involving irregular warfare, with a very small force in a territory that has not yet been consolidated and in which the enemy troops can move wherever they want, is always complex and dangerous.

The separation – which should have been temporary – of the group commanded by Joaquín (Major Vitalio Acuña[1]) from the rest of the

---

[1] Vitalio Acuña Núñez, a major in Cuba's Rebel Army, was one of the first peasant farmers who joined the guerrillas in the Sierra Maestra Mountains. He held various military commands after the triumph of the Cuban Revolution.

guerrillas and Che's fruitless efforts to find them took precious time and forced Che and his group to stay more or less in the same area, which made it easier for the enemy to find them. The ambushing and annihilation of Joaquín's group on August 31, 1967, also meant the loss of valuable combatants. In addition, Che didn't have enough medicine to control his frequent asthma attacks, which weakened him. Finally, the group included combatants who were in very bad physical condition, which forced them to march through populated areas during the day, and this inevitably led to a clash with army forces, large numbers of whom were trying to corner the guerrilla group.

On September 26, the guerrilla vanguard was ambushed in Batán Valley, and three of the best combatants were killed. This terrible setback placed the group in a situation of extreme peril, even though Che's diary from the time doesn't show that he felt lost or considered his situation to be hopeless.

Che waged his last battle, at Yuro Ravine, on October 8, 1967. He was wounded, though not mortally; the barrel of his M-2 carbine had been put out of commission; he didn't have a magazine for his pistol; and most of the revolutionaries who had fought at his side had been killed. In this situation, he was captured by a company of Bolivian Rangers and taken to the little schoolhouse in the hamlet of La Higuera. There, the troops received orders from La Paz to kill him. A drunken sergeant major carried out the order the next day, October 9, going into the classroom where Che was tied up and killing him with a burst of his submachine gun.

The Cuban people refused to believe the reports of Che's death that came in from Bolivia until Fidel Castro went on television and presented irrefutable, detailed information convincing them that it was so. A photo showed the CIA agent and terrorist Félix Rodríguez[2] in a group of people next to Che's body, proving that the United States had taken part in Che's death.

A silent, grieving crowd bade farewell to Che in a solemn vigil held in Havana's Revolution Square.

All were aware of their immense loss, even though the extent of this loss couldn't be adequately judged at the time. Everyone now knows that the Heroic Guerrilla's dreams and revolutionary plans encompassed all of Latin America and the world. His talent as a truly critical and creative Marxist thinker placed him in the vanguard of revolutionary thinkers. The experience he had gained in building socialism in Cuba and his opinions about the achievements and defects of what had been done in other countries were extremely valuable. All of those qualities combined in his personality

---

[2] Félix Rodríguez: Since 1959, he has taken part in several plans and actions against Cuba and in covert actions in Vietnam and Central America.

as a political figure, economist, military commander, trainer of cadres and inspired writer. As Fidel Castro said some years later, "Che is much more than everything that has been written about him."

Fidel Castro also refuted reports of alleged disagreements between Major Ernesto Guevara and the other leaders of the Cuban Revolution.

"In Mexico, after he joined our movement,[3] he made me promise him that after the triumph of the revolution in Cuba, I would allow him to return to fight for his homeland or for Latin America. He remained in Cuba for several years, carrying out important responsibilities, but he always had that in mind. And when the time came I kept my word. I didn't hold him back or hamper his return; rather, I helped him do what he believed was his duty. At the time I didn't stop to think if my doing so could harm me. I faithfully kept the promise I had made, and when he said, 'I want to go on a revolutionary mission now,' I said, 'All right, I'll keep my promise.'

"Everything was done in great accord. The things that were said about alleged differences with the Cuban Revolution were infamous calumnies. He had his own personality and criteria. We used to argue fraternally on various topics, but there was always harmony, communication, complete unity on everything, and excellent relations, because he also had a great sense of discipline."[4]

For 30 years, the place where Che's body was buried remained a secret; but, in 1997, the Cuban people were finally able to pay tribute to and express their admiration for him by placing his remains and those of a group of the comrades who died with him in Bolivia at the base of the monument to Che that was built in Santa Clara, in the central part of the island, where he had carried out one of his greatest feats during Cuba's War of Liberation.

A necessary introduction

(This Introduction by Fidel Castro appeared in the Cuban and international editions of Che Guevara's Bolivian Diary when it was first published in Cuba in 1968)

It was Che's custom during his days as a guerrilla [during the Cuban Revolutionary War] to carefully record his daily observations in a personal diary. During long marches over rugged and difficult terrain, in the midst of damp woods, when the lines of men, always hunched over from the weight of their packs, ammunition and

---

[3] The reference is to the stage of exile in Mexico, when Fidel Castro met Ernesto Guevara and the latter joined the expedition on the cabin cruiser *Granma*.
[4] Frei Betto, *Fidel & Religion* (Melbourne: Ocean Press, 1991), 264.

weapons, would stop for a moment to rest, or when the column would receive orders to halt and set up camp at the end of an exhausting day's march, you would see Che — as he was from the beginning affectionately nicknamed by the Cubans — take out a small notebook and, with the tiny and nearly illegible handwriting of a doctor, write his notes. What he was able to save from these notes he later used in writing his magnificent historical narratives of the revolutionary war in Cuba, accounts full of revolutionary, educational and human content.

This time, thanks to his invariable habit of noting the main events of each day, we have at our disposal rigorously exact, priceless, and detailed information on the heroic final months of his life in Bolivia.

These notes, not really written for publication, served as a tool in the constant evaluation of events, situations and people. They also served as an outlet for the expression of his keenly observant and analytical spirit, often laced with a fine sense of humor. They are soberly written and form a coherent whole from beginning to end.

It should be kept in mind that they were written during those rare moments of rest in the middle of a heroic and superhuman physical effort. Also to be remembered are his exhausting obligations as leader of a guerrilla detachment in the difficult first stages of a struggle of this nature, which unfolded under incredibly harsh material conditions. This reveals once more his way of working, his will of steel.

[Che's Bolivian] Diary, in the course of analyzing in detail the incidents of each day, takes note of the shortcomings, critical assessments and recriminations that are inevitable in the development of a revolutionary guerrilla struggle.

Inside a guerrilla detachment such assessments must take place incessantly. This is especially true in the stage in which it consists of a small nucleus facing extremely adverse material conditions and an enemy infinitely superior in number, when the slightest negligence or the most insignificant mistake can be fatal. The leader must be extremely demanding. He must use each event or episode, no matter how insignificant it may seem, to educate the combatants and future cadres of new guerrilla detachments.

The process of training a guerrilla force is a constant appeal to each man's consciousness and honor. Che knew how to touch the most sensitive fibers in revolutionaries. When Marcos, after being repeatedly admonished by Che, was warned that he could be dishonorably discharged from the guerrilla unit, he replied, "I would rather be shot!" Later he gave his life heroically. Similar behavior could be noted among all those Che placed confidence in and whom he had to admonish for one reason or another in the course of the struggle. He was a fraternal and humane leader, but he also knew how to be demanding and, at times, severe. But above all, and even more so than with the others, Che was severe with himself. He based discipline on the guerrilla's moral consciousness and on the tremendous force of his own example.

The diary also contains numerous references to [Régis] Debray. It reflects the enormous concern Che felt over the arrest and imprisonment of the revolutionary writer who had been given a mission to carry out in Europe — although, at heart, Che would have preferred him to have stayed with the guerrilla unit. That is why Che shows a certain lack of patience and, on occasion, some doubts about his behavior.

Che had no way of knowing the odyssey Debray lived through in the hands of the repressive forces, or the firm and courageous attitude he maintained in face of his captors and torturers. He noted, however, the enormous political significance of the trial and on October 3, six days before his death, in the middle of bitter and tense events, he wrote: "We heard an interview with Debray, very courageous when faced with a student provocateur." That was his last reference to the writer.

The Cuban Revolution and its relation to the guerrilla movement are repeatedly referred to in the diary. Some may interpret our decision to publish it as an act of provocation that will give the enemies of the revolution — the Yankee imperialists and their allies, the Latin American oligarchs — arguments for redoubling their efforts to blockade, isolate, and attack Cuba.

Those who judge the facts this way should remember that Yankee imperialism has never needed a pretext to carry out its crimes anywhere in the world, and that its efforts to crush the Cuban Revolution began as soon as our country passed its first revolutionary law. This stems from the obvious and well-known fact that imperialism is the policeman of world reaction, the systematic supporter of counterrevolution, and the protector of the most backward and inhuman social structures that remain in the world.

Solidarity with a revolutionary movement may be taken as a pretext for Yankee aggression, but it will never be the real cause. To deny solidarity in order to avoid giving a pretext is a ridiculous, ostrich-like policy that has nothing to do with the internationalist character of the social revolutions of today. To abandon solidarity with a revolutionary movement not only does not avoid providing a pretext, but in effect serves to show solidarity with Yankee imperialism and its policy of dominating and enslaving the world.

Cuba is a small country, economically underdeveloped as are countries dominated and exploited for centuries by colonialism and imperialism. It is located only 90 miles from the coast of the United States, has a Yankee naval base on its territory [Guantánamo], and faces numerous obstacles in attaining socioeconomic development. Grave dangers have threatened our country since the triumph of the revolution. But imperialism will never make us yield for these reasons, because the difficulties that flow from a consistently revolutionary line of action are of no importance to us.

From the revolutionary point of view, there is no alternative but to publish Che's Bolivian diary. It fell into the hands of [Bolivian dictator René] Barrientos, who immediately sent copies to the CIA, the Pentagon, and the U.S. Government. Journalists connected with the CIA had access to the document inside Bolivia. Having made photocopies of it, they promised that they would refrain, for the moment, from publishing it.

The Barrientos Government and the top-ranking military officers have more than enough reasons not to publish the diary. It reveals the immense incapacity of their army and the countless defeats they were dealt by a handful of determined guerrillas who, in a matter of weeks, took nearly 200 weapons from them in combat. Furthermore, Che describes Barrientos and his regime in terms they deserve, with words that cannot be erased from history.

Imperialism also had its own reasons. Che and the extraordinary example he set are gaining increasing force in the world. His ideas, image and name are banners of struggle against the injustices suffered by the oppressed and exploited. They evoke impassioned interest among students and intellectuals the world over.

In the United States itself, the Black movement and progressive students, both of which are continuing to grow in numbers, have made Che's figure their own. In the most combative demonstrations for civil rights and against the aggression in Vietnam, his image is brandished as a symbol of struggle. Few times in history, perhaps never before, has a figure, a name, an example become a universal symbol so quickly and with such impassioned force. This is because Che embodies, in its purest and most selfless form, the internationalist spirit that marks the world of today and that will characterize even more the world of tomorrow.

Out of a continent yesterday oppressed by colonial powers, today exploited and held in backwardness and the most iniquitous underdevelopment by Yankee imperialism, there has emerged this singular figure who has become the universal symbol of revolutionary struggle, even in the metropolitan centers of the imperialists and colonialists.

The Yankee imperialists fear the power of this example and everything that may help to spread it. The diary is the living expression of an extraordinary personality; a lesson in guerrilla warfare written in the heat and tension of daily events, as flammable as gunpowder; a demonstration in life that the people of Latin America are not powerless in face of the enslavers of entire peoples and of their mercenary armies. That is its intrinsic value, and that is what has kept them from publishing it up until now.

Also among those who may be interested in keeping the diary unpublished are the pseudo-revolutionaries, opportunists and charlatans of every stripe. These people call themselves Marxists, communists and other such titles. They have not, however, hesitated to call Che a mistaken adventurer or, when they speak more benignly, an idealist whose death marked the swan song of revolutionary armed struggle in Latin America. "If Che himself," they say, "the greatest exponent of these ideas and an experienced guerrilla fighter, died in the guerrilla struggle and his movement failed to free Bolivia, it only shows how mistaken he was ... !" How many of these miserable creatures were happy with the death of Che and have not even blushed at the thought that their positions and reasoning completely coincide with those of imperialism and the most reactionary oligarchs!

That is how they justify themselves. That is how they justify their treacherous leaders who, at a given moment, did not hesitate to play at armed struggle with the underlying intention as could be seen later — of destroying the guerrilla detachments, putting the brakes on revolutionary action, and imposing their own shameful and ridiculous political schemes, because they were absolutely incapable of carrying out any other line. That is how they justify those who do not want to fight, who will never fight for the people and their liberation. That is how they justify those who have made a caricature of revolutionary ideas, turning them into an opium-like dogma with neither content nor message for the masses; those who have converted the organizations of popular struggle into instruments of conciliation with domestic and foreign exploiters; and those who advocate policies that have nothing to do with the genuine interests of the exploited peoples of this continent.

Che thought of his death as something natural and probable in the process. He made an effort to stress, especially in his last writings, that this eventuality would not hold back the inevitable march of the revolution in Latin America. In his *Message to the Tricontinental,* he reiterated this thought: "Our every action is a battle cry against imperialism... Wherever death may surprise us, let it be welcome if our battle cry has reached even one receptive ear, if another hand reaches out to take up our arms."

Che considered himself a soldier in the revolution, with absolutely no concern as to whether he would survive it. Those who see the outcome of his struggle in Bolivia as marking the failure of his ideas can, with the same oversimplification, deny the validity of the ideas and struggles of all the great revolutionary precursors and thinkers. This includes the founders of Marxism, who were themselves unable to complete the task and to view in life the fruits of their noble efforts.

In Cuba, Martí and Maceo were killed in combat; Yankee intervention followed, ending the war of independence and frustrating the immediate objectives of their struggle. Brilliant advocates of socialist revolution like Julio Antonio Mella have been killed, murdered by agents in the service of imperialism. But these deaths could not, in the long run, block the triumph of a process that began 100 years ago. And absolutely nothing can call into question the profound justice of the cause and line of struggle of those eminent fighters, nor the timeliness of their basic ideas, which have always inspired Cuban Revolutionaries.

In Che's diary, from the notes he wrote, you can see how real the possibilities of success were, how extraordinary the catalyzing power of the guerrilla struggle. On one occasion, in face of evident signs of the Bolivian regime's weakness and rapid deterioration, he wrote: "The government is disintegrating rapidly. It's a shame we don't have 100 more men right now."

Che knew from his experience in Cuba how often our small guerrilla detachment had been on the verge of being wiped out. Whether such things happen depends almost entirely on chance and the imponderables of war. But would such an eventuality have given anyone the right to consider our line erroneous, and in addition to take it as an example to discourage revolution and inculcate a sense of powerlessness among the peoples? Many times in history revolutionary processes have been preceded by adverse episodes. We ourselves in Cuba, didn't we have the experience of Moncada just six years before the definitive triumph of the people's armed struggle?

From July 26, 1953 — the attack on the Moncada garrison in Santiago de Cuba — to December 2, 1956 — the landing of the *Granma* — revolutionary struggle in Cuba in the face of a modern, well-equipped army seemed to many people to lack any prospect for success. The action of a handful of fighters was seen as a chimera of idealists and dreamers "who were deeply mistaken." The crushing defeat and total dispersal of the inexperienced guerrilla detachment on December 5, 1956, seemed to confirm entirely those pessimistic forebodings. But only 25 months later the remnants of that guerrilla unit had already developed the strength and experience necessary to annihilate that same army.

In all epochs and under all circumstances, there will always be an abundance of pretexts for not fighting; but not fighting is the only way to never attain freedom. Che did not live as long as his ideas; he fertilized them with his blood. It is certain, on the other hand, that his pseudo-revolutionary critics, with all their political cowardice and eternal lack of action, will outlive by far the evidence of their own stupidity.

To be noted, as can be seen in the diary, are the actions of one of those revolutionary specimens that are becoming typical in Latin America these days. Mario Monje, brandishing the title of Secretary of the Communist Party of Bolivia, sought to dispute with Che the political and military leadership of the movement. Monje claimed, moreover, that he had intended to resign his party post to take on this responsibility; in his opinion, obviously, it was enough to have once held that title to claim such a prerogative.

Mario Monje, naturally, had no experience in guerrilla warfare and had never been in combat. In addition, the fact that he considered himself a communist should at least have obliged him to dispense with the gross and mundane chauvinism that had already been overcome by those who fought for Bolivia's first independence.

With such a conception of what an anti-imperialist struggle on this continent should be, "communist leaders" of this type do not even surpass the level of internationalism of the aboriginal tribes subjugated by the European colonizers in the epoch of the conquest.

Bolivia and its historical capital, Sucre, were named after the country's first liberators [Simon Bolívar and Antonio José de Sucre], both of whom were Venezuelan. And in this country, in a struggle for the definitive liberation of his people, the leader of the Communist Party had the possibility of enlisting the cooperation of the political, organizational, and military talent of a genuine revolutionary titan, of a person whose cause was not limited by the narrow and artificial — not to mention unjust borders of Bolivia. Yet he did nothing but engage in disgraceful, ridiculous and unmerited claims to leadership.

Bolivia does not have an outlet to the sea. For its own liberation, to avoid exposure to a cruel blockade, it more than any other country needs revolutionary victories by its neighbors. Che, because of his enormous authority, ability and experience, was the person who could have accelerated this process.

In the period before a split occurred in the Bolivian Communist Party, Che had established relations with leaders and members of it, soliciting their help for the revolutionary movement in South America. Under authorization from the party, some members worked with Che for years on various assignments. When the split occurred, it created a special situation, given that a number of the people who had been working with him ended up in one or another group. But Che did not see the struggle in Bolivia as an isolated occurrence, rather as part of a revolutionary liberation movement that would soon extend to other countries in South America. He sought to organize a movement free of sectarianism, one that could be joined by anyone who wanted to fight for the liberation of Bolivia and of all the other peoples of Latin America subjugated by imperialism.

In the initial phase of preparing a base for the guerrilla unit, however, Che depended for the most part on the help of a group of courageous and discreet collaborators who, at the time of the split, remained in the party headed by Monje. Although he certainly felt no sympathy toward Monje, in deference to them he invited Monje to visit his camp first. He then invited Moisés Guevara, a leader of the miners and a political leader. Moisés Guevara had left the party to join in the formation of another organization, the one led by Oscar Zamora. He later left that group as well because of differences with Zamora. Zamora was another Monje. He had once promised Che he would help in organizing the armed guerrilla struggle in Bolivia. He later backed away from that commitment and cowardly folded his arms at the hour of action. After Che's death, Zamora became one of his most venomous "Marxist-Leninist" critics. Moisés Guevara joined Che without hesitation, as he had sought to do long before Che arrived in Bolivia. He offered his support and gave his life heroically for the revolutionary cause.

The group of Bolivian guerrillas who until then had stayed with Monje's organization also joined Che. Led by Inti and Coco Peredo, who proved to be courageous, outstanding fighters, they left Monje and decisively backed Che. But Monje, seeking revenge, began to sabotage the movement. In La Paz he intercepted well-trained communist militants who were on their way to join the guerrillas. These facts demonstrate that within the ranks of revolutionaries, men who meet all the conditions necessary for struggle can be criminally frustrated in their development by incapable, maneuvering and charlatan-like leaders.

Che was a person never interested in posts, leadership, or honors. But he believed revolutionary guerrilla warfare was the fundamental form of action for the liberation of the peoples of Latin America, given the economic, political and social situation of nearly all Latin American countries. And he was firmly convinced that the military and political leadership of the guerrilla struggle had to be unified. He also believed the struggle could be led only from the guerrilla unit itself, and not from the comfortable offices of bureaucrats in the cities. So he was not prepared to give up leadership of a guerrilla nucleus that, at a later stage of its development, was intended to develop into a struggle of broad dimensions in Latin America. And he certainly was not prepared to turn over such leadership to an inexperienced empty head with narrow chauvinist views. Such chauvinism often infects even revolutionary elements of various countries in Latin America. Che believed that it must be fought because it represents reactionary, ridiculous and sterile thinking.

"And let us develop genuine proletarian internationalism..." he said in his *Message to the Tricontinental*. "Let the flag under which we fight be the sacred cause of the liberation of humanity, so that to die under the colors of Vietnam, Venezuela, Guatemala, Laos, Guinea, Colombia, Bolivia... to mention only the current scenes of armed struggle, will be equally glorious and desirable for a Latin American, an Asian, an African and even a European.

"Every drop of blood spilled in a land under whose flag one was not born is experience gathered by the survivor to be applied later in the struggle for liberation of one's own country. And every people that liberates itself is a step in the battle for the liberation of one's own people."

In the same way, Che believed fighters from various Latin American countries would participate in the guerrilla detachment, that the guerrilla struggle in Bolivia would be a school in which revolutionaries would serve their apprenticeship in combat. To help him with this task he wanted to have, together with the Bolivians, a small nucleus of experienced guerrilla fighters, nearly all of whom had been comrades of his in the Sierra Maestra during the revolutionary struggle in Cuba. These were men whose abilities, courage and spirit of self-sacrifice were known by Che. None of them hesitated to respond to his call, none of them abandoned him, none of them surrendered.

In the Bolivian campaign Che acted with his proverbial tenacity, skill, stoicism and exemplary attitude. It might be said that he was consumed with the importance of the mission he had assigned himself, and at all times he proceeded with a spirit of irreproachable responsibility. When the guerrilla unit committed an error of carelessness, he quickly called attention to it, corrected it, and noted it in his diary.

Adverse factors built up against him unbelievably. One example was the separation — supposed to last for just a few days — of part of the guerrilla detachment. That unit included a courageous group of men, some of them sick or convalescent. Once contact between the two groups was lost in very rough terrain, separation continued, and for endless months Che was occupied with the effort to find them. In this period his asthma, an ailment easily treated with simple medication, but one that, lacking the medication, became a terrible enemy — attacked him relentlessly. It became a serious problem since the medical supplies that had been accumulated by the guerrillas beforehand had been discovered and captured by the enemy. This fact, along with the annihilation at the end of August of the part of the guerrilla detachment he had lost contact with, were factors that weighed considerably in the development of events. But Che, with his iron will, overcame his physical difficulties and never for an instant cut back his activity or let his spirits fall.

Che had many contacts with the Bolivian peasants. Their character — highly suspicious and cautious — would have come as no surprise to Che, who knew their mentality perfectly well because he had dealt with them on other occasions. He knew that winning them over to the cause required long, arduous and patient work, but he had no doubt that in the long run they would obtain the support of the peasants.

If we follow the thread of events carefully, it becomes clear that even when the number of men on whom Che could count was quite small — in the month of September, a few weeks before his death — the guerrilla unit still retained its capacity to develop. It also still had a few Bolivian cadres, such as the brothers Inti and Coco Peredo, who were already beginning to show magnificent leadership potential.

It was the ambush in La Higuera [on September 26, 1967] — the sole successful action by the army against the detachment led by Che — that created a situation they could not overcome. In that ambush, in broad daylight, the advance guard was killed and several more men were wounded as they headed toward a peasant area with a higher level of political development — an objective that does not appear to have been noted in the diary but that was known to the survivors. It was without doubt dangerous to advance by daylight along the same route they had been following for days, with inevitably broad contact with the residents of an area they were crossing for the first time. It was obvious and certain that the army would intercept them at some point. But Che, fully conscious of this, decided to run the risk in order to help the doctor [Octavio de la Concepción de la Pedreja (Moro)], who was in very poor physical condition.

The day before the ambush, he wrote: "We reached Pujio but there were people who had seen us down below the day before, which means we are being announced ahead of time by Radio Bemba [word of mouth]... The march with mules is becoming dangerous, but I want the doctor to travel in the best possible way because he is very weak."

The following day he wrote: "At 13:00 the advance guard set out to try to reach Jagüey and to make a decision there about the mules and the doctor." That is, he was seeking a solution for the sick, so as to get off the road and take the necessary precautions. But that same afternoon, before the advance guard reached Jagüey, the fatal ambush occurred, leaving the detachment in an untenable situation.

A few days later, encircled in the El Yuro ravine, Che fought his final battle.

Recalling the feat carried out by this handful of revolutionaries touches one deeply. The struggle against the hostile natural environment in which their action took place constitutes by itself an insurmountable page of heroism. Never in history has so small a number of men set out on such a gigantic task. Their faith and absolute conviction that the immense revolutionary capacity of the peoples of Latin America could be awakened, their confidence in themselves and the determination with which they took on this objective — those things give us a just measure of these men.

One day Che said to the guerrilla fighters in Bolivia: "This type of struggle gives us the opportunity to become revolutionaries, the highest form of the human species, and it also enables us to become men. Those who cannot reach either of these two stages should say so and leave the struggle."

Those who fought with him until the end have become worthy of such honored terms. They symbolize the type of revolutionary and the type of person history is now calling on for a truly stubborn and difficult task — the revolutionary transformation of Latin America.

The enemy our forefathers faced in the first struggle for independence was a decadent colonial power. Revolutionaries of today have as their enemy the most powerful bulwark of the imperialist camp, equipped with the most modern technology and industry. This enemy not only organized and equipped a new army for Bolivia — where the people had destroyed the previous repressive military apparatus — and immediately sent weapons and advisers to help in the struggle against the guerrillas. It has also provided military and technical support on the same scale to every repressive force on the continent. And when these methods are not enough, it has intervened directly with its troops, as in the Dominican Republic.

Fighting this enemy requires the type of revolutionaries and men Che spoke of. Without this type of revolutionary and men, ready to do what they did; without the spirit to confront the enormous obstacles they faced; without the readiness to die that accompanied them at every moment; without their deeply held conviction in the justice of their cause and their unyielding faith in the invincible force of the peoples, against a power like Yankee imperialism, whose military, technical and economic resources are felt throughout the entire world — without these, the liberation of the peoples of this continent will not be attained.

The people of the United States themselves are beginning to become aware that the monstrous political superstructure that reigns in their country has for some time no longer been the idyllic bourgeois republic the country's founders established nearly 200 years ago. They are increasingly subjected to the moral barbarism of an irrational, alienating, dehumanized and brutal system that takes from the people of the United States a growing number of victims in its wars of aggression, its political crimes, its racial aberrations, the miserable hierarchy it has established for human beings, its repugnant waste of economic, scientific and human resources on its enormous, reactionary and repressive military apparatus — in the midst of a world where three-quarters of humanity lives in underdevelopment and hunger.

Only the revolutionary transformation of Latin America will enable the people of the United States to settle their own accounts with imperialism. At the same time, and in the same way, the growing struggle of the people of the United States against imperialist policy can become a decisive ally of the revolutionary movement in Latin America.

An enormous differentiation and imbalance occurred in the Americas at the beginning of this century. On one side a powerful and rapidly industrializing nation, in accordance with the very law of its social and economic dynamics, was marching toward imperial heights. On the other side, the weak and stagnant countries in the Balkanized remainder of the Americas were kept under the boot of feudal oligarchies and their reactionary armies. If this part of the hemisphere does not undergo a profound revolutionary transformation, that earlier gap will seem but a pale reflection of not just the enormous present unevenness in finance, science and technology, but rather of the horrible imbalance that, at an increasingly accelerated rate, the imperialist superstructure will impose on the peoples of Latin America in the next 20 years.

If we stay on this road, we will be increasingly poor, weak, dependent and enslaved to imperialism. This gloomy perspective also confronts, to an equal degree, all the underdeveloped nations of Africa and Asia. If the industrialized and educated nations of Europe, with their Common Market and supranational scientific institutions, are worried about the possibility of being left behind and contemplate with fear the perspective of being converted into economic colonies of Yankee imperialism — what does the future have in store for the peoples of Latin America?

This is unquestionably the real situation that decisively affects the destiny of our peoples. What is urgently needed is a deep-going revolutionary transformation that can gather together all the moral, material and human forces in this part of the world and launch them forward so as to overcome the economic, scientific and technological backwardness of centuries; a backwardness that is greater still when compared with the industrialized world to which we are tributaries and will continue to be to an even greater degree, especially to the United States. If some liberal or bourgeois reformist, or some pseudo-revolutionary charlatan, incapable of action, has a different answer; and if, in addition, he can provide the formula, the magic road to carrying it out, that is different from Che's conception; one that can sweep away the oligarchs, despots and petty politicians — that is to say, the servants — and the Yankee monopolies — that is, the masters — and can do it with all the urgency the circumstances require; then let him stand up to challenge Che.

But no one really has an honest answer or a consistent policy that will bring genuine hope to the nearly 300 million human beings who make up the population of Latin America. Devastatingly poor in their overwhelming majority and increasing in number to 600 million within 25 years, they have the right to the material things of life, to culture and to civilization. So the most dignified thing would be to remain silent in face of the action of Che and those who fell with him, courageously defending their ideas. The feat carried out by this handful of men, guided by the noble idea of redeeming a continent, will remain the greatest proof of what determination, heroism and human greatness can accomplish. It is an example that will illuminate the consciousness and preside over the struggle of the peoples of Latin America. Che's heroic cry will reach the receptive ear of the poor and exploited for whom he gave his life; many hands will come forward to take up arms to win their definitive liberation.

On October 7, Che wrote his last lines. The following day, at 1:00 in the afternoon, in a narrow ravine where he proposed waiting until nightfall in order to break out of the encirclement, a large enemy force made contact with them. The small group of men who now made up the detachment fought heroically until dusk. From individual positions located on the bottom of the ravine, and on the top edges, they faced a mass of soldiers who surrounded and attacked them. There were no survivors among those who fought in the positions closest to Che. Since beside him were the doctor in the grave state of health mentioned before, and a Peruvian guerrilla who was also in very poor physical condition, everything seems to indicate that until he fell wounded, Che did his utmost to safeguard the withdrawal of these comrades to a safer place. The doctor was not killed in the same battle, but rather several days later at a place not far from the El Yuro ravine. The ruggedness of the rocky, irregular terrain made it difficult — at times impossible — for the guerrillas to maintain visual contact. Those defending positions at the other entrance to the ravine, some hundreds of meters from Che, among them Inti Peredo, resisted the attack until dark, when they managed to lose the enemy and head toward the previously agreed point of regroupment.

It has been possible to establish that Che continued fighting despite being wounded, until a shot destroyed the barrel of his M-2 rifle, making it totally useless. The pistol he carried had no magazine. These incredible circumstances explain how he could have been captured alive. The wounds in his legs kept him from walking without help, but they were not fatal.

Moved to the town of La Higuera, he remained alive some 24 hours. He refused to exchange a single word with his captors, and a drunken officer who tried to annoy him received a slap across the face.

At a meeting in La Paz, Barrientos, Ovando, and other high military leaders coldly made the decision to murder Che. Details are known of the way in which the treacherous agreement was made and carried out in the school at Higuera. Major Miguel Ayoroa and Colonel Andrés Selnich, Rangers trained by the Yankees, ordered Warrant Officer Mario Terán to proceed with the murder. Terán, completely drunk, entered the school yard. When Che, who heard the shots that had just killed a Bolivian [Simón Cuba (Willy)] and a Peruvian guerrilla fighter [Juan Pablo Chang (Chino)], saw the executioner hesitate, he said firmly, "Shoot! Don't be afraid!" Terán left, and again it was necessary for his superiors, Ayoroa and Selnich, to repeat the order. He then proceeded to carry it out, firing a machine-gun burst from the belt down. A version had already been given out that Che died a few hours after combat; therefore, the executioners had orders not to shoot him in the chest or head, so as not to induce immediately fatal wounds. This cruelly prolonged Che's agony until a sergeant, also drunk, killed him with a pistol shot to the left side. Such a procedure contrasts brutally with the respect shown by Che, without a single exception, toward the lives of the many officers and soldiers of the Bolivian Army he took prisoner.

The final hours of his existence in the hands of his contemptible enemies must have been very bitter for him. But no person was better prepared than Che to be put to such a test.

The way in which the diary came into our hands cannot be told at this time; suffice it to say it required no monetary payment. It contains all the notes he wrote from November 7, 1966, the day Che arrived in Ñancahuazú, until October 7, 1967, the evening before the battle in the El Yuro ravine. There are a few pages missing, pages that have not yet arrived in our hands; but they correspond to dates on which nothing of any importance happened, and therefore do not alter the content of the diary in any way.

Although the document itself offers not the slightest doubt as to its authenticity, all photocopies have been subjected to a rigorous examination to establish not only its authenticity but also to check on any possible alteration, no matter how slight. The dates were compared with the diary of one of the surviving guerrilla fighters; both documents coincided in every aspect. Detailed testimony of the other surviving guerrilla fighters, who were witnesses to each one of the events, also contributed to establishing the document's authenticity. In short, it has been established with absolute certainty that all the photostats were faithful copies of Che's diary.

It was a tiring job to decipher the small and difficult handwriting, a task that was carried out with the tireless assistance of his *compañera*, Aleida March de Guevara.

The diary will be published almost simultaneously in France by the publishing house of Francois Maspero; in Italy by Feltrinelli publishers; in the Federal Republic of Germany by Trikont Verlag; in the United States by *Ramparts* magazine; in France, in a Spanish edition, by Ediciones Ruedo Ibérico; in Chile by the magazine *Punto Final;* in Mexico by Editorial Siglo XXI; and in other countries.

Hasta la victoria siempre! [Ever onward to victory!]

Fidel Castro

24

100TH ANNIVERSARY OF THE UPRISING AT LA DEMAJAGUA

October 10, 1968

It is not easy to establish dates for the development of an idea. As a rule, ideas take shape in the course of processes that don't always emerge publicly and that imply theoretical reflection, social practice and step-by-step progress toward conceptualization and definition. But, if one day, one moment, in the history of Cuban revolutionary thinking over the past 40 years had to be chosen to show the theses that defined the essence of the Cuban experience with particular clarity, it would be October 10, 1968.

That date was the 100th anniversary of the uprising headed by Bayamo lawyer Carlos Manuel de Céspedes,[1] who, after conspiring with other aristocrats in the eastern part of Cuba against Spanish colonial rule, decided to take up arms and free his slaves rather than be discovered and imprisoned. He carried out that decision at the La Demajagua Sugar Mill at dawn on October 10, 1868.

The Ten Years' War, which he began, was the crucible in which the Cuban nation was forged. It was the cradle of patriotic, pro-independence traditions that have been handed down to us and the medium that produced

---

[1] Carlos Manuel de Céspedes (1819-74). He studied in Europe and was the first to take up arms against Spanish colonial rule. First President of the Republic of Cuba in Arms. Surprised by an enemy force at San Lorenzo in the Sierra Maestra Mountains, he was killed in battle on February 27, 1874. Cuba honors him as the Father of his Country.

such other great figures as Ignacio Agramonte,[2] Máximo Gómez[3] and Antonio Maceo.[4]

That effort was also the first great political school for Cuban Revolutionaries. Alone, and in the limited compass of a small island, the Cuban people opposed a colonialist military power that was larger than the forces against which the armies of liberation fought at the beginning of the 19th century in the larger field of South America. Their glories and failure in 1878, when the war ended without achieving sovereignty or the emancipation of the slaves, taught the patriots of all times – and particularly José Martí, the brilliant organizer of the War of 1895 – the importance of unity and of political leadership for the triumph of the revolution.

As was only logical, the observance of that 100th anniversary – in the wake of the victorious Cuban Revolution, which had already amassed considerable experience in its struggle for survival and in the transition toward socialism – was an appropriate moment for analyzing several key issues.

One of these was the relationship between Cuba's history and the progressive values and traditions of the country's culture, including political thinking, on the one hand, and socialism at the international level and the ideas of Marx, Engels, Lenin and other fighters and theoreticians, on the other.

The world communist and workers' movement hadn't been exempt from sectarianism and dogmatism. They had been conditioned by diverse circumstances, in which patriotism was set against internationalism, the tradition of advanced national thinking was set against Marxism-Leninism, and the great figures of the country's history were set against international leaders of the working class and socialism.

This didn't happen in the case of Cuba, whose first Communist Party had been struggling against the most pernicious schemes of the Third

---

[2] Ignacio Agramonte y Loynaz. One of the main political and military leaders of the Ten Years' War (1868-78). Representative of Camagüey (where he took up arms on November 4, 1868) to the Constitutional Assembly of Guáimaro. Head of the famous Camagüey cavalry. He was killed in battle at Jimaguayú on May 11, 1873.

[3] Máximo Gómez Báez (18??-1906). A citizen of the Dominican Republic. He joined in the Ten Years' War at its beginning and was the first to teach Cubans the technique of machete charges. Major General of the Liberation Army, he helped José Martí organize the new War of 1895, in which he served as General in Chief of the Liberation Army.

[4] Antonio Maceo y Grajales (1845-96). Second in command of the Liberation Army, he came from a heroic family of AfroCuban farmers. He won all his promotions in combat. He fought in the Ten Years' War and in the War of 1895 — in which, together with Máximo Gómez, his commanding officer and teacher, he carried out the military feat of extending the fighting to the western part of the country. He was also an outstanding political figure and revolutionary. He was killed in battle on December 7, 1896.

International ever since the mid-1930s and where such outstanding intellectuals and political leaders as Carlos Rafael Rodríguez,[5] Juan Marinello[6] and Blas Roca[7] made the dialectics of national liberation and the democratic and socialist revolution an integral part of its Communist Party. Even so, confusion, narrow criteria and puerile dogmatism persisted, stemming in many cases from ignorance of Cuba's history.

The address that Fidel Castro gave on the night of October 10, 1968, at the ruins of the La Demajagua Sugar Mill, which the Cuban people venerate as a symbol of honor and patriotism, marked a definitive step in the formation of Cuban culture and political awareness. As he had already done on other occasions, Fidel Castro resolutely divorced himself from dogmas that resulted from a narrow reading of Marxism and Leninism and helped to define the Cuban essence of the revolution — and, especially, Cuba's determination to think for itself.

We are defending the work of 100 years
(Excerpts of a speech by Fidel Castro in La Demajagua on October 10, 1968)

What does October 10, 1868, signify for our people? What does this glorious date mean for the revolutionaries of our nation? It simply signifies the beginning of 100 years of struggle, the beginning of the revolution in Cuba, because in Cuba there has been one revolution:

---

[5] Carlos Rafael Rodríguez (1913-97). Outstanding intellectual, political figure and communist revolutionary. He took part in the struggles against the Machado dictatorship in 1930 and was a representative of the Popular Socialist Party (PSP) in the Sierra Maestra Mountains. He held several important posts in the Cuban Government, including as a member of the Political Bureau of the Cuban Communist Party and Vice-President of the Council of State. He wrote many works on history, economics, philosophy, art and politics.

[6] Juan Marinello Vidaurreta (1898-1977). Outstanding essayist, poet, professor and Cuban communist. He took part in the Protest of 13 in 1923, fought against the Machado dictatorship and was imprisoned. He was a leader of the first Marxist-Leninist Party and a delegate to the Constitutional Assembly of 1940. After the triumph of the Cuban Revolution, he held several important political, cultural and diplomatic posts.

[7] Blas Roca Calderío (1908-85). Labor leader and communist. Elected General Secretary of Cuba's first Marxist-Leninist party in 1934, he held that position until it became part of the Integrated Revolutionary Organizations (ORI). He was a delegate to the Constitutional Assembly of 1940 and a member of parliament. A member of the Central Committee of the Communist Party since its founding in 1965, he later became a member of its Secretariat and of the Political Bureau. He served as President of the National Assembly of People's Power from 1976 to 1981.

that which was begun by Carlos Manuel de Céspedes on October 10, 1868, the revolution that our people are carrying forward.

There is, of course, no doubt that Céspedes symbolized the spirit of the Cubans of that time. He symbolized the dignity and rebelliousness of a people — still heterogeneous in nature — which began to take shape as a nation in the course of history...

Today, perhaps that decision seems simple, but that decision to end slavery was the most revolutionary measure — the most radical, revolutionary measure — that could have been adopted in a society which was truly pro-slavery.

For this reason, what makes Céspedes a great man is not only his firm and resolute decision to take up arms, but the deed that followed that decision — the first act after the proclamation of independence — the emancipation of his own slaves. At the same time he proclaimed his attitude towards slavery, his desire to end slavery in our country, although at first that proclamation was made in the hope of drawing the greatest possible support from the rest of the Cuban landowners.

In Camagüey, the revolutionaries proclaimed the abolition of slavery from the very beginning, and the Guáimaro Constitution of April 10, 1869, established the right of all Cubans to freedom, completely abolishing the hateful, centuries-old institution of slavery...

While our sister nations of Latin America — which had freed themselves from Spanish domination some decades before — were living under servitude, under the tyranny of the social interests in those nations that replaced the Spanish tyranny, our country, absolutely alone and single-handedly — and not the whole country, but a small portion of that country — fought for 10 years against a still powerful European power which had — and used — an army of hundreds of thousands of perfectly armed men to combat the Cuban Revolutionaries.

It is a known fact that Cuba received virtually no help from abroad. We all know the story of the schisms abroad, which obstructed and finally blocked the aid of the exiles to the Cubans in arms.

Nevertheless, our people — making incredible sacrifices, and heroically carrying the weight of that war, overcoming difficult situations — succeeded in learning the art of war and in organizing a small army, which armed itself with the enemy's weapons.

And from the ranks of the poor people, from the ranks of the fighters who came from the people, from the ranks of the peasants and the emancipated slaves, for the first time, officers and leaders of the revolutionary movement rose from the ranks of the people. The most worthy patriots, the most outstanding fighters, began to emerge, and this is how the Maceo brothers came to the fore, to cite the model of these exceptional men.

At the end of 10 years this heroic struggle was defeated — not by Spanish arms but by one of the worst enemies the Cuban Revolutionary movement has ever had, by dissention among the Cubans themselves. Defeated by quarrels, by regionalism, by caudillism; in other words, this was the enemy which was permanently present in the revolutionary process that ruined that struggle...

But, when the Cuban forces had been weakened by the disagreements, and the enemy stepped up its offensive, those elements that had less revolutionary firmness began to vacillate. And it was at that time — at the time of the Zanjón Pact, which ended that heroic war — when the truest representative of the people, the truest representatives of Cuba in that war, who came from the most humble ranks of the people, Antonio Maceo, rose with all his strength and his exceptional greatness...

That war brought to the fore many leaders from among the ranks of the people, but that war also inspired the man who was, without doubt, the most brilliant and most universal of Cuban political figures, José Martí.

Martí was very young when the Ten Years' War broke out. He was to suffer imprisonment and exile. His health was not good, but he had an extraordinarily brilliant mind. In his student years he was a champion of the cause of independence and, when barely 20 years old, he wrote some of the finest documents to come out of the political history of our country.

After the Cuban forces were defeated, for the above reasons, in 1878, Martí unquestionably became the theoretician and champion of revolutionary ideas. He took up the banners of Céspedes, Agramonte and the heroes who fell in that 10-year-struggle, and brought the Cuban Revolutionary ideas of that period to their highest level. Martí understood the factors that brought about the failure of the Ten Years' War. He profoundly analyzed the causes and dedicated his energies to preparing for a new war. He planned this war for almost 20 years without ever becoming discouraged, developing his revolutionary theory, uniting wills, rallying the veterans of the Ten Years' War, once again combating — in the field of ideas — the autonomist current, that opposed the revolutionary current, and also combating the annexationist current, which, taking advantage of the defeat in the Ten Years' War, once again reappeared in the Cuban political arena.

Martí advocated this idea constantly and organized the emigrants; in fact, Martí organized the first revolutionary party — that is, the first party to lead a revolution, the first party that united all the revolutionaries. With outstanding tenacity, moral courage and heroism, with no resources other than his intelligence, his convictions and his correct position, he dedicated himself to that task.

We can state that our country has the privilege of having at its disposal one of the richest political treasures, one of the most valuable sources of political education and knowledge, in the thought, writings, books, speeches and all the other extraordinary works of José Martí…

Cubans had fought for 30 years; tens of thousands of Cubans had died on the battlefields; hundreds of thousands perished in that struggle, while the Yankees lost only a few hundred soldiers in Santiago de Cuba. But they seized Puerto Rico; they seized Cuba, although with a different arrangement; they seized the Philippine archipelago, 6,000 miles from the United States; and they seized other possessions. This was something that Martí and Maceo feared most. Political consciousness and revolutionary thought had already developed to such an extent that the key leaders of the War of 1895 had very clear, absolutely clear, ideas about the objectives, and rejected with all their hearts the ideas of annexation — and not just annexation, but even U.S. intervention in that war…

It is possible that ignorance, or forgetfulness, or the euphoria of present achievements led the present generation to an underestimation of how much our people owe those fighters.

They were the ones who paved the way; they were the ones who created the conditions; and they were the ones who had to swallow the most bitter dregs: the bitter draft that was the Zanjón Pact, the end of the struggle in 1878; the even more bitter draft that was Yankee intervention, the bitter draft of the conversion of this country into a colonial establishment and a strategic pontoon — as Martí had feared; the bitter draft of seeing opportunists and corrupt politicians, the enemies of the revolution, allied with the imperialists, ruling the country…

It is necessary to go to the archives, to exhume the documents, so that our people, our present generation, may have a clear idea of how the imperialists governed. How, through memorandums and papers, and with great insolence, the United States governed this country — a country they pretended to call a "free," "independent" and "sovereign" nation — so that our people may know what kind of liberators these were and the crude and repugnant procedures they used in their relations with this country. Our present generation must be informed about all of this because, if it is not informed, its revolutionary awareness will not be sufficiently developed. If this country's origins and history are not known the political culture of our masses will not be sufficiently well developed. We could not even understand Marxism, could not even call ourselves Marxists, if we didn't begin with an understanding of our own revolutionary process and of the process of development of awareness and political and revolutionary thought in our country over the period of 100 years. If we don't understand that we can know nothing of politics...

As revolutionaries, when we say it is our duty to defend this land, to defend this country, to defend this revolution, we must realize that we are not defending the efforts of just 10 years; we must realize that we are not just defending the revolution of this generation. We must realize that we are defending the efforts of 100 years. We must realize that we are defending not just that for which thousands of our comrades fell, but that for which hundreds of thousands of Cubans fell during these past hundred years!

With the advent of the victory of 1959, fundamental questions in the life of our people once again presented themselves — this time on a much higher plane. In 1868, one of the matters under discussion was whether or not to abolish slavery, to abolish the ownership of one human being by another, in our era, in our century, with the advent of our revolution, the fundamental question, the essential question, that which would define the revolutionary nature of this era and of this revolution, was no longer the question of man's ownership of other human beings, but that of man's ownership of other's means of earning a living...

The revolution is the result of 100 years of struggle, the result of the development of the political movement and revolutionary awareness, armed with the most up-to-date political thinking, armed with the most up-to-date, scientific concept of society, history and economics — which is Marxism-Leninism — the weapon that rounded out the wealth, the arsenal of revolutionary experience and the history of our country.

Not only are our people armed with the experience and that awareness. They are also a people that has been able to overcome the factions that divided it, caudillism and regionalism, to become one undivided revolutionary people. Because when we speak of the people we speak of revolutionaries; when we speak of a people ready to fight and to die, we are not thinking of the *gusanos,* of the few fainthearted individuals who are still around. We are thinking of those who have the legitimate right to be called Cubans and the Cuban people — the same legitimate right our combatants and our *mambises* had. A people integrated, united and led by a revolutionary party. A party that constitutes a militant vanguard.

What did Martí do, in order to make the revolution, but to organize the party of the revolution, organize the party of the revolutionaries? There was only one party of revolutionaries! Those who were not in the party of the revolutionaries were in the party of the Spanish colonialists, in the party of the annexationists or in the party of the autonomists.

In the same way today, the people, with their party, which is their vanguard, armed with the most up-to-date concepts, armed with the experiences of 100 years or struggle, having developed their revolutionary political and patriotic awareness to the highest level, have succeeded in overcoming age-old vices and have built up this unity and this power of the revolution...

The banners that flew over Yara, La Demajagua, Baire, Baraguá and Guáimaro; the banners that presided over the solemn event when slavery was eradicated; and the banners that have led the way throughout the revolutionary history of our country will never be lowered. Those banners and what they represent will be defended by our people to the last drop of blood...

We are no longer the people that abolished slavery 100 years ago; we are no longer the last to abolish slavery — the ownership of man by man — today, we are the first people of this continent to abolish the exploitation of man by man! It is true that we were the last to begin, but it is also true that we have gone further than anybody else. We have eradicated the capitalist system of exploitation; we have made the people the true owners of their future and their wealth. We were the last to break the chains of colonialism, but we have been the first to throw off the chains of imperialism.

25

10-MILLION-TON SUGAR HARVEST

May 18, 1970

Cuba's failure to bring in a record, 10-million-ton sugarcane harvest in 1970 had both immediate and medium-term repercussions in all aspects of the nation's life.

That goal was both a strategy and a necessity, and it should be understood in context. The U.S. Government was subjecting the Cuban economy to a harsh blockade; it was also waging a dirty war against the island, forcing it to maintain the mobilization of large military forces. Therefore, it had not been possible to concentrate efforts on economic development during the first few years of the Cuban Revolution. It became absolutely necessary to do this, however, for the population was growing, and its demands in all areas were multiplying. Resources were badly needed.

Cooperation with the Soviet Union and other socialist countries had not yet reached its peak, so the advantages this offered were not as great as they would later on be.

That cooperation was reduced as a result of differences with the Soviet Union following the 1962 Missile Crisis and differences on the Latin American revolutionary movements. Even so, the balance of trade between the two countries — which was, obviously, one-sided — resulted in Cuba's acquiring a growing debt to the Soviet Union. The leaders of the Cuban Government felt morally bound to pay this debt and also aspired to greater independence that would allow them to diversify their economic relations with other markets.

This was the background for Cuba's adoption of the unquestionably correct position of promoting the sugar industry, the country's main resource in those years, and of turning it into the country's basic source of finance.

Thus, an intensive process of investment in that sector took place in the 1965-70 period, aimed at increasing the industrial capacity. This included the use of modern technology in planting and cultivating sugarcane, enlarging the areas planted with sugarcane and beginning to solve the problem of using machinery in the work of harvesting — for which, at that time, there was very little experience anywhere in the world. This task was particularly pressing for Cuba.

The disappearance of the army of the unemployed and the creation of new job options for the rural population — which had traditionally provided the workforce for the heavy work of cutting the sugarcane by hand — made it necessary to bring in the harvest by mobilizing soldiers, students and volunteers from the cities, some of whom were less than productive. This raised the cost of the harvest and created other difficulties in the workplaces from which they had come.

In those conditions, the country set about reaching that goal with great spirit and enthusiasm. A state of political and revolutionary effervescence preceded the great challenge. The country's economic and human resources were placed at the service of bringing in a 10-million-ton harvest.

However, even though enough sugarcane was grown to make the 10 million tons of sugar, the goal could not be met. Many important industrial investments, aimed at enlarging the capacities of the sugar mills, had not been completed by the time of the milling. The mechanization of the cane-cutting fell behind schedule, which made it necessary to mobilize enormous numbers of cane cutters to the fields, at the cost of paralyzing other economic activities. The organization of many aspects of the work also failed, stemming in large measure from the methods of leadership and management of the economy then in effect, which led the leadership of the revolution to severely criticize those methods later on.

On May 18, 1970, an angry crowd gathered in Havana to welcome the 11 Cuban fishermen who, a few days earlier, had been attacked and left stranded on a tiny islet in the Bahamas by counterrevolutionaries aboard pirate launches coming from Miami. Fidel Castro and all the other members of the Cuban Government took part in their welcome.

One of the fishermen said that, in the midst of their trials, they had been encouraged by the thought that the Cuban people would bring in a 10-million-ton harvest. Fidel Castro then said that he hadn't intended to talk about the sugarcane harvest that evening, but that, on hearing the fisherman, he felt he had to tell the people the sad truth: that it was impossible to bring in a 10-million-ton harvest that year. He then called on all the workers in the country to keep on doing their utmost until the harvest was over and to find the revolutionary strength to turn that setback into victory.

The 1970 sugarcane harvest wound up with 8.5 million tons of sugar, the highest sugar production figure in the history of Cuba and the greatest production figure for cane sugar in the history of the world.

It was a sad and costly setback. Many illusions were lost that evening, and the nation's economy was seriously damaged. However, people are still debating whether, if the goal had been met, it would have delayed the rectification of the errors of idealism that were being made in the economy. If so, paradoxically, the setback was positive.

The trauma caused by that blow was reflected in the July 26 ceremony that year, when Fidel Castro offered to resign as Prime Minister, and the people immediately and energetically rejected his offer. It led to deep reflection and the determination to apply more realistic and effective methods, not only in the sphere of the economy but also in the work of the party, the government, the labor unions and the other mass organizations. Viewed strictly objectively, it also contained the seed of future negative phenomena, in the form of tendencies to assimilate without criticism the experiences of socialist construction in the Soviet Union.

✳

To gain more from the setback than we would have gained from a victory

(Excerpts from Fidel Castro's May 20, 1970, appearance on television to explain the situation of the sugarcane harvest)

I would like to begin by recalling the origins of the plan for producing 10 million tons of sugar.

Our trade relations with the Soviet Union began because of attacks by the United States, which took away our sugar quota. At that time, the Soviet Union began to buy the sugar that we couldn't sell on the U.S. market.

The first few times it bought our sugar, it paid more or less the same price as that on the international market.

As you know, some of our sugar is sold on what is called the free market, and some is sold by means of agreements with various countries. The price of the sugar sold under those agreements varies. In general, it is higher than the price on the free market. A large part of our sugar is sold through such agreements.

We had to import all of the oil we needed and a range of raw materials, foodstuffs and equipment from the Soviet Union, because we had no other way of obtaining those things. Because of this, our imports from the Soviet Union grew considerably, while our payment capacities were limited. The amount of sugar that we could sell was limited, as were the amounts of some other products that we sold to the Soviet Union after the United States imposed the blockade.

Of the products we exported, sugar was the most important. It was followed by mineral exports, tobacco, etc. That is, sugar, nickel, small shipments of tobacco and rum were the main exports our country had...

Because of this and of the needs of a developing—and, I could also say, a disorganized — country (the first phase of a revolutionary process in any country entails disorganization) our trade imbalance with the Soviet Union grew ever larger year by year. At the same time, our import needs for developing the country kept growing — and had to keep growing every year, both to raise the standard of living even modestly and to develop the country's economy — we could see that our imports were going to increase considerably and that our exports couldn't grow...

Sugar was practically our only export product whose production could be quickly increased. First, because there was some underutilized industrial capacity. Second, because there were many sugar mills that, with relatively small investments, could increase their production. Some, for example, had installations for greater capacity but with various bottlenecks that prevented production from increasing. Moreover, we could extend the sugarcane harvest...

So, we proposed a long-range agreement to the Soviet Union, based on our possibilities for increasing our sugar production. The Soviet Government accepted Cuba's proposal, and we agreed to increase our exports to five million tons of sugar — which would be sold for 6.11, not 4 cents a pound. In our future plans, the value of those exports would increase from 264 million to 672 million pesos a year...

This was why we drew up a great plan for increasing our sugar exports. It wasn't the result of a whim; it wasn't aimed at testing our mettle by setting ourselves difficult goals or at covering ourselves with glory. Our production target of 10 million tons of sugar responded to a real need. Moreover, it was the only possibility our country had, the only sphere in which, by making the best possible use of the land, increasing production per hectare, using all of the installed capacity, extending the sugarcane harvest and making some investments, we could increase our annual export earnings by 400 million pesos...

Some people doubted that we could find markets for 10 million tons of sugar, but it isn't a problem of markets. Ever since our relations with the socialist camp were fully opened, in spite of the blockade — in spite of the blockade! — our country's problems haven't been those of markets, but rather have been problems of production. Our country has and can find markets for as much sugar as it can produce...

The sugar industry had never before been a limiting factor in production — always before, the limits had been set by agriculture. In fact, the reason that more sugar was not produced wasn't that the sugar mills didn't have the capacity to produce it; it has always been because there wasn't enough sugarcane. That is, there was not enough raw material to increase the amount of sugar produced...

Three factors have influenced the low yields: first, investments; second, the deficient maintenance in many other sugar mills; and third — and, really, I have to state clearly that this is the main one — the poor operation of the sugar mills...

It was low sugar yields that made us lose the battle of the 10 million tons...

I should also point out one thing that is basic to this problem of the 10 million tons, and that is that it was not the people who lost this battle. I can state with complete confidence that the people didn't lose this battle. Even though I can't say that the battle for the 10 million tons was won — because it wasn't — I can say that the people didn't lose it. We were the ones who lost that battle. The administrative apparatus and those of us who are leaders of the revolution are the ones who lost it.

The people did what was needed to produce 10 million tons of sugar and more — 11 million tons. We are the ones who didn't do what was needed to produce that much. I think that this must be said as a matter of justice, because it is the unvarnished truth...

All right: we did produce eight million tons of sugar, and, comparing that figure with the largest amount of sugar produced in the capitalist era — with the disadvantages I've already pointed out — those eight million tons are 702,000 tons more than the largest amount of sugar produced during the capitalist era, which was 7,298,000 tons. That is, it's 10 percent more than the largest amount of sugar produced in the capitalist era...

What are our main tasks? First, to take all the measures and cut all the sugarcane, to go wherever the sugarcane is and cut every bit of it. We'll try to produce nine million tons, or, if we don't manage nine million, 8.8 or 8.9 million tons—as much as we can from the sugarcane we've got. We will try to increase our record as much as possible. And, if we can increase it by a hundredth of a percent or a millionth of a percent by producing one ton more with the last field of sugarcane, we'll do that...

That is the first, immediate thing, the main watchword we should adopt. Together with this, the party and the mass organizations should prepare for a job of strengthening the revolution in all spheres. This is very important.

The party had to make a tremendous effort to raise those percentages, planting 536,000 more hectares of land to sugarcane than had been planted two years ago, and there that land is, planted to new varieties, and the other hectares of land will be planted to even better varieties.

We had to launch the party into that task, concentrating on it, so less time was dedicated to political tasks, less time to work with the masses. A task of this sort introduces administrative elements more than leadership ones, and an emergency situation always leads to orderly habits, to doing things administratively.

Why? Because we threw the party into an administrative task, both in agriculture and in industry...

We have to go back to all those questions that were raised when the sectarians were criticizing us: how should the party work? What is the function of the mass organizations? What is their importance? The party isn't a mass organization. The party is selective; the party is a vanguard. If we were to make it a mass organization... That may come one day, in a communist society, when the party, the masses and the government are nearly the same thing. But, in this phase, the party still has to select its members from among the most determined people; it has to try to keep on attracting the best workers. The party has to help develop the mass organizations, as has already been stated here. But it shouldn't become a mass organization — not yet...

We must strengthen the political apparatus. The party doesn't administer anything. It guides, directs, promotes, supports and guarantees the fulfillment of the plans that the leadership of the revolution draws up for each place.

We must strengthen the administrative apparatus and the mass organizations and, above all, strengthen the party. These are matters that I think I should take this opportunity to point out to you...

And the third watchword is to turn the setback into a victory. We must turn the setback into a victory.

That is the energetic, worthy watchword of our people. We will turn the setback into a real victory. We will work to gain more from the setback than we would have gained from a victory — in terms of concern, better work, sense of responsibility, duty and more complete dedication to the tasks of the revolution.

In this way, both now and in the months and year to come, we will get more out of the setback than we would have got from a victory.

This is what we mean by turning the setback into a victory. I'm sure we can do it; I'm absolutely certain that we will.

26

ANGOLA: OPERATION CARLOTA

November 11, 1975

The ties between the Cuban Revolution and the People's Movement for the Liberation of Angola (MPLA) were historic. They had arisen in 1965, when Che Guevara, representing the leadership of the Cuban party and government, made the first contacts with the MPLA and Dr. Agostinho Neto,[1] its main leader. Since then, Cuban combatants had helped to train members of that anti-colonialist force in Angola.

After the Carnation Revolution in Portugal, which paved the way for the independence of the Portuguese colonies in Africa, the CIA, some NATO countries and the Portuguese colonialists themselves maneuvered to give power in Angola to the puppet organizations they had created.

At the same time, imperialism's main allies in that vast area in Africa — so rich in natural resources and with great economic potential — began to move in a threatening way.

Sure enough, at the beginning of October 1975, the South African racists sent troops to occupy Cunene, in southern Angola. Forces of the regime in Zaire [Congo] and bands of mercenaries recruited in several European countries and the United States entered Angola from the north and advanced toward Luanda, its capital. Meanwhile, the two main puppet organizations, UNITA[2] and the FNLA,[3] were receiving tens of millions of

---

[1] Agostinho Neto. President of the MPLA and President of the People's Republic of Angola.

[2] UNITA: Union for the Total Independence of Angola, headed by Jonas Savimbi.

dollars in arms and financing of all kinds from the United States and its allies.

That was the situation when, in mid-October 1975, at the request of the MPLA, Cuba sent some weapons and personnel to instruct the Angolan forces in their use.

On October 23, the South African forces left their bases in Cunene and Namibia and launched a large-scale invasion of Angolan territory. Over 100 tanks, artillery and armored transport vehicles participated in the attack, advancing north toward Luanda at a rate of around 40 miles (65 kilometers) a day. Meanwhile, the regular troops of Mobutu Sese Zeko's regime and the white mercenaries that were moving south came to within 16 miles (25 kilometers) of the Angolan capital.

On November 3, the first Cuban instructors — who had joined their Angolan students from a military academy — were killed in combat against the racists near Benguela.

On November 5, at the request of the MPLA, the Cuban Government decided to provide direct support for the Angolan patriots, who were faced with mortal danger. A battalion of Special Troops of the Ministry of the Interior was the first unit sent to take part in a theater of operations nearly 7,500 miles (12,000 kilometers) from Cuba. The puppets had already printed invitations for the banquet they planned to give on November 11, the date set for the transfer of power ceremony, by which time they expected to have occupied the entire country.

The invaders who were advancing from the north suffered their first crushing defeat at Quifangondo, just outside Luanda. They were also beaten back in Cabinda, a rich oil and forestry enclave. The advance of the South African racists was also contained in the south. The imperialists' plans were frustrated. On November 11, 1975, while fighting was still going on near Luanda, Agostinho Neto proclaimed Angola's independence and became the first president of the new African nation.

Following up the first unit, Cuban regular forces whose members had volunteered for this internationalist mission began to arrive in Angola.

In some cases, they were flown in on old Cubana de Aviación Britannia planes that were adapted to increase their fuel-carrying capacity. In other cases, the soldiers and weapons were sent on ships of the Cuban merchant marine. At first, Cuba did this on its own and with its own resources. Later, an agreement was reached with the Soviet Union on cooperation in providing military support to Angola.

On March 27, 1976, the last South African units withdrew from Angolan territory, which was thus freed of aggressors.

The Cuban command called that mission of solidarity Operation

---

[3] FNLA: National Front for the Liberation of Angola, headed by Holden Roberto.

Carlota, in honor of the black African slave woman who headed two uprisings against the slave owners and colonialists in the first half of the 19th century. When she was captured in 1843, in the second attempt, her executioners cut her into pieces.

The Cubans didn't return home immediately after those months of intensive fighting, however, because attacks continued from abroad, as did threats of further invasions. The Cubans had to stay for 13 years, in the course of which over 400,000 men and women went to Angola to perform their internationalist duty. Angola was thus turned into a school of combat and had a lasting effect on the political awareness and life of the Cuban people.

"We have helped our Angolan brothers," Fidel Castro said, "first of all in response to a revolutionary principle, because we are internationalists, and, secondly, because our people are both Latin American and Latin African..."[4]

For the Yankee imperialists, Angola represents an African Bay of Pigs

[Excerpts of speech by Fidel Castro on April 19, 1976]

In commemorating this 15th anniversary of the heroic and glorious victory at the Bay of Pigs, our people have an additional reason for pride, expressed in their most beautiful internationalist sentiments and which transcends the boundaries of this continent: the historical victory of the people of Angola, to whom we offered the generous and unrestricted solidarity of our revolution.

At the Bay of Pigs, African blood was shed, blood of the selfless descendants of a people who were slaves before they became workers, and who were exploited workers before they became masters of their homeland. And in Africa, alongside that of the heroic fighters of Angola, Cuban blood also flowed, that of the sons of Martí, Maceo and Agramonte, that of the internationalist heirs of Gómez and Che Guevara. Those who once enslaved human beings and sent them to America perhaps never imagined that one of those peoples who received the slaves would one day send their fighters to struggle for freedom in Africa.

The victory in Angola was the twin sister of the victory at the Bay of Pigs. For the Yankee imperialists, Angola represents an African Bay of Pigs. At one time we said that imperialism had

---

[4] Fidel Castro, address given in Conakry, the Republic of Guinea, on March 15, 1976.

suffered its great defeats in the month of April: Bay of Pigs, Vietnam, Cambodia, etc. This time the defeat came in March. On the 27th of that month, when the last South African soldiers crossed the Namibian border, after a retreat of more than 700 kilometers, one of the most brilliant pages in the liberation of black Africa was written...

The war in Angola was really [U.S. Secretary of State Henry] Kissinger's war. Against the advice of some of his closest collaborators, he insisted on carrying out covert operations to liquidate the MPLA through the counterrevolutionary FMLA and UNITA groups, with the support of white mercenaries from Zaire and South Africa. It is said that the CIA itself warned him that such clandestine operations could not be kept secret. Aside from the fact that the FNLA was supported by the CIA from the time it was founded, a fact now publicly acknowledged, the United States invested several million dollars from the spring of 1975 on, to supply arms and instructors to the counterrevolutionary and separatist Angolan groups. Instigated by the United States, regular troops from Zaire entered Angolan territory in the summer of that same year, while South African military forces occupied the Cunene area in the month of August and sent arms and instructors to the UNITA bands.

At that time there wasn't a single Cuban instructor in Angola. The first material aid and the first Cuban instructors reached Angola at the beginning of October, at the request of the MPLA, when Angola was being insolently invaded by foreign forces. However, no Cuban military unit had been sent to Angola to participate directly in the fight nor was that projected.

On October 23, also instigated by the United States, South African regular army troops, supported by tanks and artillery, invaded Angolan territory across the Namibian border and penetrated deep into the country, advancing between 60 and 70 kilometers a day. On November 3, they had penetrated more than 500 kilometers into Angola, meeting their first resistance on the outskirts of Benguela, from the personnel of a recently organized school for Angolan recruits and from their Cuban instructors, who had virtually no means for halting the attack by South African tanks, infantry and artillery.

On November 5, 1975, at the request of the MPLA, the leadership of our party decided to send with all urgency a battalion of regular troops with antitank weapons to help the Angolan patriots resist the invasion of the South African racists. This was the first Cuban troop unit sent to Angola. When it arrived in the country, the foreign interventionists were 25 kilometers from Luanda in the north, their 140 millimeter artillery was bombing the suburbs of the capital and the South African fascists had already penetrated more than 700 kilometers into the south from the Namibian border, while Cabinda was heroically defended by MPLA fighters and a handful of Cuban instructors...

The enemy has talked about the number of Cubans in Angola. It is sufficient to say that, once the struggle began, Cuba sent the men and the weapons necessary to win that struggle. In honor to our people we must say that hundreds of thousands of fighters from our regular troops and reserves were ready to fight alongside their Angolan brothers.

Our losses were minimal. In spite of the fact that the war was fought on four fronts and our fighters fought alongside the heroic MPLA soldiers in the liberation of almost a million square kilometers that had been occupied by the interventionists and their henchmen, fewer Cuban soldiers were killed in action in more than four months of fighting in Angola, than in the three days of fighting at the Bay of Pigs.

Cuba made its decision completely on its own responsibility. The Soviet Union — which had always helped the peoples of the Portuguese colonies in the struggle for their independence — provided besieged Angola with basic aid in military equipment and collaborated with our efforts when imperialism had cut off practically all our air routes to Africa. They never requested that a single Cuban be sent to that country. The Soviet Union is extraordinarily respectful and careful in its relations with Cuba. A decision of that nature could only be made by our own party.

[U.S. President Gerald] Ford and Kissinger lie to the people of the United States and to world public opinion when they try to place responsibility for Cuba's solidarity actions in Angola on the Soviet Union.

Ford and Kissinger lie when they seek to blame the Congress of the United States for the defeat of the interventionists in Angola, because Congress failed to authorize new funds for the FNLA and UNITA counterrevolutionary groups. Congress made those decisions on December 16, 18 and 19. By that time the CIA had already supplied large amounts in arms, Zairean troops had been repulsed in Luanda, Cabinda had been saved, the South Africans were contained and demoralized on the banks of the Queve River and no shipment of arms from the CIA would have changed the already inexorable course of events. Today they would be in the hands of the revolutionary forces like many of those it supplied earlier.

Ford and Kissinger lie to the people of the United States, and especially to the black population of that country, when they hide the fact that the fascist and racist troops of South Africa criminally invaded Angolan territory long before Cuba sent any regular unit of soldiers there.

There are some other lies on the part of Ford and Kissinger in relation to Angola that need not be analyzed now. Ford and Kissinger know perfectly well that everything I say is true.

In this solemn commemoration ceremony, I am not going to say what I think of the insolent epithets Ford has used in his political campaign through the south of the United States and of other cynical aspects of his imperial policy; I will confine myself, for now, to replying that he is a vulgar liar.

True, events in Angola resemble those of Ethiopia, but in reverse. In Angola, the imperialists, the racists, the aggressors symbolized by the CIA, the South African troops and the white mercenaries, did not win victory nor did they occupy the country; victory was won by those who were attacked, the revolutionaries, the black and heroic people of Angola.

True, events in Angola resemble those of Czechoslovakia at Munich, but also in reverse; the people who were attacked received the solidarity of the revolutionary movement, and the imperialists and racists could not dismember the country nor divide up its wealth nor assassinate its finest sons. Angola is united, integrated, and today it is a bulwark of liberty and dignity in Africa. The swastika of the South African racists does not fly over the palace of Luanda.

27

FIRST CONGRESS OF THE CUBAN COMMUNIST PARTY

December 17-22, 1975

A process of basic economic recovery had been developing since the beginning of the 1970s, especially on the basis of an intensification of Cuba's ties with the Soviet Union and with the Council for Mutual Economic Assistance (CMEA) system of socialist integration — which Cuba joined in July 1972. Combined with this was the greater unity achieved in the Communist Party of Cuba and the advances made in terms of its membership, functioning and methods of work, culminating in the First Congress of the Communist Party of Cuba in December 1975.

After consolidating the defense of the revolution and achieving some degree of stability and safety, Cubans called for laying the organizational, juridical and institutional bases for continuing to build the economy more efficiently and for putting the finishing touches on the construction of the political system. This would facilitate active, democratic participation by citizens in decision-making on public affairs.

Thus, the Party Congress had to take up topics of the utmost importance:

- *the drawing up of a new Constitution of the Republic and the holding of a referendum to approve its text, which had been subjected to exhaustive consultation among the people during the initial stage of its drafting;*

- *the adoption of a new political-administrative division of the country, replacing the old division of six provinces with 14 new ones and a special municipality – the Isle of Pines, later renamed the Isle of Youth;*

- *the founding of the bodies of People's Power, by means of a free and secret vote by citizens, which would imply electing delegates in all of the voting districts in the country and then creating the corresponding municipal and provincial assemblies and the National Assembly of People's Power, with its Council of State, from which would come the authority of all the bodies of government and administration; and*

- *the adoption of a system of economic management and planning that would overcome past mistakes; make it possible for the workers and cadres to acquire real economic awareness; promote strict control and administration of resources; and constantly promote mass participation in reducing costs, raising productivity and achieving good levels of efficiency.*

The Congress would also draw up long-range definitions and programs in the spheres of socioeconomic development; education; artistic and literary culture; relations with religious institutions and believers; the country's defense; and ideological tasks in information and communication.

Beginning his Central Report, Fidel Castro said, "There are episodes in great political events that are history-making. The opening of the First Party Congress is one. We have had the privilege of living at a high point in the revolutionary life of our homeland. We couldn't have achieved it without the sacrifices made by countless sons and daughters of the Cuban nation throughout several generations. Many gave their lives for the noble cause of our people's independence, justice, dignity and progress. We dedicate our emotion-filled memories to them – to those who suffered, fought and died, whether in the wars of independence or in the ignominy of the neocolony, whether in battle against the last dictatorship or in the consolidation and defense of the revolution. Without their ideas, efforts and blood, this Congress would never have been possible."[1]

No matter what deficiencies later appeared in the application of the system of economic planning and management as well as in other areas, it is unquestionable that the First Party Congress constituted an important step in organizing the country and consolidating the revolution's achievements.

That Congress in 1975 based its philosophy on the Cuban people's

---

[1] *Informe Central, Primer Congreso del Partido Comunista de Cuba* (Central Report, First Congress of the Communist Party of Cuba) (Havana: Editorial de Ciencias Sociales, 1975), 5.

ability to collectively improve their efforts, on their political and moral commitment and also on the certainty of being able to count on the support of a socialist community headed by the Soviet Union — which seemed to be extremely stable and was attaining impressive levels of economic development, great social advances and notable scientific and technological achievements in those years.

Those external premises changed after the Second and Third Congresses. The fourth meeting of the highest-ranking body of the party, which was held in Santiago de Cuba in October 1991, was faced with the imminent collapse of the Soviet Union and the regimes that had arisen after the Red Army had liberated several countries during World War II. The Fifth Congress, held in October 1997, summed up the results of the struggle Cuba was waging in the conditions of the "special period" and laid down the main prospects for continuing the country's recovery, based on its own efforts.

These changing conditions, with their dramatic challenges, confirmed the need for the Communist Party as the organized vanguard leading the revolution and put to the test its ability to guide the ship of state through a rough and stormy sea.

Here we are at last, with everyone and for the good of everyone...

(Excerpts of the Central Report presented by Fidel Castro at the First Party Congress, December 1975)[2]

This year of the First Congress has been one of great effort for the revolutionary militants and officials, but future years will be no less tense. The work to be done in the coming years to fulfill the agreements that will have to be made at this Congress will be hard and intensive work because of the diversity of the tasks entailed and the depth and breadth of the transformations it is necessary to bring about.

But within all these issues that are to be dealt with, and on which the Congress will pronounce, those that will generate the most substantial, profound and extensive changes are those relating to the process of the country's institutionalization and the reordering of all economic activity.

The new politico-administrative division, the constitution of the organizations of People's Power throughout the country and the creation of conditions for introducing the Economic Management

---

[2] PCC Central Committee Report at the First Congress, 244–8.

System, amongst many other tasks, require organized, responsible and very hard work...

It is necessary to take the requisite steps and to take the measures that are indicated so as to ensure that the following goals are achieved:

- To hold the referendum on the Constitution and the Constitutional Transit Law on February 15 next year, 1976, and to proclaim our Socialist Constitution on February 24, the date on which the 81st anniversary of the 1895 war of independence is to be celebrated.
- To apply the new politico-administrative division in the municipal organizations in the months of April and May 1976.
- To carry out elections of delegates to local organizations of People's Power and of deputies to the National Assembly in the second half of October 1976, with the aim of holding the first meeting of the National Assembly of People's Power, the State's highest organ of power, consisting of the people's representatives who have been elected throughout the country, on December 2 next year, the 20th anniversary of the landing of the *Granma*.
- To constitute the local organizations of People's Power and turn over to them the corresponding activities in production and services of local significance, in the months of November and December 1976 and the first months of 1977.
- To reestablish relations of moneys paid in and out between companies and the state sector, in accordance with the principles of the Economic Management System, which will have to be submitted to this Congress, to apply a new National Accounting System and to bring into operation a national budget as of January 1977.
- To commence in 1978 the introduction of the Economic Management System in a group of selected experimental companies, representing different production and service activities of the country.
- In the final two years of the five-year period, the Economic Management System is to be applied in all spheres of economic activity.
- To ensure the carrying out of all these proposals, which are of extraordinary importance for the consolidation and advance of our economic development and the revolution in general, it is

essential to fulfill, with the requisite quality and within the time set, each one of the tasks contemplated in the Program of Work that has been prepared.

We know that our party will undertake and fulfill, with a firm spirit, all the obligations it must meet.

EPILOGUE

This report has now reached its conclusion. We are aware that there may be omissions, that some matters have been given too brief a treatment in the interests of time, and even that there are some superfluous details, but we have done all that is humanly possible to reflect the work of the revolution and its historic meaning. It is not easy to synthesize in a few words the antecedents of our present processes and our 17 years of revolutionary power.

What is important, dear comrades, is that in our political march forward, we have reached the point at which we presently find ourselves. It is impossible not to experience right now the satisfaction of knowing that our nation occupies today an honorable and worthy place in the worldwide revolutionary movement and that a beautiful future awaits us insofar as we are capable and deserving of it.

This Congress will be like a bright star to guide us along this path. The party, its norms, its principles, its organization, its strength, will carry us forward, invincible. There will be no difficulty that we will not be able to overcome, no error that cannot be avoided if it can be foreseen, nor that cannot promptly be rectified if it should be committed.

How could we not remember at this point those extraordinary people who accompanied us in our struggle and who today are not physically with us at this Congress: Abel Santamaría,[3] Juan Manuel Márquez,[4] Ñico López,[5] Frank País,[6] José Antonio Echeverría, Che,

---

[3] Abel Santamaría Cuadrado, second in command of the movement that attacked the Moncada Barracks on July 26, 1953. He was captured and atrociously tortured and murdered after this action.

[4] Juan Manuel Márquez, second in command on the *Granma* expedition. He was captured by Batista's army and murdered after landing, in December 1956.

[5] Antonio López, an outstanding revolutionary, who participated in the actions of July 26, 1953, and was captured and murdered after participating in the *Granma* expedition.

[6] Frank País García, one of the great figures of the Cuban Revolution and a clandestine fighter, was discovered and murdered by Batista's forces in his birthplace, Santiago de Cuba, on July 30, 1957.

Camilo, Lázaro Peña[7] and other such commendable constructors of our country's present? How could we not remember the Central Committee members who gave their lives to the internationalist cause: Vilo Acuña,[8] Eliseo Reyes,[9] and Antonio Sánchez Díaz[10]? How could we not remember those who today are fulfilling these duties, many of them militants of our party, and many even elected deputies of this Congress, who are not with us right now?[11]

Presiding over this gathering today, next to the portraits of Che and Camilo, that of the legendary figure of Julio Antonio Mella[12] reminds us of the self-sacrificing fighters who dreamed of and died for a day like today.

The images of Martí, Gómez and Maceo, next to those of Marx, Engels and Lenin, symbolize those who fought for our country of Cuba along with those who wanted to make a great country of all humanity. The Republic must be with everyone, and for the good of everyone, the hero of our independence exclaimed one day, and his words resound in this hall as an echo of the formidable call with which the founders of scientific socialism rocked the world: "Proletarians of the world, unite!" Here we are at last, with everyone and for the good of everyone and with us are representatives of the worldwide revolutionary movement expressing the encouragement and solidarity of communists and progressive people from all around the world to our small country; with this are forged the ties of unity between the proletarians of the world as an impressive demonstration that those earlier visionaries knew how to recognize the future of humanity.

What is happening here, just as what happened yesterday in the heart of the czarist empire, and in so many other countries of the world, is a symbol of the world's future.

---

[7] Lázaro Peña González, Communist and workers' leader, founder in 1939 of the Cuban Workers' Confederation. At the time of his death in 1974, he was secretary general of the Cuban Trade Union Confederation.

[8] Vitalio Acuña Núñez, Commander of the Rebel Army, one of the first peasants to join the guerrillas in Sierra Maestra, was killed in Bolivia on August 31, 1967.

[9] Eliseo Reyes Rodríguez, combatant in the Rebel Army, was killed in Bolivia as part of Ernesto Che Guevara's internationalist guerrilla group.

[10] Antonio Sánchez Díaz, combatant in the Rebel Army, was killed in Bolivia as part of Ernesto Che Guevara's internationalist guerrilla group.

[11] Fidel Castro is referring to the international contingent that was then in Angola, helping to resist the invasion of the racist forces of South Africa and other mercenary forces, at the time the congress was being held in December 1975.

[12] Julio Antonio Mella, a student fighter and founder, in August 1925, of the first Communist Party of Cuba. Exiled to Mexico because of his opposition to the tyrant Machado, he was murdered by agents of the latter on January 10, 1929.

To all Cuban communists, to all our comrades in the revolution, we would like to express our gratitude for your confidence and the love with which you have accompanied your leaders in these heroic and decisive years of our country.

May the most absolute honesty, limitless fidelity to principles, altruism, capacity for sacrifice, revolutionary purity, the spirit of overcoming, heroism and merit, forever prevail in our party.

28

THE SOCIALIST CONSTITUTION

February 24, 1976

With the aim of completing the organization of Cuban society as projected by the First Party Congress, a referendum was held on February 15, 1976, in which the texts of a new Constitution of the Republic and of the Law of Constitutional Transition were approved. They were proclaimed a few days later, on February 24, 1976, the 81st anniversary of the 1895 declaration of independence.

In an unprecedented demonstration of popular participation, 98 percent of all citizens 16 years old and over voted, and 97.7 percent of them — 5.5 million people — voted for the new constitution.

However, the people's participation in the preparation of the constitution had not begun that day. The drafting commission, headed by Blas Roca Calderío, had considered the suggestions and criteria of many leaders, jurists and outstanding figures from all spheres of the nation's life.

The draft had then been submitted to a process of popular consultation in which around six million workers, armed forces personnel, students and others took part; as a result, the preamble and 60 of the 141 articles of the draft were modified.

Thus, the text that was submitted to the referendum was the result of consensus reached by democratic methods and with the active participation of nearly all the Cuban population over 16.

"Never before in the history of our homeland or of Latin America," Raúl Castro said in proclaiming the constitution, "has a constitution of such progressive and revolutionary content been approved. It is a constitution

that responds in such a great degree to the interests of the homeland and the people, consecrating and guaranteeing the principles of equality and social justice and the rights of the individual in harmony with the interests of all society and in close correspondence to the socioeconomic reality.

"Unquestionably, the constitution that we proclaim today is the manifestation of our people's will and views, expressed by means of a process of direct democracy, exercised to its fullest extent."[1]

The socialist constitution of 1976 was the seventh constitution adopted in the country. The first four had been constitutions of the mambí fighters for Cuba's independence from Spain in the 19th century: the Constitution of Guáimaro, which followed the uprisings of 1868; the Constitution of Baraguá, fruit of the history-making protest of Antonio Maceo;[2] the Constitution of Jimaguayú, of September 16, 1895, which was aimed at giving order to the new War of Independence that had begun that year; and the Constitution of La Yaya, of October 29, 1897.

These were followed by the Constitution of 1901, which marked the birth of neocolonial Cuba, shackled by the Platt Amendment; the Constitution of 1940, heir to some extent of the revolutionary struggles of the 1930s, some of whose articles — thanks largely to the role played by the Communist delegates to the Constitutional Assembly of 1940. These articles of the 1940 Constitution were progressive and advanced, but were turned into a dead letter by the prevailing system. Only the 1959 revolution was at last able to make the principles of social justice expressed in that text a reality.

Of course, the 1959 revolution could not retain the liberal-bourgeois framework of the Constitution of 1940. Advancing toward deeper structural transformation — recovering that part of the nation's patrimony that had been usurped by monopolies and large landowners, and entering fully into socialist construction — the country needed a constitution that would provide a legal framework for the important changes to be wrought on the island and that would also serve as a basis for all of the other laws and regulations that had to be drawn up and put into effect.

"The Constitution," Raúl Castro emphasized, "is, therefore, the most important document governing the process of institutionalization of the revolution.

"By discussing the draft of our constitution and then voting for it, our people have been making decisions about the socioeconomic regime in which

---

[1] Raúl Castro, "Discurso en la proclamación de la Constitución de la República de Cuba, 24 de febrero de 1976" (Address on the Proclamation of the Constitution of the Republic of Cuba, February 24, 1976), *Raúl Castro, selección de discursos y artículos, 1976-1986* (Havana: Editora Política, 1988), 3.

[2] General Antonio Maceo protested at Mangos de Baraguá on March 15, 1878, against the peace that had been agreed to at Zanjón — a peace that brought neither independence nor the emancipation of the slaves — and declared his determination to continue the war.

they want to live; about the institutions through which they believe they should organize their activities and direct their social development; about the role, powers and functions of those institutions; about the rights and freedoms of citizens; and about the rights of all.

"In short, with complete freedom and full awareness, they have been making decisions about their lives and future. They have been fully exercising their right to govern, which is only possible when the people own the resources and basic means of production, when they are really in power, when they are truly sovereign and hold the present and future of their homeland in their hands."[3]

In 1992, after the constitution had been in effect for 16 years, the National Assembly of People's Power, availing itself of its powers, modified some of the articles of the constitution, to adjust its norms to the new situation created in the world at the beginning of that decade and to provide legal bases for the economic reforms and transformations that Cuba had to effect in order to achieve its reinsertion in the international scene.

Cuba is a workers' socialist state

(Excerpts from the Constitution of the Republic of Cuba, text approved by the National Assembly in 1992)[4]

Chapter I
Political, Social and Economic Bases of the Government

ARTICLE 1. Cuba is an independent, sovereign, workers' socialist state organized with all and for the good of all as a united, democratic republic for the enjoyment of political freedom, individual and collective well-being and human solidarity.

ARTICLE 2. The name of the Cuban state is the Republic of Cuba, the official language is Spanish and its capital is Havana.

ARTICLE 3. In the Republic of Cuba, sovereignty resides in the people, from whom all of the government's power comes. That power is exercised directly or through the Assemblies of People's Power and the government bodies that are subordinate to them, in the way and according to the norms established by the Constitution and the law.

All citizens have the right to use all means — including armed struggle, when they have no other recourse — to oppose any attempt

---

[3] Raúl Castro, *Selección de discursos*, 6-7.
[4] *Constitución de la República de Cuba* (Constitution of the Republic of Cuba) (Havana: Editora Política, 1992), 4-15.

to overthrow the political, social and economic order established by this Constitution.

ARTICLE 4. The nation's symbols are those that have, for more than 100 years, reigned over Cuba's struggles for independence, for the people's rights and for social progress:

- the flag with the single star,
- the Hymn of Bayamo and
- the coat of arms with the royal palm.

ARTICLE 5. The Marxist-Leninist Communist Party of Cuba, which is based on the ideas of José Martí and is the organized vanguard of the Cuban nation, is the supreme guiding force in society and the Government. It organizes and directs joint efforts to achieve the high purpose of the construction of socialism and the advance toward communist society.

ARTICLE 6. The Union of Young Communists (UJC), the organization of the vanguard Cuban young people, is recognized and supported by the Government in its primary function of promoting active participation by the masses of young people in the tasks of socialist construction and of preparing young people to be politically aware citizens capable of assuming ever greater responsibilities for the benefit of our society.

ARTICLE 7. The socialist Cuban Government recognizes and stimulates the mass and social organizations that were created in the historic process of our people's struggle and which group various sectors of the population; represent their specific interests; and incorporate them in the tasks of building, consolidating and defending our socialist society.

ARTICLE 8. The Government recognizes, respects and guarantees religious freedom.

In the Republic of Cuba, the religious institutions are separate from the Government.

The various beliefs and religions have equal consideration.

ARTICLE 9. The Government
a) carries out the will of the working people and
  a) guides the nation's efforts in the construction of socialism;
  b) maintains and defends our homeland's integrity and sovereignty;
  c) guarantees the freedom and full dignity of the individual, the enjoyment of their rights, the exercise and fulfillment of

their duties and the integral development of their personality;

d) supports the ideology of and the norms of coexistence and conduct proper to a society free of the exploitation of man by man;

e) protects the people's creative work and the property and wealth of the socialist nation;

f) directs the national economy in a planned way; and

g) ensures the country's educational, scientific, technical and cultural progress;

b) guarantees, as the people's power at the service of the people, that

a) every man and woman who is able to work has the opportunity to get a job with which they can contribute to the purposes of society and to meeting their own needs;

b) every person who is incapacitated for work has the means for a decent way of life;

c) everyone who is sick has medical treatment;

d) every child has a school to attend, food and clothing;

e) every young person has the opportunity to study; and

f) everyone has access to study, culture and sports;

c) works to provide every family with comfortable housing.

ARTICLE 10. Each of the bodies of the Government and of their leaders, officials and staff acts within the limits of their respective legal authority and has the obligation to observe strictly socialist legality and to see to it that it is respected in the life of all society.

ARTICLE 11. The Government exercises its sovereignty over

a) all of national territory, comprising the island of Cuba, the Isle of Youth, the adjacent cays and islands, the interior waters, the territorial seas to the extension set by law and the airspace over them;

b) the country's natural resources and environment; and

c) the natural resources, both living and nonliving, of the waters, ocean bed and subsoil of the maritime economic zone of the Republic, to the extension set by law, in accordance with international practice.

The Republic of Cuba repudiates and considers illegal and invalid the treaties, pacts and/or concessions agreed to in conditions of inequality and/or which ignore or reduce its sovereignty and territorial integrity.

ARTICLE 12. The Republic of Cuba endorses anti-imperialist and internationalist principles and

a) ratifies its aspiration to a worthy, true peace valid for all nations, both large and small, both weak and powerful, based on respect for the independence and sovereignty of the peoples and the right to self-determination;

b) bases its international relations on the principles of equal rights, free determination by the peoples, territorial integrity, the independence of nations, international cooperation to the benefit of equitable mutual interest, the peaceful settlement of controversies on a basis of equality and respect and the other principles proclaimed in the Charter of the United Nations and in other international treaties that Cuba has signed;

c) reaffirms its willingness to join and cooperate with the other Latin American and Caribbean countries, whose shared identity and historic need to advance together toward economic and political integration in order to achieve true independence would allow us to take our rightful place in the world;

d) advocates the unity of all Third World countries in the face of imperialist and neocolonialist policies that seek to limit or subordinate our peoples' sovereignty and to exacerbate the economic conditions of exploitation and oppression of the underdeveloped nations;

e) denounces imperialism, which promotes and supports all manifestations of fascism, colonialism, neocolonialism and racism, as the main force of aggression and of war and the worst enemy of the peoples;

f) repudiates direct and/or indirect intervention in the internal and/or external affairs of any nation — and, therefore, armed aggression, economic blockade and any other form of economic or political coercion, physical violence against people living in other countries and any other kind of meddling with and/or threat to the integrity of nations and of the political, economic and cultural aspects of nations;

g) rejects the violation of the intrinsic, sovereign right of every nation to regulate the use and benefits of telecommunications in its territory in accord with universal practice and with the international agreements which it has signed;

h) considers wars of aggression and conquest to be international crimes, recognizes the legitimacy of struggles for national liberation and armed resistance to aggression, and considers it an internationalist duty to express solidarity with those who are attacked and with the peoples that are fighting for their liberation and self-determination;

i) bases its relations with other countries that are building socialism on fraternal friendship, cooperation and mutual assistance, based on the shared objectives of the construction of a new society; and

j) maintains relations of friendship with countries that, although they have different political, social and economic regimes, respect its sovereignty, observe the norms of coexistence among nations, uphold the principles of mutual benefit and adopt a reciprocal attitude toward our country.

ARTICLE 13. The Republic of Cuba grants asylum to those who are persecuted for their ideals and for their struggles for democratic rights against imperialism, fascism, colonialism and neo-colonialism; against discrimination and racism; for national liberation; for the rights and demands of the workers, farmers and students; for their progressive political, scientific, artistic and literary activities; and for socialism and peace.

ARTICLE 14. The Republic of Cuba is governed by the economic system based on all the people's socialist ownership of the basic means of production and on the suppression of the exploitation of man by man.

It is also governed by the principle of socialist distribution: "from each according to their capacity, to each according to their work." The law establishes regulations that guarantee that this principle is observed.

ARTICLE 15. The following are owned by the socialist Government of all the people:
a) land that does not belong to small farmers or to cooperatives composed of small farmers; the subsoil; the mines; living and nonliving natural resources in the maritime economic area of the Republic; the forests; the water and the means of communication and

b) the sugar mills; the factories; the basic means of transportation; all of the companies, banks and other installations that have been nationalized and expropriated from the imperialists, large land-owners and bourgeoisie; and all of the factories, enterprises, economic installations and scientific, social, cultural and sports centers that have been built, promoted or acquired by the Government and those which may be built, promoted or acquired in the future.

The ownership of these assets may not be transferred to individuals or bodies corporate, except in rare cases — after approval by the Council of Ministers or its Executive Committee — in which the partial or total transfer of the ownership of an economic entity is beneficial to the country's development and doesn't adversely affect the political, social and economic bases of the nation.

The provisions of the law will be observed regarding the transfer of other rights over these assets to government enterprises and/or other authorized entities, to achieve their purposes.

ARTICLE 16. The Government organizes, directs and controls the activities of the national economy, in accord with a plan which guarantees the country's programmed development, in order to strengthen the socialist system, meet the material and cultural needs of society and of the citizens to an ever greater extent, and promote the development and dignity of individuals and the country's advance and security.

Workers from all branches of the economy and other spheres of social life play an active part in drawing up and implementing the production and development programs.

ARTICLE 17. The Government directly administers the assets that constitute the socialist property of all the people; it can create and set up enterprises and entities in charge of their administration, whose structure, attributes and functions and the system of their relations are governed by law.

Within the limits established by the law, these enterprises and entities use their own financial resources to meet their obligations. The Government is not responsible for the obligations contracted by the enterprises, entities or other bodies corporate, nor are they responsible for its obligations.

ARTICLE 18. The Government directs and controls foreign trade.

The law establishes the government authorities and institutions that are empowered to

• create foreign trade enterprises,

- regulate export and import operations and
- determine which individuals and/or bodies corporate have the legal capacity to carry out these export and import operations and enter into trade agreements.

ARTICLE 19. The Government recognizes the small farmers' ownership of the land to which they have legal title and their right to the other real estate and personal property that they need to carry out their activities, in accordance with the provisions of the law.

When authorized by the pertinent government agency and while complying with the other legal requisites, small farmers may make their land a part of agricultural production cooperatives. In those cases, forms and conditions established by the law, they may also sell, exchange and/or transfer it by other means to the Government and/or to agricultural production cooperatives or to small farmers without prejudice to the Government's prior claim to its acquisition by means of payment of its fair price.

This land may not be leased, sharecropped, mortgaged or subjected to any other action that implies obligations or the ceding to individuals of the rights arising from the small farmers' ownership of their land.

The Government supports individual production by the small farmers who contribute to the national economy.

ARTICLE 20. Small farmers have the right to join together in the way and with the prerequisites established by the law, both for purposes of agricultural production and for those of obtaining credits and services from the Government.

The organization of agricultural production cooperatives is authorized in those cases and forms established by the law. Cooperative ownership is recognized by the Government and constitutes an advanced, efficient form of socialist production.

Agricultural production cooperatives administer, possess and dispose of the assets they own, in accordance with the provisions of the law and its regulations.

The land of the cooperatives cannot be garnisheed or encumbered, and its ownership can be transferred to other cooperatives or to the Government, for the causes and following the procedures established by the law.

The Government offers all possible assistance to this form of agricultural production.

ARTICLE 21. Personal ownership is guaranteed of income and

savings resulting from individual work, of housing owned with fair title in fee simple and of the other assets and objects that serve to meet the material and cultural needs of the individual.

Likewise, ownership of the means and instruments of personal and/or family work — which may not be used to obtain income coming from the exploitation of the work of others — is also guaranteed.

The law establishes the amount of personal property that may be garnisheed.

ARTICLE 22. The Government recognizes the political, mass and social organizations' ownership of the assets used for achieving their purposes.

ARTICLE 23. The Government recognizes the property of the joint ventures, companies and economic associations that are established in accordance with the law.

The use, possession and disposal of the assets belonging to the capital of the above entities is governed by the provisions of the law, by agreements and by their own statutes and regulations.

ARTICLE 24. The Government recognizes the right of inheritance to privately owned housing and other personal assets.

The land and other assets linked to production that constitute the property of small farmers may be inherited and are only awarded to those heirs who work the land and following the procedures established by the law.

The law establishes the cases, conditions and form in which assets that are owned cooperatively may be inherited.

ARTICLE 25. The expropriation of assets is authorized for reasons of public utility or social interest, with due compensation.

The law establishes the procedures for expropriation, the bases for determining its utility and need, and the form of compensation, considering the interests and socioeconomic needs of the expropriated.

ARTICLE 26. Anyone who suffers undue damage or prejudice caused by officials or agents of the Government in the exercise of the functions of their positions has the right to claim and obtain the corresponding redress or compensation in the form established by law.

ARTICLE 27. The Government protects the environment and the country's natural resources. It recognizes their close link to sustainable socioeconomic development for making human life more rational and ensuring the survival, well-being and safety of the present and future generations. The pertinent agencies apply this policy.

Citizens have the duty to contribute to the protection of the water and atmosphere and to the conservation of the soil, flora, fauna and all the rich potential of nature.

29

PEOPLE'S POWER

December 2, 1976

On December 2, 1976, the process of the country's institutionalization culminated in the creation of the National Assembly of People's Power; the election of the members of the Council of State and President, First Vice-President and other Vice-Presidents; and the ratification of the members of the Council of Ministers. Thus, a new stage in the nation's political life began.

That project, which was outlined in the Constitution that went into effect on February 24, 1976, included the establishment of a new political-administrative division of the country; the nomination of candidates for delegates at the grass roots level by the people living in each voting district; the election of delegates; the subsequent creation of the municipal assemblies and their administrative bodies; the election of delegates to the provincial assemblies and of the national deputies; the creation of the provincial assemblies; and, finally, the creation of the National Assembly as the highest-ranking governing body, endowed with constitutional and legislative powers.

People's Power was the fruit of many years of thought, effort and experience.

In the initial stage of the revolution, when the principal task was to dismantle the instruments and bases of the old power and, at the same time, to defend the new workers' and farmers' democracy, it was necessary to have a flexible, cohesive government apparatus that concentrated the legislative, executive and administrative powers and was able to respond rapidly to the deep radical changes that were being instituted.

The people's democratic participation was expressed directly in that stage in their incorporation in a wide range of tasks, in the political and military mobilizations in which they participated and in the role they played in the revolutionary organizations. As Raúl Castro pointed out, "There may not be any other case in history in which a revolution, the leaders of a revolution, have had such massive, total support from the people; such inexhaustible and constant confidence and revolutionary enthusiasm by the masses; and such complete unity as [the Cuban] people have offered their revolution."[1]

The Cuban leaders had always been aware of how important it was — in addition to having these means of participation — to create representative institutions that would enable all citizens to take systematic part in the governing of society.

The first attempt to solve problems of local government was the creation of the Coordination, Implementation and Inspection Boards (*Juntas de Coordinación, Ejecución e Inspección, JUCEI*), in the 1960s.

Various factors, including the great effort to bring in the gigantic sugarcane harvest of 1970, led to the postponement of that task. Following the difficult experience of that year, the determination to institutionalize the country was given a big boost. The labor unions and mass organizations were strengthened. In 1972, the Council of Ministers was restructured, and its Executive Committee was created. In 1973, the party apparatus was strengthened in the same way, from the grassroots all the way up to the Central Committee.

In the course of that process, concepts based on the Soviet experience were introduced, which later combined with endogenous mistakes to create new problems, such as the top-heavy nature of the administrative superstructure, its virtual duplication in the party apparatus and the party's Secretariat control of the day to day running of the government. But the result, considered as a whole, was an advance toward more efficient, more democratic leadership.

People's Power was tried out first in Matanzas Province in 1974, to see what adjustments should be made and as a means to consider its later extension to the rest of the country.

The proposed system was based on several principles: the people, not the party, nominate and elect candidates, and the party has no veto power; the party's role in the process is to see that all norms are strictly upheld; voting is free and secret, and all citizens 16 years old and over, including members of the Armed Forces, have the right to vote and to be elected; those who are

---

[1] Raúl Castro, "Discurso ante los delegados del Poder Popular en Matanzas, 22 de agosto de 1974" (Address to the Delegates of People's Power in Matanzas, August 22, 1974), *Selección de discursos*, 206.

elected must report back periodically to their electors, who may vote them out of office at any time; and the norms of democratic centralism, collective leadership and individual responsibility govern all the levels of People's Power.

Fidel Castro had warned of the danger that the merely administrative procedures of the early years of the revolution might turn into bureaucratic procedures. Likewise, there was a risk that the centralism inherent in the Revolutionary Government at the beginning might become an obstacle to the administration of production and services at the local level and to initiatives of those exercising functions of government at that level.

Therefore, the creation of People's Power in 1976 meant not only the establishment of a system of representative institutions that were the product of democratic elections, giving the administrative authorities at each level their power, but also an important decentralization of tasks and powers, transferring them from the central government and its ministries to the local bodies in the provinces and municipalities.

This made many activities more rational and effective. In many cases, the central leadership retained the powers of deciding on methodology, establishing norms and making inspections, and the local bodies took over the direct administration of the country.

In July 1992, the National Assembly adopted changes in the constitution that, among other things, recognized the People's Councils (Consejos Populares) to be important links for coordinating and promoting the tasks of government and modified the electoral law, establishing that the deputies to the National Assembly and delegates to the provincial assemblies of People's Power — who, up until then, had been elected by the members of the level of government immediately inferior to them — should, like the delegates to the municipal assemblies, be elected by the people in a free, direct and secret vote.

Improving our democracy

(Excerpts from the address by Raúl Castro, First Vice-President of the Cuban Government, to the first delegates of People's Power)[2]

During the first few years after the triumph of the revolution, we didn't have adequate conditions for creating these institutions [the bodies of People's Power]. Moreover, there was no pressing, vital or decisive need to do so in order to carry out the tasks with which our revolutionary process was confronted in that early period.

Those early years were characterized by thoroughgoing, radical,

---

[2] Ibid, 202-42

accelerated, rapid revolutionary changes. During those first few years, we had to confront successive, ever more violent attacks by imperialism and the domestic counterrevolution.

To develop in that situation and to take up the tasks of that period, Cuba needed a government apparatus that could act quickly and effectively; exercise a workers' dictatorship; concentrate the legislative, executive and administrative powers in a single body; and make quick decisions.

Our Revolutionary Government, which has concentrated the legislative, executive and administrative powers in itself throughout those years, carried out its functions well. In the first phase of the struggle for survival, it ended exploitation in our country and successfully waged a political struggle against attacks both from abroad and from within the country.

During those early years, the shortage of material means held back the organization of People's Power, for the country lacked even the minimum resources for carrying out its tasks, which included housing, maintenance and repairs for which the people were clamoring.

It was feared that limited resources would make it too difficult for People's Power to carry out its tasks and that the idea of its creation, which was basically correct, could be discredited. Moreover, in the first few years after the triumph of the revolution, we weren't sufficiently prepared to create those representative institutions. At that time, we didn't yet have a strong party, the mass organizations hadn't developed enough and we didn't have all of the organizational tools that we have now...

The establishment of the representative institutions of our government is an extremely important step forward in our revolutionary process. They complete the elements of our proletarian government. During the first few years of the struggle for survival, they were neither indispensable nor vital — and might even have proved a hindrance to the speed with which the government had to act at that time. Now, in the conditions that have been created, they have become a pressing need, a basic element of our government with which the people's participation will be given a standard, real and systematic institutional form.

Naturally, this doesn't mean that the revolution and its leaders have ever been above the people, that the people have been forgotten or that the masses have ever withdrawn their support from the revolution. To the contrary, because the masses of workers and the rest of the people have always supported the revolution and its leaders, the insurrectional struggle was carried out successfully, the [Batista] dictatorship was overthrown, a general strike was held and attempted coups were put down. The thoroughgoing revolutionary changes that were carried out could only be effected with the support of the people and their massive, enthusiastic participation in them...

Even before the representative institutions were created, our revolutionary government was and has always been democratic.

No matter what its form and structure, a government such as ours is more democratic than any other kind of government that has ever existed in the history of the world, because it represents the interests of the workers; and a government that represents the workers, a government that is building socialism, is — no matter what its form — a government of the majority, whereas all of the earlier governments have been governments representing exploiting minorities...

Therefore, our government has been and is an essentially democratic one — a government of, by and for the ordinary people, a government of and for all the workers. Therefore, the creation of the representative institutions is simply an improvement on our government, giving it a complete and definitive structure and improving our democracy.

Socialist representative institutions embody the express will of the people, through their votes. They are a means by which the people not only are represented by the government but, in fact, form a direct part of that government and participate directly and systematically in its decisions. Since the conditions for the creation of these institutions now exist, it is absolutely necessary to create them immediately...

We should remember that, as Fidel said on the 10th anniversary of the founding of the Federation of Cuban Women (FMC) when referring to this subject, it is a matter of "replacing the purely administrative habits of the early years of the revolution with democratic procedures that replace the administrative procedures which are threatening to become bureaucratic."

The existence and functioning of the bodies of People's Power — the representative institutions of our socialist government and the highest-ranking bodies of government power in the territories over which they will exercise their jurisdiction — should, without fail, lead to the total eradication of those purely administrative habits and to the complete replacement of those procedures, which threaten to become or that, in many — very many — cases, have already become bureaucratic.

The bodies of People's Power at the municipal, regional and provincial levels are taking over the administration of many important activities, which have been centrally administered so far. However, the most important thing about these institutions isn't the role they are playing in the administrative sphere; rather, it is the fact that they are the basic bodies of government power, bodies composed of representatives who have been democratically elected by the masses. They are bodies through which the people have the possibility of participating directly in governing social matters. The existence of the bodies of People's Power should, necessarily, eliminate the bureaucratic centralism that still exists in many parts of our government apparatus, replacing it with democratic centralism, which is the Marxist-Leninist basis on which they should function...

You should educate your electors, the masses, in every electoral district about the problems we have, explaining which of them can and which can't yet be solved. You should explain to them that the bodies of People's Power aren't going to come up with miraculous solutions.

We should ensure that false hopes aren't raised among the masses. At the same time, you have the responsibility to struggle not to defraud the masses in things that they can logically expect of you. You must manage the people's resources more efficiently, using the same amount of resources to produce more — and better — products and services than in the past. It is within our power to do this. We must strive for greater efficiency, higher productivity, better quality, rigorous controls in the management of resources, less bureaucracy, solutions for the problems that we can solve and proposed solutions for others that we can't solve but which can be solved at other levels. We must also strive for the correct functioning of the bodies of People's Power and seek the best specific forms that these institutions should have in our country.

30

INTERNATIONALIST POLICY

October 12, 1979

In spite of intensive communication with leaders and other international figures who visited Cuba in the 1960s, the Cuban Revolution somehow remained relatively isolated in that period. In Latin America, after the United States had forced Cuba's expulsion from the Organization of American States (OAS), only Mexico maintained diplomatic relations with Cuba. The Caribbean nations weren't yet — or had just become — independent. With the Soviet Union, there was a period of differences, which didn't end until after the events in Czechoslovakia in the spring of 1968.

In the early 1970s, Cuba began to open its doors to a changing world and its international outreach grew very strong in Latin America and the Caribbean, the Third World and nonaligned countries, and the socialist community centered around the Soviet Union.

In 1970, Salvador Allende's victory in the Chilean election renewed hopes for change in Latin America. In November of that year, on being inaugurated, the Chilean Socialist leader reestablished diplomatic relations with Cuba and dealt the first powerful blow to the fundamentalist doctrine of the OAS, which had been used as a pretext for Cuba's expulsion from that forum. Later on, in 1975, the OAS was forced to adopt the principle of ideological pluralism.

Between November 10 and December 4, 1971, Fidel Castro made a long trip through Chile, always in close contact with the Chilean people, which enabled him not only to contribute to the consolidation of that process but *also to outline his views on the most strategic problems of Latin America and the world.*

In May, June and July 1972, Fidel Castro made a 63-day tour of several African and Arab countries and the Central and Eastern European socialist countries, concluding with a stay in the Soviet Union.

On December 8 of that year, in an admirable gesture of dignity and independence, the governments of Jamaica, Barbados, Guyana and Trinidad and Tobago made a collective decision to establish diplomatic relations with Cuba.

In September 1973, for the first time, Fidel Castro attended a Nonaligned Summit held in Algiers. After the meeting, he flew to Vietnam. During the flight, he heard the tragic news of the fascist coup in Chile and President Allende's death.

On January 28, 1974, Soviet leader Leonid Ilyich Brezhnev visited Cuba.

In this period, several Latin American governments, including that of Omar Torrijos in Panama, changed their policies and decided to reestablish diplomatic relations with Cuba. Many important figures on the international political scene visited Havana.

Between February 22 and March 16, 1976, Fidel Castro made another trip to the Soviet Union, Yugoslavia, Bulgaria, Algeria and Guinea. In Conakry, capital of Guinea, he met with Ahmed Sékou Touré of Guinea, Luis Cabral of Guinea-Bissau and Agostinho Neto of Angola.

Between March 1 and April 8, 1977, the Cuban President visited Libya, Southern Yemen, Somalia, Ethiopia, Tanzania, Mozambique, Angola and Algeria. The most important aspects of the trip included his efforts to find a negotiated solution for the Ogaden conflict between Somalia and the new Ethiopian leadership, his rebuttal of Mobuto's accusation that Cubans had taken part in the rebellion in Katanga and his meeting in Luanda with the national liberation leaders of South Africa and Namibia. The trip wound up with visits to the German Democratic Republic and the Soviet Union.

That same year, in October, Fidel Castro visited Jamaica for the first time.

In December 1977, Cuban forces were sent to Ethiopia and helped to push back and defeat the invasion of the Ogaden desert by Somalian troops backed by the reactionary governments in the region and by Western powers.

The 11th World Festival of Youth and Students, in which 18,500 delegates from 145 countries participated, was held in Havana from July 28 through August 5, 1978. The next month Fidel Castro made another visit to Ethiopia, Libya and Algeria.

On May 17, 1979, the President of Cuba went to Cozumel, Mexico, where he met with Mexican President José López Portillo.

The Sandinista Revolution triumphed in Nicaragua on July 19, 1979, after a bloody people's struggle with which the Cuban Revolution had expressed its solidarity in various ways. A few days later, the two governments decided to renew their diplomatic relations and to cooperate actively in Nicaragua's recovery.

On September 3, 1979, Havana hosted the Sixth Summit of the Nonaligned Movement. Delegations attended from 138 countries – including representatives of 94 governments and liberation movements that were full members of the movement. It was the largest and most representative Nonaligned Summit held up until then. Marshal Josip Broz Tito, President of Yugoslavia and one of the founders of the movement, was one of those attending. In his inaugural address, Fidel Castro denied charges that Cuba was trying to turn the movement into a tool of Soviet policy, reaffirmed the timeliness of its historic principles and called on the meeting to express "a firm determination to struggle and to implement specific plans of action. Actions, not just words!"

More heads of state and/or government gathered on Cuban soil to attend that meeting than ever before or since.

As President of the Movement of Nonaligned Countries, between the Sixth and Seventh Summits, Fidel Castro went to the United Nations in New York and there, on October 12, 1979, presented his report to the General Assembly.

I speak on behalf of all the children in the world who have no bread to eat

(Excerpts from the address by Fidel Castro to the General Assembly of the United Nations on October 12, 1979, representing the Movement of Nonaligned Countries)

On more than one occasion, it has been said that we were forced into underdevelopment by colonization and imperialist neo-colonization. Therefore, the task of helping us to emerge from underdevelopment is, first and foremost, a historic and moral obligation for those who benefited from the plunder of our wealth and the exploitation of our men and women for decades and for centuries. But it is, at the same time, the task of humankind as a whole, as was stated at the Sixth Summit...

Therefore, we must mobilize the resources for development. This is our joint obligation...

In addition to the resources already mobilized by various banks, loan organizations, international bodies and private finance agencies, we must discuss and decide on the strategy for the next development decade. In that strategy we will need an additional contribution of at least $200 billion at 1977 real values to be invested in the underdeveloped countries and to be made in yearly installments of at least $25 billion from the very beginning. This aid should be in the form of donations and long-term, moderate- and low-interest credits.

It is imperative that these additional funds be mobilized as the contribution of the developed world and of other countries with resources to the underdeveloped world over the next 10 years. These resources are required for peace. If there are no resources for development, there will be no peace. Some may think that we are asking too much, but I think that the figure is still modest. According to statistical information, as I stated in the inaugural session of the Sixth Summit of Nonaligned Countries, the world's annual military expenditures amount to more than $300 billion.

In one year, with $300 billion, you could build 600,000 schools with a capacity for 400 million children; 60 million comfortable homes for 300 million people; 30,000 hospitals with 18 million beds; or 20,000 factories with jobs for more than 20 million workers. Or you could build irrigation systems to water 150 million hectares of land — which, with appropriate technology, could feed a billion people. Humankind wastes this much every year on its military spending.

Moreover, consider the enormous waste of young human resources, technicians, scientists, fuel, raw materials and other items. This is the high price of preventing a true climate of peace and security from existing in the world.

The United States, alone, will spend six times this much on military activities in the 1980s.

We are requesting less for 10 years of development than is spent in a single year by the ministries of war, and much less than a tenth of what will be spent for military purposes in 10 years.

Some may consider our demand irrational, but what is truly irrational is the world's madness in our era and the peril that threatens humanity...

As revolutionaries, we are not afraid of confrontation. We have placed our trust in history and in the peoples. But, as the spokesperson and interpreter of the feelings of 95 nations, I have the duty to strive to achieve cooperation among people. That cooperation, if obtained on a new and fair basis, will benefit all of the countries in the international community and will especially improve the prospects for world peace.

In the short term, development may be a task involving apparent sacrifices and even donations that may appear irrecoverable. However, if the vast world now living in backwardness — with no purchasing power and with extremely limited consumer capacity — is developed, it will add a flood of hundreds of millions of consumers and producers to the international economy. This is the only way to rehabilitate the international economy and the economies of the developed countries, which now generate and suffer from economic crises...

This is why, speaking on behalf of the developing countries, we advocate our countries' cause and ask you to support it. We aren't asking for a gift. If we don't come up with effective solutions, we will all be victims of the catastrophe.

Mr. President and distinguished representatives, people often speak of human rights, but we must also speak of the rights of humanity.

Why should some people go barefoot so that others can ride in expensive cars? Why should some live only 35 years so that others can live 70? Why should some be miserably poor so that others can be exaggeratedly rich?

I speak on behalf of all the children in the world who have no bread to eat. I speak on behalf of the sick who lack medicine. I speak on behalf of those who have been denied the right to life and to human dignity.

Some countries are by the sea; others are not. Some have energy resources; others do not. Some have plenty of land on which to grow food; others do not. Some are so glutted with machinery and factories that the very air is poisoned and cannot be breathed; others have only their own emaciated arms with which to earn their daily bread.

In short, some countries have abundant resources, while others have nothing. What is their fate? To starve? To be eternally poor? What good, then, is civilization? What good is the conscience of man? What good is the United Nations? What good is the world? You cannot speak of peace on behalf of tens of millions of human beings all over the world who are starving to death or dying of curable diseases. You cannot speak of peace on behalf of 900 million illiterates.

The exploitation of the poor countries by the rich countries must cease.   I know that there are both exploiters and exploited in many poor countries, as well.

I ask the rich nations to contribute, and I ask the poor nations to distribute.

Enough of words! We need deeds. Enough of abstractions! We need concrete action. Enough of talking about a speculative new international economic order that nobody understands. Now, we must talk of a real, objective order that everybody understands.

I haven't come here as a prophet of revolution. I haven't come here to ask or to wish that the world be violently convulsed. I have come to speak of peace and cooperation among the peoples and to warn that, if we don't peacefully and wisely solve and do away with the injustices that exist in the world, the future will be apocalyptic.

The sound of weapons, threatening language and overbearing behavior in the international arena must cease. Enough of the illusion that the problems of the world can be solved by means of nuclear weapons. Bombs may kill the hungry, the sick and the ignorant, but bombs cannot kill hunger, disease and ignorance. Nor can bombs kill the peoples' justified rebelliousness. And, in the holocaust, the rich — who are the ones who have the most to lose in this world — will also die.

Let us say a farewell to arms, and let us, in a civilized manner, dedicate ourselves to solving the most pressing problems of our times. This is the responsibility, the most sacred duty, of the world's leaders. Moreover, it is the basic premise for human survival.

31

THE MARIEL CRISIS

April 1, 1980

Starting in 1973, the U.S. Government stepped up its policy of using Cuban emigration as a weapon in its efforts to create internal difficulties for the revolution.

Cuba had freed thousands of prisoners who had served time for having committed counterrevolutionary crimes. Most of them wanted to go to Miami as quickly as possible. In addition, there were tens of thousands of people in Havana and other cities who had been waiting for years to get visas so they could join their relatives in the United States. There were others who wanted to emigrate for economic reasons, along with many criminal, marginal and classless individuals who also wanted to leave Cuba.

The U.S. Government refused to give them visas through normal channels but urged them to commit acts of violence and to go to the United States illegally — which, though dangerous for them, would boost the anti-Cuba propaganda.

Thus, they were incited to force their way into embassies, the plan being to place the Cuban Government in a difficult position and, in fact, to blackmail it. Certain Latin American governments and embassies lent themselves to these maneuvers.

A decisive moment occurred on April 1, 1980. A group of individuals drove a bus into the gates of the Peruvian Embassy on the corner of Fifth Avenue and 72nd Streets, in Miramar, Havana. Pedro Ortiz Cabrera, a young Cuban guard, was killed during the break-in.

Instead of expelling the intruders, who had no right to request asylum, the Peruvian Government allowed them to stay. On April 4, Cuba decided to withdraw its guards from around the Embassy. The Peruvian Chargé d'Affaires announced that anyone who wished to enter could do so, and a noisy, disorderly mob of thousands crammed into the mansion, overflowing into its grounds and onto its roof. Chaos reigned there in the following days, since there was no control over the antisocial elements' behavior.

The first groups of emigrants via the Peruvian Embassy went to Costa Rica; others went to Lima, where they lived in tents put up in a park and were ignored by the government for many years.

In fact, none of the would-be emigrés wanted to go to Third World countries. They all had their sights set on the United States. On April 18, 1980, an editorial in Granma, *official organ of the Communist Party of Cuba, stated clearly that Cuba wouldn't oppose those who wanted to go to the United States, and they could do so directly and safely, in boats sent by their relatives to the port of Mariel. Thus, the crisis boomeranged on the country that had instigated it, the United States.*

The following day, while over a million people marched past the Peruvian Embassy, preparations began for what would be the largest migratory bridge in the history of the conflict between the United States and Cuba. Between April 21, when the first yachts and other vessels from Florida arrived in Mariel, and the end of May, around 125,000 people went to Miami.

On May Day, 1980, the people marched through Havana's Revolution Square. Referring to current events, Fidel Castro said, "One of our key ideas is that the work of a revolution and the construction of socialism are the tasks of absolutely free volunteers, both men and women."

On May 17, five million Cubans took part in the second people's march in Havana and in other marches in different parts of the country. In the capital, the enormous column marched past the U.S. Interests Section, on Havana's Malecón, where some of those opposed to the revolution — most of them former prisoners who had staged a riot near the diplomatic site and forced their way in on May 2 — still remained.

The events at the Peruvian Embassy and at Mariel, from which Cuba emerged the victor, plunged the Carter Administration into a crisis. The proposals of the "new right" in the United States gained ground with a much more aggressive and dangerous anti-Cuba policy.

When a powerful nation's policy is unprincipled and its rulers are immoral

(Editorial published in Granma *on May 19, 1980)*

A few days ago, U.S. President [Jimmy] Carter publicly appealed to Cuba to establish what he called an orderly sea or air shuttle for taking Cubans who wanted to emigrate from Cuba to the United States. After that, naturally, he set a series of limitations, saying that only those who already had relatives in the United States could live there. Nobody knows what other country, if any, is willing to accept the others. In short, the U.S. Government wants to pick and choose — if possible, to take away skilled people with no criminal record, unless they are counterrevolutionary, and leave us the rest of those who are hostile to the well-being of society.

However, the lumpen elements and all the others who are hostile to the well-being of society in general want to emigrate to the United States. None of them want to go to Haiti, Santo Domingo, Brazil, Colombia, Ecuador or Peru; nor do they want to go to India, Bangladesh, Pakistan, Nigeria, Zaire or the Ivory Coast — in short, to any underdeveloped country in Latin America, Asia or Africa. All of them want to go to the United States — or at least to a developed European country.

Some of those who went to Costa Rica tried to hijack a plane that would take them to Miami; others, in Peru, tried to stow away on a ship that was going to the United States.

This makes us think that some of those governments that agreed to accept "refugees" weren't very serious about it.

The main thing isn't the means the Cubans who leave Cuba use or the route they take to get to the United States. The main thing is to analyze and remove the causes that generated those elements and the Cuban emigration to that country.

Generally, emigration from underdeveloped to developed countries for economic reasons is a result of the poverty that the brutal system of colonial and imperialist exploitation has caused in the Third World nations. Millions of Mexicans have emigrated to the United States for that reason, and people say that a million cross the border every year, most of them heading for that part of the United States that used to belong to Mexico and which the United States took by means of force. For that reason, too, millions of Haitians have tried to emigrate to the United States. Innumerable millions from the rest of Latin America want to do so, as well, to escape from the dreadful socioeconomic conditions in which they live. It doesn't occur to anybody to call them dissidents. Is this or isn't it a result of imperialist rule and exploitation in our hemisphere?

Prior to the triumph of the revolution, people also emigrated from Cuba for economic reasons, but the United States maintained a strict limit on the number of Cubans who could enter that country.

During the past 21 years, no other country in this hemisphere has done more than Cuba to do away with unemployment, poverty, ignorance, disease, gambling, drugs and prostitution. No other country in the hemisphere has done more to remove the socio-economic factors that cause people to become lumpen elements and to emigrate. No other country has struggled as selflessly to overcome socioeconomic underdevelopment. We have performed our most sacred duty as a nation for the good of Cuban children.

However, the United States has made the greatest effort known to history to sabotage our economic plans and our tenacious struggle in the sphere of social development. It wants to keep our country submerged in underdevelopment and poverty, to destabilize the Revolutionary Government and to starve us into submission.

Following the triumph of the revolution, a new immigration policy with strictly counterrevolutionary purposes was applied to Cuba.

It all began when masses of Batista's torturers and other criminals were granted asylum in the United States. Now, U.S. officials express concern about the possibility that common criminals who have committed crimes of violence might enter that country, but in 1959 they gave a warm welcome to Ventura, Masferrer, Calviño and hundreds of other assassins and torturers who had killed many thousands of Cubans. They welcomed all of Batista's henchmen, including officials who had plundered the treasury, stealing hundreds of millions of pesos from the people. Then they opened their doors to all of the large landowners, urban landlords, capitalists and all kinds of despicable people and urged doctors, engineers, architects, accountants, artists, professors, teachers at all levels and intellectual workers of all kinds to leave Cuba.

Of the 6,000 doctors in Cuba at the time of the triumph of the revolution, they took 3,000 away from a country that was beginning an epic battle against disease. They opened their doors wide, to deprive Cuba not only of its university-educated professionals but even of its skilled workers and production technicians. Never before or since has such an enormous, systematic effort been made to deprive a country of its skilled personnel, to destroy its economy and to destabilize it politically within the framework of a counterrevolutionary strategy. This was what created the basis of a veritable community of residents of Cuban origin in the United States, dividing countless families who later tried to be reunited in that country.

An abrupt change occurred in October 1962. The United States suspended all flights. Why? To generate discontent and promote counterrevolutionary activities by hundreds of thousands of people who were still in Cuba with their passports ready.

The opening of the port of Camarioca and the Cuban Government's willingness to negotiate created a partial solution for that situation.

However, the United States still maintained a destabilizing, counterrevolutionary policy regarding our country. Once again, it clamped restrictions on emigration. Much worse, it encouraged illegal departures from Cuba as a tool of dirty imperialist propaganda. Any criminal or lumpen element or anyone else hostile to the well-being of society — to whom it wouldn't normally give a visa — who arrived illegally was given a hero's welcome and lots of publicity. Sometimes such people hijacked vessels and took their crews hostage. The U.S. Government was warned several times of the negative consequences of such behavior.

Our streets teemed with thousands of former counterrevolutionary prisoners, and the United States, which had urged and led them to commit counterrevolutionary acts, refused to accept them even though the Cuban Government authorized them and their families to leave.

The U.S. actions against Cuba weren't limited to immigration policies. A tight economic blockade was imposed to keep our country from emerging from underdevelopment and poverty and to defeat our socioeconomic plans. Moreover, the arsenal of criminal measures that imperialism used against our homeland also included mercenary invasions, pirate attacks, actions by armed groups, acts of terrorism, acts of sabotage in our industries and plagues in agriculture.

The United States did its utmost to deprive us of participation in the international credit agencies and to shut off our access to credits from international commercial banks.

The United States forced our country to invest enormous amounts of economic resources and human energy in the nation's defense against its constant military threats.

The United States still has a naval base in our territory against our will, which goes against all principles of international law. That base, which has no global military value, constitutes an enemy beachhead in our homeland and is a deliberate, flagrant attempt to humiliate us.

The United States arrogates to itself the right to violate our airspace whenever it wants to, making use and abuse of its technical resources and thumbing its nose at international regulations.

In contrast, Cuba has — several times — demonstrated its willingness to seek settlements, even if partial ones. At the time of the departures from Camarioca, we achieved a discussion and a partial solution. When skyjacking began to proliferate (for which the United States was responsible, as it had used that tactic against Cuba just after the triumph of the revolution) we again agreed to a partial solution of our problems and signed an agreement — which was ended because of the monstrous act of sabotage which blew up a Cuban plane in the air near Barbados [in 1976].

What good have those partial solutions been?

Our country's socioeconomic conditions still, unfortunately, create lumpen elements and emigration.

Seven thousand families in Havana are living in dormitories because their homes were destroyed in natural disasters; 43,000 houses have been propped up to keep them from collapsing; and tens of thousands of families, many of them exemplary, self-sacrificing poor families, live in overcrowded conditions. And that's only in the capital.

In spite of our enormous efforts and admirable advances in education and health and in spite of our struggle against unemployment, begging, prostitution, gambling and drugs, our country is still underdeveloped, and underdevelopment engenders lumpen elements and emigration. Developed capitalism also produces lumpen elements — and on a much larger scale — but capitalism, with its corruption and its vices, is the natural medium of lumpen elements; socialism isn't.

Right now, the United States is making enormous efforts to hinder our development plans. Throughout the 21 years since the triumph of the revolution, the United States has maintained its cruel blockade, which prevents sales of even food and medicines to Cuba.

Now, it isn't doctors, engineers, architects, artists, teachers and technicians who want to emigrate to the United States. The revolution has trained many of them. To their honor and to the pride of our homeland, their attitude en masse is to struggle firmly alongside the people. The few exceptions only serve to prove the rule. Now, almost no former large landowners, urban landlords or refined bourgeois remain. There are only a few vacillating petty bourgeois. Now, the only allies imperialism has in our country are the lumpen elements and those who are hostile to the well-being of society — those who, though not strictly lumpen elements, lack all national feeling and love of their homeland. We are not averse to their going to live in the U.S. "paradise."

The imperialist blockade against Cuba generates lumpen elements and, therefore, emigration.

The systematic, sustained hostility of the United States against Cuba hinders our socioeconomic development and generates lumpen elements and, therefore, emigration.

The imperialist policy of terror against Cuba generates fear, difficulties, lumpen elements, and, therefore, emigration.

The imperialist monopolies' exploitation of Cuba for nearly 60 years generated poverty and underdevelopment — and, therefore, lumpen elements and emigration.

The U.S. counterrevolutionary policy against Cuba encourages lumpen elements and, therefore, their emigration to the United States.

Why does the United States discuss the means of emigrating from Cuba to the United States rather than the deep-rooted causes that gave rise to the problem?

We are willing to discuss and negotiate our problems and global relations with the United States — but not isolated, partial problems, which are of interest only to that country and its strategy against Cuba.

The Mariel-Florida route has proved to be efficient, serious and safe. Even though there were as many as 1,800 vessels in that harbor at times, the operation was perfectly organized. To say anything else is to engage in demagogy. For our part, we aren't breaking any laws: entries in and departures from the port are free. If the United States wants to impose its jurisdiction, it should do so in Florida; it can't do anything in Mariel.

We understand that the United States is in the midst of a period of electoral demagogy, but other people should understand the difficulties a small country has in dealing with a powerful neighbor whose government is unprincipled and whose leaders are immoral.

We have nothing personal against Carter or for Reagan. That would be inconceivable. Not long ago, a prominent U.S. black leader told a representative of Cuba that Reagan was an extreme reactionary, crazy, a fascist, and that, if Reagan won the election, the U.S. black leaders might have to seek refuge in Cuba.

Reagan is one of those who has talked of imposing a naval blockade of Cuba, but that wouldn't be our problem. We can hold out against any blockade and repulse any attack. If the people of the United States elect a fascist or a crazy person, that's their business. Hitler, too, was "crazy," and look where that got him.

Should we help [U.S. President] Carter solve the problem of the

Mariel shuttles — which was created by the far from brilliant earlier policy and which has used counterrevolutionary former prisoners to stage acts of provocation — as he wants, considering only the internal situation of the United States?

Who can guarantee that Carter will win? And, if Carter wins, who can guarantee that he will really effect a change in policy toward Cuba?

Moreover, even if we wanted to do so, how could we gloss over the fact that the United States has arrogated to itself the prerogative to grant the right of asylum even though, historically, it has refused to sign the corresponding agreement? What will happen if the other Western capitalist nations do the same?

We feel no panic or fear with regard to Reagan or anybody else. We have already struggled against six U.S. presidents, and none of them has frightened or will ever be able to frighten us. We aren't going to lower our banners, renounce our legitimate demands — that the blockade be lifted, that the U.S. troops be withdrawn from the [Guantánamo naval] base and that the spy flights be ended — or make concessions to help the domestic situation in the United States in the hope that its leaders will become more sensible or that better times will come.

People who are willing to fight to the death don't beg for their rights.

We don't want to be inflexible, but neither do we want to interfere or be used in internal struggles in the United States. We are even willing to continue analyzing the important matter of the implications which that country's present electoral period have in its foreign policy, but we are duty-bound to set forth our position very clearly.

32

THE PANDORA CASE

September 15, 1981

In January 1981, Ronald Reagan was sworn in as president of the United States. His entire electoral campaign had promoted the idea of a much more active and energetic anticommunist policy that would wipe out the "Vietnam syndrome" and reestablish U.S. leadership in the "free world."

The public platform of the new administration on Latin America — and especially Cuba — was contained in a document called the Santa Fe Document, a New Inter-American Policy for the Decade of the Eighties,[1] which stated that the Americas were under attack by the Soviet Union, which was using Cuba as a vassal state. It recommended that a series of measures be taken against Cuba — including the installation of a broadcasting station to beam counterrevolutionary information and other programs to Cuba (this was the origin, in 1985, of Radio Martí) — and said that troops should be sent to intervene militarily in Cuba if those actions weren't effective.

Logically enough, those threats caused the Cuban leadership to take counter measures.

During the preceding 20 years, the Revolutionary Armed Forces of Cuba had been working hard to make it unfeasible for the United States to launch a direct attack on Cuba. The Soviet Union's provision of weapons

---

[1] The Santa Fe Committee, which wrote the document, had been linked to Ronald Reagan from the time he was Governor of California. Its members were Francis Bouchey, Roger Fontaine, David C. Jordan and General Gordon Sumner, Jr.

free of charge and the advice of its military specialists unquestionably contributed to the level of organization and strength achieved. Cuba managed to create the strongest armed forces in Latin America, organized as a regular army and ready to wage modern − though conventional − warfare. Cuba has never been dependent for its defense on the might of the Soviet Union or the other Warsaw Pact countries, but it felt that the solidarity of its allies should always be an important factor in containing its enemy's potential.

The new situation that was created after Reagan took office repeated, to some extent, the moment of serious pressures and tensions preceding the 1962 October Missile Crisis. This time, Raúl Castro, Minister of the Revolutionary Armed Forces and the second most important figure in the Cuban Government and Communist Party, made another trip to Moscow.

Raúl Castro met with Leonid Ilyich Brezhnev, the top Soviet leader, on September 15, 1981 − which wasn't made public until over a decade later, after the Soviet Union had collapsed. When the representative of the Cuban leadership suggested that the aggressiveness of the new U.S. administration could be curbed by an official Soviet declaration that the Soviet Union would not tolerate an attack on Cuba, Brezhnev's reply was categorical: "We can't fight in Cuba, because you're 11,000 kilometers away from us. We'd only get a thrashing."

For years, that bitter revelation was a secret that Raúl Castro shared only with Fidel. The Cuban President expressed his attitude toward it indirectly, emphasizing in one of his later addresses that the people would defend Cuba with their own lives.

On the one hand, the certainty that the Soviet Union wouldn't run any risks for Cuba reflected the deep process of retreat and internal deterioration that was occurring in that immense country; on the other, it reaffirmed the idea that Cuba couldn't base its defense on anything but its own forces. In view of Cuba's overwhelming disadvantage in terms of combatants and technology in the case of an eventual large-scale military attack by the United States, that struggle shouldn't be considered only as a confrontation between two regular armies.

Thus, the process of rectification began in the Revolutionary Armed Forces at an early date, before the imminent and far from glorious end of the Soviet Union and of the European socialist community could be discerned.

A new military doctrine emerged: that of a war of all the people, based on the criterion that, even though the United States could destroy the country with technological warfare, to achieve its aims it would necessarily have to try to occupy it with human forces. In those conditions, the Cuban people − organized in the cities, mountains and other defense areas throughout the country, with tunnels and caves in which to preserve human lives and weapons, and with officers prepared to act in a decentralized way − would begin a war of annihilation and attrition that the invaders would never survive in the long run.

The idea of the troops' self-sufficiency in food and a proposal that was even more ambitious − the effort to have the Revolutionary Armed Forces gradually finance themselves − were soon added to those concepts.

The adoption of the doctrine of a war of all the people was the beginning of a long, intensive, sustained effort. During the following years, special attention was paid to organizing the Territorial Troop Militias and defense areas; preparing the theater of military operations; carrying out protection projects, in which hundreds of thousands of members of the Armed Forces and workers took part; and, in short, setting up a system linking the political and military leaderships at every level, the regular and people's forces, defense and production.

We would only get a thrashing

(Excerpt from the interview between Raúl Castro, First Vice-President of Cuba and Minister of the Revolutionary Armed Forces, and Mexican journalist Mario Vázquez Raña)[2]

Raúl Castro is a man of power because he is a man of secrets. For more than a decade, he kept a priceless secret of strategic value about the former Soviet Union's abandonment of its military alliance with Cuba when it said it wouldn't participate in Cuba's active defense if the United States should decide to invade the island during the belligerent stage at the beginning of Ronald Reagan's first term of office.

The U.S. intelligence services didn't become aware of the situation because of the smoke screen that both Moscow and Havana created with previously prepared symbolic acts, but the fact was that the Soviet Union had unforgivably changed its military stand concerning its ally.

Now, 12 years later, Raúl Castro tells us about it.

Mario Vázquez Raña: General, now that some secret files of the former Soviet Union's have been made public, you told me that you would make some comments about Cuba's relations with that country. What is it all about?

Raúl Castro: Early in the 1980s, I visited the Soviet Union and had an official meeting with the President of the Supreme Soviet and

---

[2] *Granma*, October 23, 1993.

General Secretary of the Communist Party of the Soviet Union, in which the Minister of Defense and the Secretary for Foreign Relations of the Central Committee also took part. At their request, I went alone. The translator was Soviet.

In view of the Reagan Administration's aggressiveness toward Cuba, which started a few weeks after Reagan took office, the purpose of my visit to Moscow was to give the Soviet leaders our opinion about the urgency of carrying out special diplomatic and political actions so as to brake the U.S. Government's renewed intentions of attacking Cuba militarily.

I suggested that such actions might consist of an official Soviet statement to the United States that the Soviet Union would not tolerate an attack on Cuba and a demand that Washington abide by its pledge not to attack Cuba, which it had made at the time of the 1962 October Missile Crisis. All this could be backed up with gestures that would show the increased closeness of the political and military ties between Cuba and the Soviet Union.

The response the top Soviet leader made was categorical: "In case of U.S. aggression against Cuba, we can't fight in Cuba" — those were his exact words — "because you're 11,000 kilometers away from us. We'd only get a thrashing."

The Soviets informed me that they weren't willing to give the United States any kind of warning about Cuba or even to remind Washington of the pledge Kennedy had made in October 1962, which was placed in doubt by each new U.S. administration.

Of course, the Soviet Union offered to always give us its political and moral support and to supply us with armaments, under the five-year program then in effect.

As you will remember, that was the most virulent period of the first Reagan Administration, and his arrogant Secretary of State Haig, a former general and supreme commander of NATO, was insisting in no uncertain terms that the United States had to crush the revolutions in Central America and to wipe out their source — which, according to him, was Cuba.

Although I had felt for a long time that the Soviet Union wouldn't go to war for Cuba and knew that we had only ourselves to depend on for our defense, it was precisely at that moment of greatest danger that the Soviet leaders told me solemnly, clearly and officially that Cuba would be dramatically alone in the case of military attack by the Pentagon.

As you can imagine, if the United States had found out about the Soviet position and had known that it had complete immunity, it would have been spurred to attack.

This led to two things: I guarded the secret with the utmost care, so as not to give the enemy any encouragement, and we redoubled our preparations for waging a war of all the people if imperialism forced it upon us.

That is why, after my return from Moscow, Comrade Fidel stated in the meeting of the [Communist Party] Political Bureau in which a general report of the trip was presented, that there was one thing that was so bitter and that would be of such crucial importance if made known that, up until then, only he and I knew it. He proposed to the members of the Political Bureau that they agree that knowledge and handling of the issue be restricted to the First and Second Secretaries [of the Communist Party] for as long as we thought necessary, and all of them agreed to this.

Mario Vázquez Raña: Minister, didn't the Soviet Union's admitted abandonment of Cuba in case of foreign aggression produce a cooling of relations between the two countries?

Raúl Castro: Publicly, relations remained the same as always, and some gestures of closer ties were even made, which helped to disinform the enemy about the real Soviet position.

Privately, Fidel and I — and some other comrades who had to be told about this development (which we called "the Pandora case") because of their work — suffered in silence from the bitterness. We assimilated the experience and drew new energy from it for preparing ourselves to assume our historic mission alone — alone, as we had always waged our wars of independence.

The fact that the Soviet Union had told us of its decision to do nothing militarily if Cuba were attacked in no way lessened the dangers we were exposed to because of East-West tensions. For example, even though we were never in favor of the Soviets' intervention in Afghanistan — which could have led the United States to act in the same way, though with inadmissible purposes, in its own "sphere of influence" — we refused to add our voice to the hypocritical imperialist chorus that denounced it.

Another example: a "new Afghanistan" in Poland sponsored by the Soviet Union — which, luckily, never came about — would also have considerably increased the danger for Cuba.

In short, we were running the risk of being wiped out because of the ongoing confrontation and would have suffered from any conflict between the United States and the Soviet Union, yet the latter wasn't willing to run any risks for Cuba.

Mario Vázquez Raña: What measures did Cuba adopt at that time, General?

Raúl Castro: We took a series of measures that enabled us to increase our military reserves of all kinds to the maximum, and we began to create government reserves, modernize and complete our military industry, improve and modernize the quality of the materiel of our regular troops and acquire the armaments and other things required to supply 100 percent of all the units of the Territorial Troop Militias, so as to have everything needed for waging a war of all the people — which might last for 100 years, if need be — without any help from outside.

Mario Vázquez Raña: What you have just told me is extraordinary.

Raúl Castro: As I was explaining, in our doctrine, land troops were the decisive forces, since, once the enemy had landed, the fighting would be waged on our soil, soldier to soldier, a rifle shot apart. In those conditions, those defending their homeland would have tremendous moral superiority over the hated invaders.

Knowledge of the terrain, which we have studied and prepared, also gave us a great advantage.

We had millions of trained and armed men and women. Faced with that wasps' nest, could the enemy outnumber us?

The effectiveness of the enemy aviation would be partially wiped out when its soldiers and ours were close together on the field of battle.

In a prolonged war, if one out of every two or three of our snipers (and we had tens of thousands of them) killed a U.S. soldier — preferably an officer — could the invaders absorb so many casualties and keep on fighting? The same could be said of our special troops.

If only 20 percent of our millions of armed and organized fellow citizens fought — and I am sure that the proportion of the brave ones is infinitely higher — the aggressors would be bound to lose the war.

The struggle would be waged without any defined front or rear guard — all over the country. In addition to the regular troops, we could also call on the Territorial Troop Militias and on the Production and Defense Brigades, which had been set up in every province and in each of the 169 municipalities. The fighting would take place in the more than 1,400 defense zones if the enemy were up to it — which was not likely because that would require millions of soldiers. They would be extremely weak, running the risk of stepping on mines or of being wiped out by bullets or grenades, and our ambushes would be a nightmare for them. The ground would burn under their feet, and, after their air strikes, our fighters would come out from the bowels of the earth to settle accounts on the sacred soil of our homeland, which repulses the boots of invaders. In short, revolutionary power would spring up again.

Even if they seized the capital — which they could do only by paying a very high price — that wouldn't solve the problem; to the contrary, new problems would begin for them, and this would be repeated in every town and city throughout the island.

Our defenses in those conditions couldn't be destroyed; they would be invincible.

I'm not talking about big battles, about large-scale classical confrontations. I'm talking about battles consisting of thousands of small strikes that come at any time of day or night, wherever it seems propitious, using all kinds of light and heavy weapons.

These include actions both by regular troops and by the Militias and Production and Defense Brigades. For that purpose, fortified regions (points and centers) are being carefully prepared, in all possible directions of action.

Keep in mind, Mario, that we manufacture all kinds of mines: antitank, antipersonnel and naval. A patriotic grandmother — or grandchild — can lay a mine. Some mines can be triggered at a considerable distance, using a device that we make, as well.

The Cuban people are descendents of the mambí fighters for Cuba's independence against Spain in the 19th century, the sons and daughters of members of the Rebel Army and of internationalist combatants. They have learned heroism at their mothers' knee, listening to tales of struggle in distant jungles, fighting shoulder to shoulder with other peoples. Hundreds of thousands of our men and women have victorious fighting experience. Keep in mind that most of our regular troops and a large part of our reserves were toughened in victorious combat while carrying out internationalist missions. More than 300,000 fighters were in the People's Republic of Angola. Any attacker should take this factor into consideration when weighing the balance of forces.

Moreover, I haven't mentioned the mountains that we have turned into impregnable bastions by applying a program of socioeconomic development we call Plan Turquino, named after the highest mountain in Cuba. The program has three main aspects: electrification, with electricity already supplied to more than 95 percent of the homes; the building of a network of all weather roads;

and housing construction.

In the first two years, we managed to halt the exodus of people from those regions. If we hadn't done this, it would have been impossible to get the support bases needed to ensure the economic development of the mountain areas, which is required in the case of a prolonged war.

The mountain areas would not only provide material support for the troops that would be defending themselves there but would also serve as support for those who would be continuing the struggle on the plains. From there, unquestionably, after bleeding the enemy white and wearing it down, we would descend victoriously, as we did on January 1, 1959.

33

FOREIGN DEBT CRISIS

August 3, 1985

Many dates in this year, 1985, could be chosen as the beginning of one of the biggest political battles ever headed by the Cuban Revolution as a whole and by Fidel Castro as an individual. August 3 may be the best date to select, because that was the day on which the Cuban President gave his final address in the Meeting on the Foreign Debt of Latin America and the Caribbean, one of the largest and most representative of the meetings held in Havana at the time.

In any case, the exact date isn't really important. In the life of a revolution such as the Cuban Revolution, a time comes when its great deeds cannot be associated with a precise instant, a specific date, because they reflect processes of a political, economic, intellectual or cultural nature which take place over several years.

This is what happened with regard to the foreign debt. When the price of oil soared following the 1973 Arab-Israeli war and the United States' inflationary financing of its war in Vietnam caused convulsions in the world economy, the results were a rising cost of energy, the exacerbation of unequal terms of trade and the concentration in the Western banks of large amounts of money that were lent liberally to a large number of poor countries. This led Cuba to keep a close eye on the consequences for the economies of the underdeveloped countries. This topic was taken up thoroughly in the Sixth Summit of Nonaligned Countries, which was held in Havana in 1979.

On October 12 of that year, in his address to the UN General Assembly, *speaking as President of the Movement of Nonaligned Countries, Fidel Castro said, "We see that, while the inequality in international relations is increasing the foreign debt accumulated in the developing countries to over $300 billion, the international financial bodies and private banks are raising the interest rates, shortening the amortization periods of debts and therefore strangling the developing countries financially...*

"The debts of the countries with lesser relative development and in disadvantageous situations are intolerable and have no solution. They should be cancelled."[1]

In the following years, the foreign debt grew geometrically, and, finally, it could be seen that, far from being transitory, it was becoming a permanent mechanism that the transnational economy of capitalism and imperialism was employing to superexploit the poor countries.

However, as a paradox of history, the debtor countries in this way obtained a weapon that might have been decisive, if the problem had been approached as the political problem it was, rather than viewed from the purely economic or technocratic prism. Above all, the countries most heavily burdened by debt could have decided to create a great, broad front – a cartel of debtor nations that would force the financial powers to negotiate with them as a group and to take into consideration the legitimate demands of those countries, whose economies and people were being crushed.

It was an historic opportunity, which statesmen with vision who were truly concerned about the destiny of their peoples could have used to obtain the cancellation of the debt and the establishment of a new international economic order.

In view of the inaction of other Latin American governments, Cuba, represented by Fidel Castro, took the initiative and headed the struggle to unite all the Latin American and Caribbean countries. The arguments, as was shown over and over again, were irrefutable. The foreign debt was morally indefensible and economically unpayable and could be repudiated politically. Most of the capital in the region had wound up in the hands of repressive military regimes, had been stolen or was sitting in private accounts in foreign banks. The people, who had not benefited in any way, should not be forced to pay the consequences.

That opportunity, however, was let slip. Even though public opinion was mobilized and broad political, labor union, religious, intellectual and social sectors worked hard to obtain a response in each country, the fact is that most of the Latin American governments – which were used to

---

[1] Fidel Castro Ruz, *Discurso en el XXXIV Período de Sesiones de la Asamblea General de la Organización de las Naciones Unidas. 12 de octubre de 1979* (Address in the 34th Period of Sessions of the General Assembly of the United Nations, October 12, 1979) (Havana: Editorial de Ciencias Sociales, 1979), 42 and 54.

obeying, consulting and in no way challenging Washington — proved incapable of taking steps toward combined action.

They preferred the U.S. formula of bilateral negotiation, in which they were bound to lose, to the formula of Latin American unity and solidarity, which would have given them a new voice and authority for discussing their problems with the United States and the rest of the industrialized world.

Debt is a cancer that requires surgical removal

(Excerpts of a speech made by Fidel Castro, at the closing ceremony of the Conference on the External Debt of Latin America and the Caribbean, August 3, 1985)[2]

The problem must be properly understood: debt is a cancer in the sense that it is a cancer that is multiplying, one that is destroying the organism, that will finish with the organism. It is a cancer that requires surgical removal. Any other attempt to deal with it that is not surgical, I assure you, will not solve the problem. Not a single malignant cell can be left. If malignant cells are left, metastases form and the tumor is reproduced and it soon finishes off the organism. This has to be understood. It is by now an incurable disease...

Imperialism has created this disease, imperialism has created this cancer and it must be extirpated surgically, and totally. I do not see that there can be any other solution. Any approach that differs from this idea is simply not in touch with reality, and whatever technical formula is used to confront this reality, whatever the palliative may be, rather than bringing about any improvement, it tends to make the disease worse.

On the other hand, the unequal exchange is increasingly unequal. I think that even a child in his first year at school can see this when they teach him to count a little and he gets an idea of what a million means.

This is demonstrated by any analysis that is made of the situation.

So, how do we resolve it? We know there's a cancer and we ask ourselves how we are going to pay for this operation, and this was the first thing I wondered myself when I began to ponder the question. Where are the means to do it? It is clear that, in the world,

[2] Fidel Castro, *Closing Speech at the Conference on the External Debt of Latin America and the Caribbean*, (Havana: Editora Política, 1985).

there are resources that can cure this cancer that is affecting the lives of thousands of millions of people...

So, are there resources then? Yes, there are resources. What are they used for? To bring about people's deaths; for war, the arms race, military expenditure. A million million! In a single year, the world threw away, on war games and military expenditure, a million million dollars, more than the external debt of all the Third World countries put together. Isn't there a basic logic here? Can't it be understood by any human being? Can't any citizen, no matter what his ideology, understand that it would be a good idea to write off this debt using a small part of this military expenditure? Because we are not just speaking of Latin America's debt, we are speaking of the debt of the entire Third World. At the very most, and depending on interest rates, 12% of this military expenditure would be sufficient.

Moreover, in this military expenditure, we have the resources to create a new international economic order, to be able to establish a system of more just prices for all the products coming from the Third World, to put an end to the ignominious system of unequal exchange. How much would all this cost?

At a rough approximation, it would amount to some $300 billion per year. The acquisitive power of Third World countries would increase because they are not going to put the money away, because they are too hungry, there are too many needs for them to put the money away. They are going to invest in industries and they will spend it one way or another. There would still be $700 billion left for military spending, and this would be enough to destroy the world several times over, unfortunately, and it is all utter madness. These expenditures exist in the world. We must be aware that these resources exist so that we can cure this terrible cancer, which is killing tens of millions, which is disabling so many people each year and which is ruining the existence of so many millions of people. This is why we associate these two questions: the problem is not going be solved just by annulling the debt, by abolishing the debt. We would only be going back to square one, because the determining factors of this situation are still present. And we have proposed these two closely associated factors: abolishing the debt and the establishment of a new international economic order.

We also have other ideas to propose because this must be implemented. How can it be implemented? People must be made aware of it and first we need to create awareness amongst our own people, in the countries of Latin America and the Caribbean. But people must be made aware of it not just in our own circles but also in the Third World countries — and this is what can give us strength — and we can even create this awareness in the industrialized countries. The message must be taken to public opinion in the industrialized countries to show them that what is happening is total madness. The message must be conveyed to the workers to students, to intellectuals, to women, to the middle classes. They have different problems, and perhaps resolving our problem will help to resolve some of their problems.

It is very important to convey to public opinion in the industrialized countries that these formulas we are proposing here are not going to affect them adversely, are not going to mean increased levies or taxes for them because it won't be necessary if the resources for military spending are used.

We need to send a message to people who are depositing money in the banks. When they say that any of these formulas will ruin the world financial system, they must be told, "No! That's a lie." If the resources for resolving the problem of debt and establishing the new economic order are taken from military spending, then nobody who is depositing money in the banks is going to lose it.

We must not forget that there are millions of these people in the industrialized capitalist world, including workers, the middle classes, professionals, a lot of people, and they are being told that the formulas we are proposing are going to bring down the whole banking system and that people who have money deposited in the banks are going to lose it.

The message must be taken to the workers whose scourge is unemployment, for this is the scourge of Europe, and the scourge of the United States, and they must be told, "This formula will raise the acquisitive power of the Third World countries, so the industries will be more active and there will be more employment in the industrialized countries"...

I have no doubt at all that the socialist countries will support this cause. And now it is very important that we are aware that this is not a struggle of Latin America alone, but it must also be a struggle of all the Third World countries, because this is what gives us strength. They have the same problems and some have worse problems than we do, but Latin America is the zone that can lead this struggle, because it has more social development, and even more political development, a better social structure, millions of intellectuals, professionals, tens of millions of workers, of peasants, a certain level of political training, and the same language is spoken.

People in Africa are in a more desperate situation. They owe almost $200 billion, but it is even worse than that because they are more dependent on the food that is sent to them from time to time when they are in the midst of desperate famines — a situation even more terrible, if such a thing is possible, than that of Latin America. But all the Third World countries, those that are struggling in the United Nations, in the Group of 77, that are fighting for a new world economic order, are aware of these problems...

These are basic principles. It is not one idea alone, the single idea of abolishing debt, but it comes in association with the idea of the new order. In Latin America it is also associated with the idea of integration, because even if we manage to have the debt abolished, even if the new economic order is attained, without integration we continue to be dependent countries forever. If Europe cannot conceive of living without integration, how can these countries conceive of it, these numerous countries of different sizes and levels of development, some older than others. Brazil, of course, has more possibilities but even Brazil needs this integration. Brazil needs the rest of Latin America and the Caribbean, and the rest of Latin America and the Caribbean needs Brazil. All the countries of this hemisphere need this integration and so economic integration is under discussion here, as another of the points we have raised. It is essential, fundamental.

These are basic ideas. The problem of when and how all this might be implemented is another story. I believe that, to the extent that these ideas are now coming down from the ivory towers, to the extent that these ideas are becoming those of the masses, of public opinion, of the people, to the extent that these ideas are becoming ideas of the workers, of the peasants, of the students and of the intellectuals and the middle classes of Latin America, these ideas will triumph sooner or later and amongst them will be the idea of economic integration...

Another essential idea is the following, and this is the idea of unity which we have been proposing from the start: unity within the countries and unity between the countries. I mean unity within the countries where there are minimal conditions for unity, and, fortunately, the conditions do exist today in the majority of the countries of Latin America, but not in all as I have carefully explained. Nobody can think about unity with a tyranny like Pinochet's[3] or like Stroessner's[4], and there are some other cases,

---

[3] Augusto Pinochet, the Chilean dictator at the time.

though not so many of them. This is the idea of internal unity, because inner strength is needed to fight this fight, and then there is the unity between all the countries of Latin America and between all the countries of the Third World because strength from outside is also needed. Unity needs to be sought with certain of the industrialized countries and I am sure that this struggle could even count on their help, that of many industrialized countries those which are not at the center of world power and which, in one way or another, have also been affected by the mercenary monetarist policies of the present administration of the U. S. Government...

We have not just been proposing subversive slogans. We have not been proposing social revolution but we have said, on the contrary, that we cannot wait for socialism to arrive first in order to resolve the problem. This is an urgent and immediate problem and it has to be resolved. In order to resolve it, everybody must come together, at all levels, except for the insignificant minority that has sold out to international finance capital, that has sold out to imperialism.

Here there is room for everyone, including the industrialists who have spoken in this hall, or bankers, businessmen or farmers. There is room for everyone. It is precisely what is good about this struggle, that it can be and must be a very broad-based struggle in order to resolve these problems that cannot wait until our peoples have a socialist awareness, until all the subjective factors, which are behind the objective factors right now, come together, though we are advancing fast and, in my judgment, it would not be prudent to wait at a time when the decisive battle for the independence of our peoples is already being fought. Because, how could a government and a country, which has to go every month to discuss with the International Monetary Fund what it must do at home, be called independent? This is a make-believe independence, and we see this as a struggle for national liberation, which can truly bring together, for the first time in the history of our hemisphere, all the social strata in a struggle to attain their true independence.

We cannot plan this with socialism as a prerequisite.

We are not recommending socialism, of course, but neither are we advising against it, do you understand me? It does not seem correct to me to make it the center of the struggle. I think that, in any case, this profound crisis is going to raise awareness amongst our peoples. I do not believe we are moving away from socialism, given

---

[4] Alfredo Stroessner, the Paraguayan dictator at the time.

that the masses are aware, but I think that, whatever the case, we are approaching the vision of a more just society, though it would be an error now to propose socialism as the objective, because this is an urgent problem which must be resolved. I think that if there is awareness, if the workers, peasants, students, intellectuals, business people have a clear idea of the problem, it will be possible to isolate the traitors, those who are in the service of imperialism, and it will be possible to win this battle.

34

RECTIFICATION

April 19, 1986

The late 1970s was a period when Cuba's hard-currency income was falling for several reasons — unequal terms of trade, the drop in the price of sugar, the devaluation of the dollar and rising oil prices. These external factors coincided with negative trends growing within Cuban society. These internal problems were directly related to mistakes made in the application of the economic planning and management system that the First Party Congress had approved in 1975.

That system, based on the experience of the Soviet Union and other European socialist countries, was weighed down from the beginning by concepts and formulas that proved to be inefficient, even in the countries that had developed them. The main difficulties, however, lay not in whether the system that was applied was backward or not, but in the fact that it was applied badly, in a fragmentary, incomplete and unsystematic manner without any controls.

The main mistake lay in the economist concept that it was enough to create certain mechanisms and to apply such categories as economic calculus, income-yield capacity and profit to have all enterprises begin to function smoothly.

In other words, political work was ignored; the role of ideology was played down; the party's function of political leadership and control was undervalued; and spontaneity and, in many cases, irresponsibility were given free rein.

This was shown in various ways: agricultural cooperatives that dedicated themselves to producing handicrafts that weren't linked to use of the land and the production of foodstuffs but which gave them higher profits; companies that gave their workers too many bonuses without their being justified by increased production; the replacement, in construction, of the concepts of finished projects and created use value with those of financial values, which led to doing the jobs that produced greater income for the companies and putting off the finishing work; and lack of attention to building housing, hospitals, polyclinics, children's day-care centers and old people's homes.

Behind it all, this situation showed a tendency of some functionaries to blindly copy the experiences and practices applied in the Soviet Union and other European socialist countries.

On April 19, 1986, in his address on the 25th anniversary of the victory at the Bay of Pigs, President Fidel Castro denounced these phenomena and outlined the strategy to be followed, in line with the idea of returning to the experiences and traditions of the Cuban Revolution; giving more weight to national realities — both positive and negative — in the future; and revitalizing Cuba's original, creative interpretations of socialism and Marxism-Leninism.

The process that began then — of rectifying errors — had, among its virtues, that of trying to dig down to the root causes of problems rather than limiting itself to the most immediate or obvious problems. "Rectification," Fidel Castro said, "means seeking new solutions for old problems."

Thus, Cuba's rectification arose autonomously and was different from the processes appearing in other socialist countries at the time, in the mid-1980s, such as the Soviet perestroika. Cuba wanted to deepen and improve socialism by defending its history and the work and ideas of the revolution. Thanks to that effort, the country was better prepared, both materially and morally, for meeting the incredible challenge that would come three or four years later, when the Soviet Union and the rest of the European socialist countries collapsed.

Problems must also be resolved morally, honorably and with principles...

(Excerpts from a speech by Fidel Castro on April 19, 1986)[1]

In the party congress, very precise lines were drawn. Tough, acute

---

[1] Fidel Castro, April 19, 1986, on the 25th anniversary of the Bay of Pigs victory. In "Por el camino correcto", (Havana: Editora Política, Havana, 1987, 1-17.

criticisms were made of the enduring problems, and we made a commitment to struggle against these problems, to detect them, one by one, and to fight them. We are debating the [Communist Party] Program, as we were saying before. Without the problems to which I refer, this line mapped out by the Congress would still have to be complied with, but today, with the greater difficulties that we are going to have, it is much more important to comply with this line. We need to be much more ruthless against anything that is badly done, against anything that is not correct, and we have to wage a much more consistent struggle against the problems that are still with us and the new problems that will develop...

Some of the factors that have given rise to these problems have been created by ourselves and we must also know how to rectify such problems in an appropriate manner, because, lamentably, there are people who confuse income earned through work with what can be got through speculation and that which comes from shady deals that verge on robbery or which amount to real robbery.

Again, there are some of our company directors who have become businessmen who are doing nicely for themselves, like good capitalists. But the first thing a revolutionary official, a socialist official, a communist official, must ask themselves is not whether the business is earning more, but how to earn more for the country. As soon as we have these supposed businesspeople who are more concerned about the business itself than the country's interests, we have full-blown capitalists. This is not why the Department for Managing and Planning the Economy was formed, to start playing at capitalism, and there are some who are playing at capitalism in a degrading fashion. We know this and we see this. These things have to be rectified.

It also happens with those who raise prices because they want to earn profits and to give bonuses, charging any price they like for whatever it may be. In this way, anything can be profitable, can't it?...

We cannot adapt ourselves to things that are badly done. We cannot be a party to such confusions. Might there be somebody here who is making some shady deals without the people seeing, without the masses seeing it? We do not want, and I repeat this, we do not want to turn the masses against those who are responsible, so that the masses themselves can put an end to such activities, because we have the party, we have the young people, we have our organizations. What we have to do is to carry out a systematic, serious and tenacious struggle, applying pressure from the top down. And from the bottom up! And firmly, too...

There are some who think that socialism can be brought about without political work and, as a matter of fact, there are even some who think it can be done without physical work...

I believe that the problems must be resolved morally, honorably and with principles, that we need to appeal — and it would be demagogic not to do so — to the sense of duty of our compatriots and of our workers...

The revolution has marched ahead, and has made great advances, has had great successes; but those who believe that the new generations will not have the same tasks or even greater tasks than those that the Bay of Pigs generation had, and those who went before them had, are mistaken. They are mistaken! The struggle will be long, hard and will go on for a long time. These 25 years teach us, the record of imperialist crimes demonstrates it to us, because we are faced with an imperialism that is more and more aggressive, ever more arrogant, ever more flagrant...

Faced with these external enemies and the danger that besets us from outside the country, we want to say to our heroes and martyrs as well, to those who gave their all for the revolution and to those who, through their sacrifices, brought suffering to their nearest and dearest: the revolution will not only know how to defend itself against these weaknesses, its own weaknesses, but it will know how to defend itself against its external enemies, and this country will never go back to capitalism, and this country will never again be imperialist property.

35

THE BATTLE OF CUITO CUANAVALE

March 23, 1988

It may well be that the powerful mass media had never before made such efforts to silence, black out or twist reports of such an important event, with so many implications for the future of a region and a continent, as at the time of the great victory of the Cuban-Angolan forces and of the South West African People's Organization (SWAPO), of Namibia, at Cuito Cuanavale, on the western front of Angola's southern flank.

In spite of that effort, however, many Africans, Cubans and an ever growing number of other informed, aware people in the world consider that strategic operation to have been the most important turning point in the recent history of the Southern Cone of Africa.

For 13 years after 1975, in response to a request by the legitimate government of Angola, internationalist forces of Cuban volunteers had helped to defend that country's independence. Angola's independence had been threatened by constant attacks by South African racists who used bases of operations in the illegally occupied territory of Namibia and were supported inside Angola by bands of fighters whom they had armed and financed with the backing of the main Western powers, headed by the United States.

In the last few months of 1987, acting on the advice of Soviet military advisers — who tended to mechanically apply the concept of large-scale operations using conventional forces to the situation in Angola — the leaders of the People's Liberation Armed Forces of Angola (FAPLA) launched a large number of troops toward the distant, inhospitable, sandy territory of the extreme southeastern part of Angola in a strike against the general headquarters and leadership of the UNITA bands.

With their fuel and other provisions running out, far from their sources of supplies, the Angolan troops had to fall back on Cuito Cuanavale without having achieved their objective and were trapped in an encirclement.

Aware of the situation, the South African military command quickly mobilized, sending a large number of troops, long-range artillery and other war materiel toward the area. Its aim was to surround and destroy the Angolan forces, certain that the Angolan Government wouldn't be able to survive such a disaster.

Thus, an extremely serious military crisis was created that also endangered the small Cuban forces, which, in accord with the agreements that had been made, were defending a line deep in Angolan territory far from the area where those events were taking place.

In those conditions, the Angolan Government sent an urgent request for assistance to the Cuban Government. Soldiers and weaponry were immediately mobilized to try to reinforce the besieged units and to reorganize the lines of defense, which were unstable.

On November 15, 1987, the Cuban leadership decided to do whatever was needed to guarantee that the invaders would be repulsed and to seek a definitive solution that would ensure Angola's safety. In Cuba's philosophy, this meant guaranteeing superiority in forces and materiel, so as to give the fighters as much protection as possible and to carry out the mission.

As a result of this decision, the Cuban internationalist contingent in Angola was increased to over 50,000 men, with around 1,000 tanks, over 600 armored transport vehicles and 1,600 pieces of artillery, mortars and means of anti-aircraft defense. The fighter planes ensured control of the air and dealt decisive blows to the enemy.

On March 23, 1988 — one of several dates that might be chosen to symbolize this event — an extremely intensive battle was fought at Cuito Cuanavale, in which the aggressors were repulsed and defeated.

The operation wasn't limited to saving the Angolans who were besieged in the southeastern-most part of the country. Along the southwestern front, a powerful force of over 40,000 Cubans, 30,000 Angolans and SWAPO patriotic forces advanced unstoppably toward the border with Namibia.

At that time, the Pretoria regime had seven nuclear weapons. The troops had to be spread out along the southern front in such a way that losses would be minimal if the enemy, maddened by its defeats, should decide to use those arms.

The Battle of Cuito Cuanavale put an end to the racists' incursions in Angola, paved the way for Namibia's independence and helped to seal the fate of apartheid in South Africa. It deserves to be included among the important events of this century and to be considered one of the greatest feats of the Cuban people and their armed forces in the past 40 years.

Communiqué from the Ministry of the Revolutionary Armed Forces[1]

A substantial change has been wrought in Angola's situation. For the last three and a half months, using infantry of the counter-revolutionary UNITA organization, troops of the so-called Territorial Forces of Namibia and regular units of its own army, South Africa has been fruitlessly trying to occupy the town of Cuito Cuanavale, located west of the river of the same name in southeastern Angola. Cuito Cuanavale is 125 miles (200 kilometers) from Menongue, at the left end of the line that Cuban troops are defending in southern Angola. In view of the large-scale South African escalation that took place in October to prevent the defeat of UNITA in the Mavinga region, around 93 miles (150 kilometers) southeast of Cuito Cuanavale, a group of Angolan brigades fell back toward Cuito Cuanavale, which has an airport, in November.

The South Africans intervened with extensive use of infantry, tanks, long-range heavy artillery and planes. Their final objective in Cuito Cuanavale was to wipe out the group of Angolan troops that had taken part in the offensive against UNITA to the southeast.

There were no Cuban advisers, combat units or military personnel at all at Cuito Cuanavale.

At the request of the Angolan Government, Cuban advisers for the People's Liberation Armed Forces of Angola (FAPLA) infantry, artillery and tanks began to be flown in to Cuito Cuanavale starting in early December, as were some specialists in artillery and tanks.

At almost the same time, the Cuban Air Force in Angola was reinforced with a group of our most experienced pilots.

In mid-January, in view of South Africa's persistence in its aim of occupying Cuito Cuanavale, Cuban armored infantry, tank and artillery units were sent there to reinforce the heroic FAPLA combatants, who, with the cooperation of a limited number of Cuban advisers and specialists, were defending that position.

From the beginning of December up today (March 17), all enemy attacks have been repulsed by the firm Angolan-Cuban resistance.

---

[1] *Granma*, March 18, 1988.

During this period, the South African long-range, heavy-caliber artillery launched over 20,000 155-millimeter shells against the Cuito Cuanavale area, but they have failed to weaken the defenders' tenacious resistance.

Every attempt that the South African troops and their allies have made to occupy Cuito Cuanavale has met with a hail of artillery fire and air strikes. The Cuban-Angolan aviation has played a brilliant, heroic role in the course of the fighting. The pilots have carried out veritable feats, attacking the enemy columns and units without letup. Their actions have been decisive.

South Africa has shattered its forces against the iron resistance at Cuito Cuanavale, whose capture the enemy had announced on January 23, nearly two months ago.

The Angolan soldiers have demonstrated admirable courage. Since they constitute the bulk of the defending forces, they have done most of the fighting.

Their units have had hundreds of losses (dead and wounded). Between December 5, when the first Cuban personnel reached Cuito Cuanavale, and March 17, the Cuban forces have had 39 losses (dead and wounded), whose relatives have been informed. Most of those losses occurred during the last two months.

According to data taken from the enemy's communications and estimates made by the Angolan and Cuban officers, the enemy has been dealt heavy losses (dead and wounded), including hundreds of soldiers of the so-called Territorial Forces of Namibia and the white regular forces of South Africa. The South Africans haven't made any more attempts to occupy Cuito Cuanavale during the last 16 days.

The South African racists have been taught a lasting lesson. By stopping the troops of racism and apartheid dead, the heroic Angolan and Cuban combatants at Cuito Cuanavale have become an outstanding symbol of the dignity of the peoples of Africa and the rest of the world.

March 17, 1988, 9 p.m.

Reply to the South African escalation[2]

As was reported on April 28, in the communiqué that informed our people of the grievous plane accident that occurred in Angola, the last large-scale South African escalation against that sister nation has

---

been practically defeated, starting with the enemy's disaster at Cuito Cuanavale and the audacious, unstoppable movements by the Cuban, Angolan and South West African People's Organization (SWAPO) forces on the western flank of the Southern Angolan Front.

As our people already know from the communiqué that the Ministry of the Revolutionary Armed Forces issued on March 17, 1988, South Africa has been unsuccessfully trying to occupy Cuito Cuanavale ever since the middle of November last year, using infantry from the counterrevolutionary UNITA organization, troops of the so-called Territorial Forces of Namibia and regular units of its own army, with artillery and air support.

After assessing the gravity of the situation created by the racists' new adventure, the leadership of our party and government, in complete agreement with the leadership of the People's Movement for the Liberation of Angola-Workers' Party (MPLA-PT) and the Angolan Government, decided to reinforce our internationalist contingent assigned to southern Angola with several dozen experienced military specialists, pilots and cadres and with the forces and weaponry needed to further guarantee the territorial integrity of that sister nation and the safety of our troops.

The reinforcement operation was carried out with great efficiency and speed. A powerful group of units of armored infantry, tanks, artillery and means of anti-aircraft defense was quickly moved to Angola, creating more favorable conditions than ever for confronting the South African aggression.

The reiterated attempts that the South African troops and their allies have made to break through the defenses of Cuito Cuanavale have been repulsed. The most recent of those attempts took place on March 23 and constituted a debacle for their forces, that, demonstrating their arrogance and impotence, have kept on harassing our positions with long-range artillery — whose fire has been returned with a hail of artillery fire and air strikes.

In view of the South Africans' stubbornness and their irrational determination to maintain their occupation of a part of the territory of the People's Republic of Angola and to continue their attacks on the Cuban-Angolan forces defending Cuito Cuanavale, the Cuban-Angolan-SWAPO forces that were stationed along the 15th parallel were ordered to begin to move toward the border with Namibia on March 11, and our troops are now more than 125 miles (200 kilometers) south of their prior position.

The courageous, coordinated, admirable action of the Cuban-Angolan troops and of the veteran SWAPO combatants in their movement has pushed the racists back almost to the border with the territory of Namibia, which they occupy. Their troops can't act with impunity in southern Angola any longer — as they had been doing in recent years, with utter contempt for the norms of international law.

The response to the South African escalation has been firm, resolute and crushing. Cuito Cuanavale has established itself as an impregnable bastion and as a history-making symbol. The Cuban combatants, together with their African brothers, will fully carry out the internationalist mission that the party and the revolution have entrusted to them.

Our Revolutionary Armed Forces, people, government and party are proud of their valiant, invincible, internationalist combatants.

The possibility of a negotiated solution gained ground

(Excerpt from a speech by Raúl Castro, Minister of the Revolutionary Armed Forces, on May 27, 1991)[3]

Toward the end of 1987, thousands of South African soldiers opposed a group of People's Liberation Armed Forces of Angola (FAPLA) combatants who were carrying out an important operation in the southeastern part of Angola. In the course of the unequal fighting, a part of the Angolan group was threatened with being surrounded and wiped out at Cuito Cuanavale. If the South Africans' designs had been fulfilled, the setback could have brought about a collapse with unforeseeable consequences.

We didn't have enough forces in Angola to handle that situation. Using the ones we had there to reinforce Cuito Cuanavale might endanger the general stability of our defenses on the Southern Front. Therefore, it was absolutely necessary to have reinforcements sent from Cuba. At the same time, we shouldn't engage in a decisive battle at Cuito, because that was the terrain chosen by the enemy, where it had all the advantages. It was absolutely necessary to organize an impregnable defense there against which the enemy would wear itself out without achieving its objective. The decisive actions should be waged at a time and place we had chosen — that is, when we were stronger and at the enemy's most vulnerable points: specifically, on the southwestern flank.

To do this, following the prescribed consultations with the

---

[3] Raúl Castro Ruz, *Discurso en el acto por la culminación de la Operación Carlota* (Address Given during the Ceremony Held to Mark the Conclusion of Operation Carlota) (Havana: Editora Política, 1991), May 27, 1991.

Angolan Government and meticulous planning by the General Staff of the Revolutionary Armed Forces (FAR) [of Cuba], directed by our Commander in Chief, the history-making decision of reinforcing our troops in the People's Republic of Angola was reached on November 15, 1987. As is known, the total number of our troops there was increased to 50,000. They had the mission of working in cooperation with the Angolan troops to defeat the invading South African troops. When the time is right, we will explain how it was possible for a Third World country such as ours to carry out that feat of logistics and morale in just a matter of weeks.

We knew that the South African command estimated that it would take us at least six months to transfer the personnel, armaments and other weaponry required for a division. The South African strategists took longer to realize that, by doubling the number of our forces and multiplying the number of them on the Southern Front several times over, we had obtained — for the first time in 12 years — control of the air. This required veritable feats of labor, such as the construction of the Cahama airport, which placed vital enemy targets within our range, in just 70 days.

We also deployed a strike force on that front which included 998 tanks; over 600 armored carriers; and 1,600 pieces of artillery, mortars and means of antiaircraft defense.

From Cuba, in daily work stints of up to 20 hours and more, Comrade Fidel — as he had done on several occasions since 1975 — personally directed the work of the General Staff of the Ministry of the Revolutionary Armed Forces, imbuing all of us with his iron determination to achieve victory with minimum losses, combining daring and heroism with the philosophy of not endangering the life of even a single man without having first exhausted all other possibilities.

That spirit prevailed throughout those 16 years. It became an ethic and a style that gave the finishing touches to combat mastery in the chiefs and was expressed in morale that brought out the confidence and courage of the combatants.

Cuito held out. All of the South Africans' attempts to advance on its approaches were repulsed. Their sophisticated long-range artillery, which never stopped firing day and night, didn't terrify the Angolan-Cuban forces and proved ineffective. Meanwhile, a powerful group, which units from the South West African People's Organization (SWAPO) had joined, seriously threatened places of strategic importance to the enemy on the southwestern flank. Clashes with detachments of scouts in Donguena and Tchipa and the air strike against their positions in Calueque persuaded the South Africans that it was impossible to achieve a military victory over Angolan sovereignty and the combined Angolan and Cuban forces. Thus, the possibility arose for a negotiated solution that would include compliance with Resolution 435/78 of the Security Council of the United Nations for the decolonization and independence of Namibia, which had been postponed several times.

The December 1988 agreements that were signed in New York — which wouldn't have been conceivable without Operation Carlota — placed the withdrawal of the Cuban internationalist troops in the context of a global solution whose key element was always the total, prior withdrawal of the South African invaders, first from Angola and then from Namibia.

36

CASES 1 AND 2

June 14, 1989

The most amazing and unforeseen events since the triumph of the revolution began to be revealed publicly on June 14, 1989. A note from the Ministry of the Revolutionary Armed Forces, which was published in Granma *on that day, announced that Major General Arnaldo Ochoa Sánchez[1] had been arrested, accused of having committed serious crimes of corruption and of dishonest management of economic resources.*

The details of the charges, which were difficult to believe at the time, came out in the following days: General Ochoa and a small group of subordinates close to him, who had been charged at first with corruption and the unlawful use, misappropriation and mismanagement of hard currency by means of illicit activities beginning when he was an officer in the Cuban military mission in Angola, were now found to have established criminal contacts with a group of officers in the Ministry of the Interior's Department MC, headed by Antonio de la Guardia,[2] who, for some time, had been linked to traffickers in drugs, using Cuban airports and jurisdictional waters — which the members of this department were empowered to use in carrying out their delicate mission — to traffic in drugs.

The details of the case, which were scrupulously published in the Cuban

---

[1] Arnaldo Ochoa Sánchez had been a combatant in the Rebel Army and had carried out several missions. He was a major general and a Hero of the Republic of Cuba.

[2] Antonio de la Guardia Font was a brigadier general in the Ministry of the Interior and head of Department MC, which had been formed to carry out actions to break the U.S. blockade.

press during the following weeks, showed irresponsible actions, such as Ochoa's having sent his aide to Colombia, where he met and negotiated personally with Pablo Escobar, the kingpin of the Medellín drug cartel.

"A true revolution will never permit impunity," the party and government leadership stated right from the start. "If serious moral or physical ills arise among individuals, absolutely nobody in our homeland — no matter how great his merits or how high his position — may violate the principles and laws of the revolution with impunity."[3]

A few days later, on June 22, Granma stated in an editorial, "The international traffic in drugs has dealt us a terrible blow. We can't even say that the big traffickers in drugs are mainly to blame. Our own people sought them out and easily accepted their first offers. However, we will pull this evil out by the roots. We are the only ones in this hemisphere who can do it, and it won't even be a difficult task. Our citizens, our border patrols and fighters in the Ministry of the Revolutionary Armed Forces and Ministry of the Interior and our party members will be much more alert from now on. After this bitter experience, it will be very difficult for new groups such as Tony de la Guardia's and for conduct such as Ochoa's and Martínez's to arise."[4]

The Cuban people were able to watch the entire process — from the meeting of the Court of Honor, composed of 47 generals of the Revolutionary Armed Forces, to the hearings of the extremely brief trial by the Special Military Court and the session of the Council of State, in which its members deliberated on the use of their powers and on whether or not to apply the death penalty to four of the accused. This was broadcast on television.

As Fidel Castro pointed out, "The revolution has been generous on many occasions, when it could be so without doing mortal damage to itself. Now, the revolution cannot be generous without doing itself serious damage." As President of the Council of State, Fidel Castro argued that the crimes committed by the defendants hurt the country at its most sensitive point: morale, its capacity to resist and its credibility before the world. They constituted a stab in the back for Cuba, precisely when it was faced with its most difficult trials.

"It is hard to think," Fidel Castro said, "that some men are going to die as a result of all this and as a result of our decision. It is hard, yes, and bitter, and it can't be pleasing to anybody at all, but I think, above all, of others who died.

"I think of those who gave their lives to build a decent country — and not only those who were killed recently but also those who gave their lives

---

[3] *Granma*, June 16, 1989.

[4] *Granma*, June 22, 1989. Jorge Martínez, a captain in the Revolutionary Armed Forces, was Arnaldo Ochoa's aide.

in the past 120 years and more, to create a republic in which law and justice would prevail, a republic where there would be no corruption, where there would be no impunity, where there would be no dishonesty; a republic where there would be no corruption, embezzlement or treason. I think of those who gave their lives for a worthy and honorable country, those who died in two wars of independence and have given their lives throughout this century; of the many, many excellent comrades who died. I think of them!"[5]

The 29 members of the Council of State unanimously decided not to exercise the constitutional right of pardon. On July 13, a note in Granma *announced that, early on the morning of that day, the death sentence by firing squad had been carried out against Arnaldo Ochoa, Jorge Martínez, Antonio de la Guardia and Amado Padrón.*

A few days later, before the echoes of Case 1 had died away, a proceeding was initiated against a group of high-ranking officers in the Ministry of the Interior, who were accused of having made incorrect use of their positions and of resources. This led to Case 2 of 1989 and to a thorough reconstruction of that ministry.

Let us learn from this and keep moving forward

(Editorial in Granma, *September 2, 1989)*

The Military Court has pronounced judgment in Case 2 of 1989. The affront to the law and ethics of the revolution has been wiped clean. The guilty parties have received their punishment. The entire nation perceives, however, that the problems confronted in the country this summer go far beyond the fate of a handful of corrupt, disloyal men. The working people, with their infallible wisdom, feel that these past months have been decisive and history-making.

Therefore, the most important aspects don't end with the court's decision. It may be only a beginning. The main things are the teachings and reflections that all of society and the party should draw from this bitter lesson.

Rectification has already achieved some very serious goals. But, unquestionably, we are now entering a much more important stage of this process. In the future, these things that have shaken the country may be seen as a turning point toward the thoroughgoing institutional, political and moral improvement of the revolution.

An essential characteristic of the situation confronting us — first with the eradication of the Ochoa-La Guardia mafia of traffickers in

---

[5] *Vindicación de Cuba* (Cuba's Vindication) (Havana: Editora Política, 1989), 446.

drugs and now with the no less repugnant or dangerous phenomenon of corruption and failure at the highest levels of the Ministry of the Interior — is that it doesn't involve activity by enemy agents; rather, it concerns that of people who have come from our own ranks. What has been cleared up isn't a confrontation between revolution and counterrevolution. The serious, harsh lesson of these facts is that it shows us that, without going over to the enemy, men who have served in our cause can inflict worse damage on us than any counterrevolutionary and, in practice, serve the purposes of imperialism, which never stops trying to destroy us.

In this regard, the first and main consequence of this process is that we have categorically reaffirmed a vital principle: respect for the law, which is applicable to all citizens equally, no matter how high their political or governmental rank.

We don't know how many countries in the world can truly — rather than just formally — assert this principle. Cuba can do so, as it has just shown courageously and eloquently.

There is no impunity, nor can there ever be, for those who violate the legal and ethical principles of the revolution, no matter what their merit or position. The greater their political or governmental responsibility, the more obliged they are to behave with dignity and honor, both publicly and privately.

Conscious observance of the law isn't merely a juridical matter. This has been said many times, and it's worth remembering now. This principle was upheld by our mambí fighters for Cuba's independence against Spain in the late 19th century, who, half naked and hungry, imposed the majesty of a Republic in Arms in the fields of free Cuba. They believed that their homeland was worth fighting and dying for; they believed in the legitimacy of fighting for freedom. In the same way, unlimited subordination to legality now constitutes the key to profound ideological and political definition. We believe in patriotism, independence, socialism and the revolution.

How could someone who doesn't respect the law or morality and who acts as if he belonged to a higher caste, above everyone and everything, be a revolutionary?

What concept of solidarity could anyone have who isn't capable of feeling solidarity with his fellow citizens?

How can anyone speak of socialism and revolution when he doesn't have the sensitivity to realize that privileges, high-handedness, abuse and distancing from the masses are some of the main causes of the difficulties now convulsing the socialist system —

a system that arose precisely to eradicate those capitalist ills?

These trials have shown something else. Since the law was broken, we have been able to face this delicate, exceptional situation in a strictly legal framework.

There hasn't been any crisis. The revolution has remained firm, sure and serene. It has been true to itself, with its exemplary history, and has placed itself above emotional reactions to these cases of betrayal and disloyalty, which are cause for indignation. The country's institutions have carried out their role with morality and authority and have managed to maintain order, punish the guilty parties and begin working to keep such vices from reappearing in the future.

The people's support has accompanied and encouraged the revolution in these months of testing. However, the revolution's actions weren't aimed at satisfying public opinion, nor could it ever have been motivated to act only in that way. Public opinion is important and should be kept in mind in informing and guiding the people, but the law cannot be manipulated or violated. In applying it, it is impossible to go beyond the limits it establishes.

At one point, public opinion temporarily leaned toward benevolence for the principal defendant in Case 1. Some unhappiness was also noted with the punishment requested for José Abrantes[6] and others who were sentenced in Case 2. In the first case, the trial itself and the session of the Council of State did away with that view. In the second case, it has been necessary to explain that the crime that could have brought a more severe punishment wasn't proved and that both the government attorney's office and the court and investigators, after examining the facts exhaustively, came to the conclusion that the former Minister of the Interior had not behaved badly with regard to the drug trafficking mafia in MC Department.

The experience of these trials, however, has helped us to understand that our laws must be improved. That is another important conclusion.

Omissions have been noted both in the penal code and in military penal law. The most important ones concern the illegal trafficking in drugs and the manipulation or suppression of information. Obviously, when those bodies of law were written, it was impossible to imagine that phenomena such as these could occur. The blows received and our interest in protecting our society from such

---

[6] José Abrantes was Minister of the Interior. He was arrested, tried and punished in Case 2.

deformations show us the need to make an example of this conduct and to punish it with exemplary severity.

As for Case 2, some people are even asking why we don't change the law and apply more severe punishments. The law is the law, and, luckily, we live in a country that is governed by laws. We cannot apply harsher punishments than those established by the law, no matter how serious the actions may be, both morally and politically, nor can changes in the law be retroactive.

The case of Abrantes has also made it necessary to consider the advisability and possibility of further increasing the punishments for the crimes of abuse of power and incorrect use of resources — even of establishing the death penalty for them in certain circumstances.

Naturally, this matter must be taken up by the pertinent bodies of the party and government, at the right time.

In view of conduct such as that of Luis Orlando Domínguez,[7] Diocles Torralbas[8] and now José Abrantes, each of whom was given the most severe punishment established by the law in effect at the time their crimes were committed, many men and women of the people are asking themselves how such things can occur without being discovered more quickly.

First of all, our people should understand the very exceptional nature of these cases, involving people who have been given authority, trust and privileges, and recognize that they are different from phenomena such as Tony de la Guardia's gang, which is an expression of the cancer that had begun to eat away at a Government institution and even its metastasis into criminal acts such as these, petty-bourgeois lifestyles, laxity, favoritism and high-handedness.

Having recognized that exceptional nature, it is absolutely necessary to admit that deeper problems affecting society underlie what happened. We cannot content ourselves with the simplification that attributes all acts of this kind to lack of control.

Good accounting and correct economic and financial controls aren't enough to prevent events such as these. We will always have to delegate a large number of decision-making and other powers to some leaders and cadres, because of the nature of their work. Far from being effective means for preventing the spread of these crimes, super-centralization and generalized distrust may lead to even worse problems.

---

[7] An official punished for corruption in an earlier period.
[8] He had been Minister of Sugar and Vice-President of the government. He was punished for crimes of corruption shortly before Case 1.

We must seek real solutions in improving our country's institutions and in establishing principles, methods, norms and mechanisms that exclude impunity and make it impossible for conditions that serve as a culture for these distortions to arise.

Let us state this clearly: several faults that, in one way or another, involve all of the institutions of the revolution contributed to what happened.

The first proof of this is that, in spite of its extremely delicate tasks, the Ministry of the Interior didn't have a system of internal controls. Our political and governmental leaders received information about the rest of the country and the world through the Ministry of the Interior, among other sources, but they didn't know very much about what was really going on in that Ministry. For their part, the leaders of the Ministry of the Interior didn't know about many of the problems that were arising in it and hid others that they were aware of, so as to present a false image of integrity and efficiency that had begun to crumble in many places.

There were moments in which the top leaders of the party noted signs that certain negative tendencies were developing in the Ministry of the Interior, and warnings were given and specific guidelines issued concerning the conduct of its cadres and officers to reinforce the measures of austerity and to turn over to People's Power the recreation centers, restaurants, polyclinics and other installations that were being created in various provinces. Express instructions were issued that they shouldn't get involved in commercial and business activities that were unrelated to the functions of the Ministry. In some cases, those instructions were only partially followed or were given no more than lip service. In other cases, no attention was paid to them whatsoever.

In addition to this defect, there were problems in the party's functioning in the Ministry. The facts show that, in practice, the role of its organizations was blocked or their leadership was placed in the hands of extremists and/or incompetents.

The attempts that some party members and leaders made in the party to denounce or seek explanations for the negative tendencies that were flourishing were pushed aside.

Naturally, the party's responsibility isn't limited to the organizations which function in the Ministry of the Interior. It is bitter to recognize that, in fact, this institution generally acted outside party control.

Deficiencies were noted in the party leaderships in the provinces — where it is absolutely necessary to find formulas that ensure compartmentalization and the secrecy of the Ministry of the Interior's work — and in the party's evaluation of the agency's activities, its vigilance concerning any phenomenon that might have political implications. In the provinces, too, the Ministry of the Interior has given rise to deformations and negative tendencies, which, generally speaking, haven't been known in party channels.

The leading function of the party at the national level must be to ensure the work of the Ministry in a more integral, deeper way, keeping in mind that, by its very nature, this agency exercises a key influence on the stability and political and moral climate of society.

This isn't limited to the Ministry of the Interior alone, however. It is also applicable to all of the other governmental agencies and political and mass organizations. The party is called upon to fully exercise its role of leadership, guidance and control, in which there can be no fissures; one of its expressions should be the establishment of norms that make it possible to regulate certain aspects of the conduct of leaders and cadres.

We have an honest, strong party. There is no place in it for corruption or sponging. As a rule, its cadres are models of austerity, dedication and modest living. This is a decisive guarantee in the process that we are developing, but serious soul-searching should bring us to the idea that the improvement of society also supposes the improvement of the party, and that it is not only the subject but also the object of correction.

The main tasks of the Ministry of the Interior are to defend the security of the revolution and to ensure the stability of domestic order.

The security of a country such as Cuba is, first of all, an ideological and political matter. It isn't limited to the technical and professional work of the combatants who work on that front, though their work is not only important but also absolutely necessary. It also includes the people's unity with the revolution; their trust in the individuals who exercise power; the leaders' prestige, morale and authority; and the example of honesty that the leaders set.

The negative phenomena discovered in the Ministry of the Interior led inexorably to a weakening of our security in all these spheres. The psychological and moral impact of these things has been even stronger because of the clash between reality and the institution's meritorious image and historic role. That image, of course, is correct, but it was sometimes promoted and exaggerated by its leaders, perhaps as a justification for giving it special material, social and political status.

This in no way denies the legitimate merits of the combatants in the security and police forces, but it is necessary to understand that, in the life of the revolution, there are things that are already a part of the combat glory of all the people — such as the Bay of Pigs, the struggle against groups of armed counterrevolutionaries in the mountains, and internationalist missions — and that there is no sense in trying to parcel them out and make isolated mention of the contribution that any agency in particular may have made to them.

We understand the embarrassment, bitterness and even momentary bewilderment that many comrades in the Ministry may be feeling.

We think of the men and women who joined that institution when they were very young and who have dedicated practically all their lives in it to the defense of the revolution. We think of the honest, self-sacrificing combatants who saw that the cadre policy that was applied was, in essence, its negation, and who witnessed with pain some individuals' meteoric promotion to ranks and responsibilities that exceeded their merits and competence, while other combatants who did deserve them were ignored. We think of the loyal comrades who witnessed the gradual corruption of chiefs and cadres but were unable to do anything to halt the deterioration of the institution and the proliferation of indulgence, favoritism and complicity and even the creation of interest groups jostling for positions of power and resources.

That mass of honorable men and women constitute the grassroots and a large part of the intermediate-level cadres of the Ministry of the Interior. They should see the answer to their real interests and motivations in the reconstruction of the Ministry now being undertaken as a sad but immediate necessity.

This isn't the moment for useless lamentation or for being depressed — much less for letting ourselves be carried away by pointless speculation, resentment and other attitudes typical of petty-bourgeois clergymen. This is a revolutionary moment and offers all loyal combatants in the Ministry a place of work and of honor.

The fraternal union of these combatants with the chiefs and cadres of the Revolutionary Armed Forces who have started working in the Ministry of the Interior as needed and as a matter of principle will be the key to that institution's recovery from the setback it has suffered and to its soon being able to respond with pride to what the people and the revolution expect of it.

Nobody should be afraid that the country's security is weakened.

The new cadres who are taking up these tasks are capable, well-prepared comrades who come from a political school that guarantees the application of truly revolutionary methods.

Our sworn enemy — the U.S. Government, with its agencies of subversion and aggression — shouldn't make mistaken calculations about what has happened in Cuba. We know that the CIA had information about Cubans participating in drug trafficking operations months before we denounced those actions, but it didn't use that information, undoubtedly waiting for the right moment to achieve maximum political impact. Likewise, it wouldn't be surprising if the U.S. special services had evidence concerning some of the cases of officers involved in the problems of corruption and breakdown in the Ministry of the Interior and were waiting for that process to get much more serious. We have acted in time. We have destroyed those expectations. If the imperialists were waiting to find a breach caused by a slackening of principles, they will now come up against an impregnable wall.

Our people have been fully informed about what has happened. Once again, the party has told them the truth, no matter how disagreeable and distressing it is, placing its trust in the people's maturity and political development. This has been and will continue to be a matter of principle of our revolution.

We have no doubts that we will emerge from this test infinitely stronger and that, from now on, our revolution will advance with growing strength in all spheres, in spite of our economic limitations and the difficult external circumstances in which we are developing.

We must understand, above all, that we are working for the 21st century. Healing society of malignant cells such as these; making our very best effort; and establishing solid institutional, ethical and political bases for Cuba in the future is a history-making task that today's generations cannot and will not leave half-done.

In our country, as Commander in Chief Fidel Castro put it, there cannot be two worlds, but only one: that of the workers. There cannot be two truths — the truth of the heroic battle that our people are waging for development and against difficulties, and the truth of privileged, venal, wasteful cliques. The great lesson of the past few months is that the party, the people and the Revolutionary Armed Forces are firmly determined to achieve that goal.

Let us learn from these things. Let every revolutionary make a rigorous analysis of his own conduct and turn these blows into renewed strength for advancing. This is what we must do.

37

ANGOLA AND
OPERATION TRIBUTE

December 7, 1989

The image belongs to history, and will not fade with time. At 3 p.m. on December 7, 1989, the 93rd anniversary of the death in combat of Major General Antonio Maceo and of his aide, Captain Francisco Gómez Toro[1] *— who symbolized the mambí*[2] *fighters for Cuba's independence in the 19th century — simultaneous funeral corteges set out in all of the 169 municipalities in the country, taking the remains of the internationalist combatants who had lost their lives in Angola during the more than 13 years of Cuba's solidarity with and assistance to that country and other sister nations, such as Ethiopia and Nicaragua.*[3] *The internationalist*

---

[1] Major General Antonio Maceo, second in command of the Liberation Army, and Captain Francisco Gómez Toro, his young aide, the son of General Máximo Gómez, were killed at Punta Brava on December 7, 1896. They were buried together in El Cacahual, Cuba's most prestigious pantheon, near Havana.

[2] According to some, *mambí* was a derisive term that the Spanish colonialists used when referring to those fighting for Cuba's independence. Now, it denotes honor. (Translator's note: The British used the term *Yankee* in much the same way back in 1776. Its meaning, too, has changed, but not to denote anything honorable.)

[3] A Cuban internationalist contingent helped Ethiopia in combating Somalia's invasion of Ogaden. Likewise, some Cuban combatants helped the Sandinista insurgents in the final stage of the war against the Somoza regime and later in Nicaragua's defense against the dirty war organized by the CIA and reactionary elements from neighboring countries.

combatants were being taken to their final rest: the Mausoleum of Defenders.

A total of 2,085 combatants lost their lives while carrying out military missions, and another 204 died on missions of a civilian nature — a total of 2,289 internationalists who were killed.

The Cuban Government and Revolutionary Armed Forces had always been scrupulous in informing relatives in Cuba of those killed in action or who died as a result of accidents or of wounds in Angola. However, it was impossible to think of repatriating their bodies and burying them in their home towns while the war was going on in distant Africa. But this was an important part of Cuban tradition and culture, linked to the pride of parents, sons, daughters, wives, brothers and sisters, for whom they had given their lives, upholding the principles of the revolution and fraternity among the peoples.

Fidel Castro had stated that, when the war was over, the Cubans would bring back from Angola only the satisfaction of duty done and the bodies of their fallen comrades. That opportunity came after the peace agreements of December 1988, which put an end to the South African racists' incursions in Angolan territory and made it possible for Namibia to become independent. The peace agreements also made an important contribution to the internal political process that, in the following years, would end the opprobrious system of apartheid.

Operation Tribute, as it was called, was a model of organization and logistical precision. A mausoleum was built in every municipality in the country to receive the remains of the fallen. In those places that lacked a band, one was created in just a few months. Solemn ceremonies unprecedented in the life of the nation were prepared in detail.

No description can do justice, in human and patriotic terms, to what happened, starting the night of December 6, when the urns and coffins, each draped with a Cuban flag and with a photograph of the internationalist who had died, were brought to public places. The members of each family reached the end of a long road of grief and hope and, surrounded by friends and relatives, gave their dead a formal farewell that had been postponed for years. Those dead ceased to be theirs alone but became a part of the entire nation, related to all fathers and mothers, all sisters and brothers, all wives and children.

When the time for the funeral cortege arrived on December 7 and the funeral march sounded, the units that served as guards of honor responded to the voice of command with a martial pace and the flags were raised gracefully, the people as a whole lined the streets to pay tribute to that part of themselves that was going along its last road, and the people as a whole shed tears of grief. Thus, the feeling of victory, the reaffirmation of the significance of an effort that helped to change the future of Africa, and grief for those who had died were joined.

Operation Tribute also embodied another essential message: It symbolized the end of one era in the life of the revolution and the beginning of another. It coincided with the already evident collapse of the European socialist countries and the unstoppable disaster in the Soviet Union, which would lead to the dismemberment and disappearance of that country two years later. Cuba had to regroup its forces for a battle in which its main internationalist mission and principal service to the revolutionary movement would be to defend itself and preserve its independence and socialism.

The main ceremony bidding farewell to the combatants who had died was held at El Cacahual, Havana Province, at the tomb of Antonio Maceo and Panchito Gómez Toro. Once more, Fidel Castro spoke on behalf of all the Cuban people.

We will follow their example!

(Excerpt of speech given by Fidel Castro on December 7, 1989, for the Cuban internationalists who fell while carrying out military and civilian missions.)

December 7, the date on which Antonio Maceo, the most illustrious of all our soldiers, and his young aide-de-camp were killed, has always been very meaningful for all Cubans. Their remains lie here, in this sacred site of their homeland.

By choosing this day for laying to rest the remains of our heroic internationalist fighters who have died in different parts of the world — mainly in Africa, the land of birth of Maceo's ancestors and many of our forebears — we make it a day for honoring all Cubans who gave their lives while defending their country and all humankind. Thus, patriotism and inter-nationalism — two of humanity's most treasured values — will be joined forever in Cuba's history.

Perhaps, some day, a monument will be erected not far from this site to honor our internationalist heroes.

The remains of all internationalists who died while carrying out their missions are being laid to rest in their home towns all over Cuba right now.

The imperialists thought we would conceal the number of our combatants killed in Angola during that complex, 14-year-long mission — as if it were a dishonor or a discredit for the revolution. For a long time they dreamed that the blood shed had been to no purpose, as if those who died for a just cause had died in vain. Even if victory were the ordinary yardstick to measure the value of human sacrifice in their legitimate struggles, they also returned victorious.

The Spartans used to tell their fighters to return with their shields or on them. Our troops are returning with their shields…

The final stage of the war in Angola was the most difficult. It demanded all of our country's determination, tenacity and fighting spirit in support of our Angolan brothers.

In fulfilling this duty of solidarity, not only to Angola but also to our own troops fighting under difficult conditions there, the revolution did not hesitate in risking everything. When the imperialist threats against our own country became very serious, we did not hesitate in sending a large part of our most modern and sophisticated military equipment to the Southern Front of the People's Republic of Angola. Over 50,000 Cuban troops were in that sister nation — a truly impressive figure, in view of the distance and our country's size and resources. It was a veritable feat by our Revolutionary Armed Forces and our people. Such chapters of altruism and international solidarity are very infrequent…

The hundreds of thousands of Cubans who carried out military or civilian internationalist missions have earned the respect of present and future generations. They have honorably upheld our people's glorious fighting and internationalist traditions.

On their return, they have found their country engaged in a tremendous struggle for development while continuing to confront the criminal imperialist blockade with exemplary dignity. This is in addition to the current crisis in the socialist camp, from which we can only expect negative economic consequences for our country.

People in most of those countries aren't talking about the anti-imperialist struggle or the principles of internationalism. Those words aren't even mentioned in their press. Such concepts have been virtually removed from their political dictionaries. Meanwhile, capitalist values are gaining unheard-of strength in those societies…

I believe that revolution cannot be imported or exported; a socialist state cannot be founded through artificial insemination or by means of an embryo transplant. A revolution requires certain conditions within society, and the people in each individual nation are the only ones who can create it. These ideas don't run counter to the solidarity that all revolutionaries can and should extend to one another. Moreover, a revolution is a process that may advance or regress, a process that may even be frustrated. But, above all, communists must be courageous and revolutionary. Communists are duty-bound to struggle under all circumstances, no matter how adverse they may be. The Paris Communards struggled and died in the defense of their ideas. The banners of the revolution and of socialism are not surrendered without a fight. Only cowards and the demoralized surrender — never communists and other revolutionaries...

In Cuba, we are engaged in a process of rectification. No revolution or truly socialist rectification is possible without a strong, disciplined, respected party. Such a process cannot be advanced by slandering socialism, destroying its values, casting slurs on the party, demoralizing its vanguard, abandoning the party's guiding role, eliminating social discipline and sowing chaos and anarchy everywhere. This may foster a counterrevolution, but not revolutionary changes.

The U.S. imperialists think that Cuba won't be able to hold out and that the new situation in the socialist community will inexorably help them to bring our revolution to its knees.

Cuba is not a country in which socialism came in the wake of the victorious divisions of the Red Army. In Cuba, our people created our socialist society in the course of a legitimate, heroic struggle. The 30 years in which we have stood firm against the most powerful empire on earth, that sought to destroy our revolution, bear witness to our political and moral strength.

Those of us in our country's leadership aren't a bunch of bumbling parvenus, new to our positions of responsibility. We come from the ranks of the old anti-imperialist fighters who followed Mella and Guiteras; who attacked the Moncada and came on the *Granma*; who fought in the Sierra Maestra, in the underground struggle and at the Bay of Pigs; who were unshaken by the October Missile Crisis; who have stood firm against imperialist aggression for 30 years; who have performed great labor feats and have carried out glorious internationalist missions. Men and women from three generations of Cubans are members and hold posts of responsibility in our battle-seasoned party, our marvelous vanguard young people's organization, our powerful mass organizations, our glorious Revolutionary Armed Forces and our Ministry of the Interior.

In Cuba, the revolution, socialism and national independence are indissolubly linked.

We owe everything we are today to the revolution and socialism. If Cuba were ever to return to capitalism, our independence and sovereignty would be lost forever; we would be an extension of

Miami, a mere appendage of US imperialism; and the repugnant prediction that a US president made in the 19th century — when that country was considering the annexation of Cuba — that our island would fall into its hands like a ripe fruit, would prove true. Our people are and always will be willing to give their lives to prevent this. Here, at Maceo's tomb, we recall his immortal phrase: "Whoever tries to take power over Cuba will get only the dust of its soil, drenched in blood, if he does not perish in the struggle"...

These men and women whom are honorably laying to rest today in the land of their birth gave their lives for the most treasured values of our history and our revolution.

They died fighting against colonialism and neocolonialism.

They died fighting against racism and apartheid.

They died fighting against the plunder and exploitation to which the Third World peoples are subjected.

They died fighting for the independence and sovereignty of those peoples.

They died fighting for the right of all peoples in the world to well-being and development.

They died fighting so there would be no hunger or begging; so that all sick people would have doctors, all children would have schools, and all human beings would have jobs, shelter and food.

They died so there would be no oppressors or oppressed, no exploiters or exploited.

They died fighting for the dignity and freedom of all men and women.

They died fighting for true peace and security for all nations.

They died defending the ideals of Céspedes and Máximo Gómez.

They died defending the ideals of Martí and Maceo.

They died defending the ideals of Marx, Engels and Lenin.

They died defending the ideals of the October Revolution and the example it set throughout the world.

They died for socialism.

They died for internationalism.

They died for the proud, revolutionary homeland that is today's Cuba.

We will follow their example!

38

THE ECONOMIC CRISIS AND THE "SPECIAL PERIOD"

January 1, 1992

The term "special period in time of war" was added to Cuban military doctrine in the 1980s. At that time, the country was making ready to confront the warlike policy of the extreme right in the United States, and one of the alternatives considered was that the U.S. administration, under any pretext that came to hand and taking advantage of its naval and air superiority, would impose a military blockade on Cuba that would make it extremely difficult for food, fuel and medicine to reach its coasts.

It was supposed that such a situation would arise only in a state of war, no matter in what form it was disguised.

However, the events which led to the collapse of the European socialist community and, finally, to the collapse and self-destruction of the Soviet Union itself — which had been not only unforeseeable but inconceivable earlier — led the "special period" (a strategy for withstanding an exceptionally serious situation) to be associated not with direct military attack by the United States but with the loss of our main allies. This is how the "special period in time of peace" arose.

The following facts help to explain what it means: at the time of the triumph of the revolution, Cuba was completely dependent on the U.S. market, on which it sold its sugar and the small quantities of other products it exported and from which it bought fuel, food, medicine, equipment and spare parts. The imposition of the blockade between 1960 and 1962 forced the island to completely redirect its foreign trade; change its technologies; and, over a period of more than three decades, structure a system of fairer, more equitable and mutually advantageous relations with its new economic partners.

The catastrophe that hit Eastern and Central Europe in the late 1980s and early 1990s — which was totally unrelated to Cuba — meant that the shield that had been protecting Cuba, to some extent, from the deadly effects sought by the U.S. blockade disappeared practically overnight.

Thus, in the short period of about 30 years, Cuba was once again faced with the pressing need to restructure and completely redirect its participation in the world economy. It did so this time with the added difficulty of receiving no solidarity from abroad (though it did have the support of the peoples and of progressive organizations) and being subject to the unfair prices of North-South trade after losing the markets and sources of supplies and financing on which its development had been based. In addition, it faced the growing hostility of the U.S. Government.

Only a revolutionary, united nation endowed with a tremendous fighting spirit could have confronted such a challenge successfully.

The acute recessive economic crisis into which the country was plunged by its loss of sources of oil, other raw materials, equipment, spare parts, food and credit had a sharp impact on development and the standard of living. The Gross Domestic Product plummeted by 35 percent in about two years. Even more revealing for a country such as Cuba, with an open economy, dependent on foreign trade to solve all kinds of needs, the island's import capacity in 1992 had been reduced to about a quarter of what it had been in 1989. That is, in a short period of time, Cuba lost close to 75 percent of its purchasing power.

It is admirable that, in this adverse situation, the nation didn't fall apart, didn't let itself be plunged into chaos, but protected all its citizens, preserved the strategic programs of the revolution and not only stood firm but also gradually, in a relatively short period of time, restored the growth capacity of its economy.

In order to do this, it was absolutely necessary, in consultation with the workers and all the people, to draw up a series of measures that placed the initial accent on putting the nation's finances on a sound footing (that is, restoring the value of the peso, which had been considerably devalued); establishing employment guarantees; ensuring supplies of basic foodstuffs for workers' families; and defending the revolution's social policies, such as public health, education and the system of social security.

At the same time, in a short period, other decisions were implemented to adapt economic management to the new realities, making the most of Cuba's natural resources and increasing hard-currency income.

Those measures included turning large state agricultural enterprises into cooperative units of a new kind, legalizing the people's possession and use of hard currency, decentralizing foreign trade, reorganizing the central administrative apparatus of the Government, promoting foreign investments, quickly developing tourism and providing greater possibilities for self-employment.

These economic mechanisms played an important role in the realistic confrontation of the crisis. They have implied making some concessions to capitalist formulas – up to a point, and only in those areas determined by the Government – but the revolutionary government has never renounced its right and duty to oversee the economy as a whole.

"Special period" policies include more than just the economic sphere. They are based, above all, on a broader, more creative and dynamic approach to political and ideological work – especially the capacity for self-sacrifice and determination of the workers and the people as a whole. They are founded on the honor, patriotism, fighting spirit and socialist awareness of the masses.

What date could be selected as the symbol of Cuba's full entry in the "special period" – and, with it, the beginning of an inevitably long phase in the history of the revolution?

It isn't easy to choose such a date in a complex, step-by-step process. Conventionally, we might adopt January 1, 1992, since it was on that date that Fidel Castro told the National Assembly of People's Power that 1992 would be "the first year of the special period."[1] The Soviet Union had just been dissolved with the stroke of a pen, there was no guarantee that any of the agreements then in effect between Cuba and the Soviet Union would be kept, and Cuba was preparing to begin the new year in conditions of tremendous uncertainty.

We have no doubts about the country's chances of going ahead...

(Excerpts from the televised speech made by Carlos Lage, secretary of the Executive Committee of the Council of Ministers, explaining the country's economic situation, November 6, 1992)[2]

We need to refer here to Fidel's speech of July 1989, on the anniversary of July 26, in Camagüey. As early as this, if we think about the vertiginous unfolding of events afterwards, [Fidel Castro]

---

[1] See *Granma*, December 31, 1991.

[2] In "El desfafío económico de Cuba" (Cuba's Economic Challenge), a televised speech made by Carlos Lage Dávila on the Cuba Television program "Hoy Mismo." (Havana, Ediciones Entorno, 1992.

warned of the dangers that could face us as a consequence of what was then occurring in the Soviet Union and in the socialist bloc.

I recall that he stated that even if one day we should receive the news that the Soviet Union had disappeared, we would continue to construct and defend socialism. Even before this date, in our internal working sessions, he warned of the dangers of some measures being taken, of some tendencies, of some currents that were starting to appear, and the consequences that their end result might have in the Soviet Union and in the economic relations between the socialist bloc and the Soviet Union with our country.

It must be said that, even though we were warned and had begun to prepare our country, the subsequent events happened so precipitously, and the disintegration, first of the socialist bloc and then of the Soviet Union, occurred so fast that it was impossible to prevent the consequences of these events being felt in our economy and in the lives of our people.

All our people know, because they have been explained, the reasons for the difficulties we are experiencing today and how we must confront them. The economic impact on our economy caused by the interruption of these relations has been explained very clearly.

It has been said that the country's import capacity has been reduced by more than $8.1 billion per year to about $2.2 billion; that is to say, $8.1 billion in 1989 when it was still possible to regard our links with the community of socialist countries as fully developing, and $2.2 billion as the estimate for the country's import capacity in 1992. This means that the country has had to live this year with 73 percent less of the imported resources that were normally sufficient for the regular functioning of the country's economy and peoples' lives.

But the consequences of the situation we are going through are not to be reduced to this. It has to be said that in addition to all this, we used to have an intense commercial exchange with the countries of the socialist community, and principally with the Soviet Union. 81 percent of our exports went to those countries while 85 percent of our imported goods came from the countries in the socialist bloc.

This means that with the rupturing of these commercial relations and the conditions in which they were developing, Cuba lost more than three-quarters of its market, both the market of our supply of primary materials for national production and consumer goods, as well as the market for our export products.

Thus, it is possible to see an additional effect: it means trying to live, all of a sudden, with less resources while the economy must keep functioning and seeking new markets.

If we make a balance sheet of what has happened in the year 1992, Cuba's commerce with the former Soviet Union and the countries of the former socialist bloc would be around $830 million in these two areas, that is both exports and imports, including an estimate for the last two months of the year. This means that our commerce will be only 7 percent of what was previously developed with these countries.

From this it might be concluded that not only have we lost Cuba's preferential conditions for commerce with the socialist countries, along with credits, prices in accordance with bilateral agreements, and with an economic order in these relations that was much more than just those in the prevailing international economic order, but also, apart from losing these conditions, we now have the fact that commerce is almost broken off, reduced to a minimum expression, almost zero.

A good part of this 7 percent I was talking about is the million tons of sugar we export to Russia in return for 1.8 million tons of petroleum. This represents more than half of the commerce I mentioned. Then, the country had to function with these reduced resources and, besides that, had to find new markets for its import and export products.

Another factor that we might indicate is that our relations with the socialist bloc were not only relations with a great volume of commerce, and the country's most important commercial relations, but they were also relations of economic integration. In other words, over the years our economy has become integrated into the economies of the countries of COMECON, the Council for Mutual Economic Aid.

Many investments, many programs, many developments that were taking place in the country, and which required considerable resources and effort, were happening in accordance with the responsibilities Cuba had to discharge within COMECON, with the commitments Cuba had to honor within COMECON, and with the market that this community of countries offered to our nation; so a tie was broken that went much deeper than a mere commercial tie but which is also related with our need, not only of finding new markets, but also of strategically orienting the development of our country's economy toward completely new circumstances.

Parenthetically, was it the correct choice to have developed this relation? Is it historically correct? What are the origins of this relation and this integration? The origin lies in the imperialist blockade at the start of the revolution.

When the blockade began, when our trade with the United States was interrupted, when pressure was applied and the Latin American countries broke political, economic and commercial relations with Cuba, the socialist bloc, and the Soviet Union in particular, appeared as an alternative for our nation's commerce and development. And not only was it a market alternative, but it must be said that it appeared as an alternative that offered increasingly advantageous and increasingly appropriate conditions for our country, because, with this, we were able to develop commercial relations in which we obtained preferential prices for our products in relation to the prices on the world market, and we obtained credits for development, which the imperialist blockade denied us in other areas of the world.

This corresponded with a policy, mainly in the solidarity shown by the Soviet Union, an internationalist policy, for which we shall be eternally grateful. In other words, historically speaking, our high degree of integration into the socialist bloc has its origins in the blockade, and Cuba obtained advantages from this alternative trade.

It has often been said outside of Cuba that our country was subsidized and that this subsidy is now lost so the problems are beginning because our economy has to confront the normal market situation. This analysis is not correct because, in fact, there was no subsidy, but rather a policy of establishing a more just international exchange, corresponding to the kind of exchange that ought to exist between the developed countries and under-developed countries, something that even the UN proclaimed. We managed to have these relations in our trade with the Soviet Union and the socialist bloc to a greater degree than other underdeveloped countries had with the rest of the community of developed countries.

This is what occurred in our relations with the Soviet Union and, at a certain point in these relations, it was agreed that, to the extent that the prices of the products we imported were increasing, the prices of the products we exported would also increase. This is why there was a time when the price of sugar went as high as $800 a ton. In other words, it was the result of this agreement with the Soviet Union, which was a just agreement, and an agreement that we appreciate because it corresponds to the needs of the under-developed world and is also a just demand coming from the underdeveloped world.

When, as we have said, these relations were broken off, these commercial exchanges were broken off, we had already been integrated into this system for 30 years. Thus, in all essential aspects, the technology of our country is socialist technology, mainly from the Soviet Union. In our equipment and machinery, if we review it all, it's obvious that all our planes are Soviet, all the mechanization of our sugar industry, its technology, its combine harvesters, are Soviet, and more than 60 percent of our electric power generation is Soviet, a good part of it coming from the socialist bloc with the Czechoslovakian technical teams now working in the thermoelectric centers.

This means that there is no branch of the economy where there isn't a significant proportion of technology from the socialist bloc, and once the economic relations were interrupted, technical assistance and our chances of obtaining spare parts for the functioning of this machinery were also cut off. This is happening and yet the conditions in which Cuba is facing the world market and relations with other countries are not normal conditions. Cuba is facing, therefore, a market where it has been fighting for thirty years against a blockade imposed by the United States.

The blockade has always been present, but there is no doubt that our relations with the Soviet Union and the socialist bloc contributed toward attenuating the effects of the blockade on our country's economy. A blockade that affects 15 percent of our economy is not the same as a blockade that affects 100 percent of our economy.

The consequences of this rupture of our relations with the socialist bloc now confront our country with a commercial sphere that is blocked to us, where our commercial relations have to function under the effects of the blockade imposed by the United States at a time when the hegemony of that nation is even stronger as a result of these same circumstances, as well as others. In other words, the U.S. capacity for pressuring us, and its capacity for successful action in imposing the blockade is greater just at the time when Cuba must confront these new commercial relations, and it is at this time when the United States decides to intensify the blockade.

The blockade has been intensified and measures are being taken against our country, one after the other, the most recent being the Torricelli Act. Pressure is exerted on governments and business people. At this juncture, pressures of all kinds are being exerted...

[Fidel Castro] has explained that 1992 is year one of a special period, in the sense that, for the first time now, in 1992, we are totally faced with the effects of these problems. In the years 1990 and 1991 the situation was becoming progressively worse but, as you will recall, it was at the end of 1991 when the Soviet Union totally disappeared. In 1991, we still had bilateral agreements with the

Soviet Union, with preferential prices for our products, not as high as previously, but still better prices than on the world market — though this did not function the whole year but only the first quarter and part of what there was of the second quarter — and, for the first time in 1992, the socialist bloc is no more, the Soviet Union is no more, there are no more agreements, no more preferential prices and the consequences of this situation, in all their harshness, are now being faced...

I believe that it is not possible to define the number of years that this special period will last and to state when it will come to an end, and it would not be serious to try to do that. I think that, if we consider it carefully, we will be aware first of all that the seriousness of the problems will not permit us to put this behind us quickly. However great the effort, however major the measures we will have to take, and we are already taking, whatever efforts we make and whatever we do, this will take time. As Fidel was saying in the Assembly: "This will take a long time."

Along with this is the idea that if we see that in these circumstances we are much more vulnerable to the influence of the international market and the international situation — and still more with the effects of the blockade imposed by the United States and the pressures exerted by the United States — we must also see that, for the duration of this special period, these external factors will play a significant role, and depending on the ways in which they affect our economy, they will have an influence throughout this special period, throughout the time we will have to be living and working with the limitations and restrictions we have today.

What we do not doubt is that our country has the possibilities we need to keep going, and I believe that the greatest proof that we have these possibilities is the fact that we are here, that we have come as far as today, and that we have resisted until today.

39

THE HELMS-BURTON ACT IS DECLARED IMMORAL

December 24, 1996

In the second half of the 1970s, under the Carter Administration, the U.S. Government was forced to reconsider and make adaptations of some of the presidential decisions that had been made in earlier eras to isolate and economically strangle the island. In part, this was proof of the blockade's failure, the solidity of Cuba's growing relations with the socialist countries and the U.S. strategy adopted at the time on "human rights" and its pretension of legalizing a "peaceful opposition" to the revolution inside Cuba.

When Reagan moved into the White House in the early 1980s, that incipient easing of tensions in the U.S.-Cuban conflict was reversed, and a long stage began that was characterized by the escalation of measures aimed at reestablishing the blockade in full strength. At the same time, there was an avalanche of propaganda, including the establishment of Radio Martí and, later, broadcasts over TV Martí.

When the Eastern and Central European countries collapsed and the Soviet Union was dismembered and dissolved in late 1991, the political forces of the ultra right in the United States, intimately linked to the most reactionary sectors of Cuban émigrés in that country, assumed that Cuba wouldn't be able to withstand the blow; that, alone, the island would fall an easy victim to U.S. policy; and that, therefore, the time had come for seizing the offensive and taking the steps needed to ensure Cuba's liquidation.

Those were the premises that gave rise to the Torricelli Bill, which President Bush signed into law in October 1992. It not only exacerbated the blockade but also brought up to date all other U.S. policies against the Cuban Revolution.

A key aim of that legislation was to cut off Cuba's trade with U.S. subsidiaries in third countries. After the collapse of the European socialist countries, that trade had nearly tripled, amounting to $705 million a year, nearly all of which were purchases of food, medicine and supplies for agriculture.

The law also tried to block the sending of merchandise of all kinds to Cuba, stating that any ship which touched a Cuban port would not be allowed to enter U.S. territory for six months.

Together with measures of this kind, which sought to kill the Cuban people through starvation and disease, the Torricelli Act gave the U.S. Executive the possibility of using "Track Two" — communications, information and ideological influence — against Cuba.

The failure of that law, in spite of the damage it did to Cuba's economy, plus the measures that President Bill Clinton decreed on August 20, 1994, stemming from the "rafters' crisis," led the extreme right entrenched in the U.S. Congress to come up with a new step, the Helms-Burton Bill, which was a synthesis of several similar proposals that were aired in that period.

Clinton, who had criticized the text as being both excessive and unnecessary, signed it after the incident of February 24, 1996, when two small planes belonging to the Brothers to the Rescue paramilitary group based in Miami — which had repeatedly violated Cuban airspace in acts of provocation — were shot down by Cuban pursuit planes.

Above all, the Helms-Burton Act established a qualitative difference in U.S. policy on Cuba by setting forth a detailed, explicit program for the recolonization of the island under U.S. trusteeship. Such policies, which had been the prerogative of the President, were transferred to Congress.

The main target of the Torricelli Act was Cuba's trade with U.S. subsidiaries. The Helms-Burton Act placed its main emphasis on discouraging, obstructing and preventing foreign investment in Cuba. For this purpose, it used the pretext of demanding compensation for the U.S. property nationalized in 1959 and 1960, arbitrarily including that of Cubans who later became U.S. citizens and whose property was expropriated after January 1, 1959 — which obviously included all of Batista's henchmen and others who had escaped revolutionary justice.

Never before in the history of the world had there been a law that so arrogantly tried to force individuals and bodies corporate of third countries to obey the laws of the United States, on pain of punishment and humiliation of various kinds.

Faced with this attempt by the United States to extend its hegemony beyond its borders, several other countries promulgated "antidote" laws. However, not all countries were consistently steadfast in standing up against the empire.

For its part, Cuba submitted the Law of Reaffirmation of Cuban Dignity and Sovereignty to the people for consultation and then, on December 24, 1996, to the National Assembly of People's Power, for its approval. Thus, legal rebuttal by the Cuban Government was added to the rest of the world's opposition to that monstrous U.S. law.

Law of Reaffirmation of Cuban Dignity and Sovereignty[1]
Republic of Cuba
National Assembly of People's Power
December 24, 1996

I, RICARDO ALARCON DE QUESADA, President of the National Assembly of People's Power of the Republic of Cuba,

MAKE KNOWN that, in its session held on December 24, 1996, Year of the 100th Anniversary of Antonio Maceo's Death in Combat, corresponding to the 7th Session of the 4th Legislature, the National Assembly of People's Power approved the following:

WHEREAS the Helms-Burton Act, whose purpose is the colonial reabsorption of the Republic of Cuba, has been put into effect in the United States of America;

WHEREAS Cuba has suffered from the imperialist policy of the United States of America, which is bent on seizing it, using various means — including attempts to purchase the island from Spain; the application of the theory of Manifest Destiny and of the ripe fruit, reflected in the Monroe Doctrine; attempts to systematically hinder our struggles for national liberation; and intervention in 1898, which frustrated the independence for which the Cubans had been fighting with machetes, courage, intelligence and bravery—and on making Cuba its colony;

WHEREAS, through the Platt Amendment and its continued interference and intervention in the internal affairs of the country, the United States of America usurped part of our national territory, where it installed the Guantánamo Naval Base; imposed corrupt and despotic regimes at its service, including the opprobrious and bloody Machado and Batista dictatorships; and, since 1959, has

---

[1] *Granma*, December 25, 1996.

systematically attacked Cuba with the ostensible purpose of putting an end to its independence, doing away with Cuban nationality and subjecting the people to slavery;

WHEREAS the Cuban people — true heirs to the legacy of the mambí fighters for Cuba's independence from Spain in the 19th century and of the workers, farmers, students and intellectuals who have opposed and will continue to oppose the pretensions of their century-long enemy — are willing to make the greatest efforts and sacrifices to maintain the sovereignty, independence and freedom which they won definitively on January 1, 1959;

WHEREAS the process of nationalization of the wealth and natural resources of the nation, which was implemented by the Revolutionary Government on behalf of the Cuban people, was carried out in accordance with the Constitution, the laws in effect and international law; without discrimination; for the public good; and with appropriate compensation provided, the amount of which was agreed to by means of bilateral negotiation with all the governments that were involved, except for that of the United States of America, which refused to negotiate because of its policy of blockade and aggression, thus seriously injuring its nationals;

WHEREAS the Cuban people will never allow the future of their country to be governed by laws dictated by any foreign power;

WHEREAS the international community has rejected the Helms-Burton Act almost unanimously because it violates the principles of international law recognized in the Charter of the United Nations and because its extraterritorial application, seeking to arbitrarily and illegally dictate rules to be obeyed by other nations, goes counter to international norms;

WHEREAS a large number of foreign businessmen have demonstrated their confidence in Cuba by investing in the country or negotiating concerning potential investments, and it is a duty to use all possible legal formulas to help to protect their interests; and

WHEREAS the National Assembly of People's Power, representing all the people, rejects the Helms-Burton Act and declares its firm decision to adopt measures within its power in response to that anti-Cuban legislation and to claim the compensation to which the Cuban Government and people are entitled,

THEREFORE, making use of the powers granted it in Article 75, Paragraph B, of the Constitution of the Republic, the National Assembly of People's Power has approved the following:

Law 80
Law of Reaffirmation of Cuban Dignity and Sovereignty
Article 1. The Helms-Burton Act is declared unlawful, inapplicable and without any legal effect whatsoever.

As a result, any claim based on it that is made by any individual or corporate body, no matter what his/its citizenship or nationality, is considered invalid.

Article 2. The resolution of the Government of the Republic of Cuba expressed in the laws of nationalization that were promulgated over 35 years ago concerning adequate, fair compensation for the assets expropriated from individuals and bodies corporate that at that time had U.S. citizenship or nationality is reaffirmed.

Article 3. The compensation for the U.S. property that was nationalized through that legitimate process — which was validated by Cuban laws and international law — referred to in the preceding article may form part of a process of negotiation that is held between the Government of the United States of America and the Government of the Republic of Cuba on the basis of equality and mutual respect.

The ratios of compensation for the nationalization of that property should be examined together with the compensation to which the Cuban Government and people are entitled, for the damage caused by the blockade and acts of aggression of all kinds for which the Government of the United States of America is responsible.

Article 4. Any individual or body corporate of the United States of America that uses or resorts to the procedures and mechanisms of the Helms-Burton Act or tries to use them to the prejudice of others will be excluded from any of the negotiations referred to in Articles 2 and 3 which may be held in the future.

Article 5. The Government of the Republic of Cuba will adopt whatever additional powers, measures and/or provisions may be required for the complete protection of current and potential foreign investments in Cuba and for the defense of their legitimate interests against actions which may stem from the Helms-Burton Act.

Article 6. The Government of the Republic of Cuba is empowered to apply and/or authorize the formulas required for the protection of foreign investments against the application of the Helms-Burton Act, including the transfer of the interests of the foreign investor to fiduciary companies, financial bodies or investment funds.

Article 7. At the request of foreign investors, the pertinent government bodies, as authorized by the Government of the Republic of Cuba and carrying out the provisions of the legal regulations in effect, will provide those investors with all available information and documentation which they need for the defense of their legitimate interests against the provisions of the Helms-Burton Act.

Likewise, they will offer all of that available information and documentation to foreign investors who request it for use in lawsuits in courts in their own countries, under the legal provisions that protect their interests or that have been issued to prevent or limit the application of the Helms-Burton Act.

Article 8. Any form of cooperation, whether direct or indirect, with the application of the Helms-Burton Act is declared illegal. Among other things, cooperation is understood to mean the following:

- seeking — for any representative of the Government of the United States of America or another person — or supplying to any such person information that may be used, either directly or indirectly, in the possible application of that law or helping another person to seek or supply such information;
- requesting, receiving, accepting and/or facilitating the distribution of, or benefiting in any way from financial, material or any other kind of resources that come from or are channeled by the Government of the United States of America, through its representatives or in any other way, whose use would promote the application of the Helms-Burton Act;
- making known, spreading and/or helping in the distribution of information, publications, documents and/or propaganda material from the Government of the United States of America, its agencies, its branches or any other source in order to promote the application of the Helms-Burton Act; and
- cooperating in any way with radio and/or television broadcasting stations and/or other mass media to promote the application of the Helms-Burton Act.

Article 9. The Government of the Republic of Cuba will present to the National Assembly of People's Power or to the Council of State, when applicable, proposed laws which are needed to penalize all of those actions which, in one way or another, involve cooperation with the purposes of the Helms-Burton Act.

Article 10. It is confirmed that remittances of money from

individuals of Cuban origin who live abroad to their relatives who live in Cuba will not be taxed. The Government of the Republic of Cuba will adopt as many measures as it deems convenient to facilitate those remittances.

Individuals of Cuban origin who live abroad may have bank accounts in convertible currency or in Cuban pesos in banks in the Republic of Cuba, and the interest they receive on those accounts will not be taxed.

Likewise, they may take out insurance policies from insurance agencies naming permanent residents in Cuba as beneficiaries. The beneficiaries may receive those benefits freely, without paying any taxes.

Article 11. The Government of the Republic of Cuba will keep up-to-date information on the compensation which the Government of the United States of America should pay for the effects of the economic, commercial and financial blockade and for its acts of aggression against Cuba and will add to these claims the damage caused by thieves, embezzlers, corrupt politicians, and the torturers and assassins of the Batista tyranny, for whose actions the Government of the United States of America has made itself responsible with the promulgation of the Helms-Burton Act.

Article 12. The individuals who have been victims of the actions sponsored or supported by the Government of the United States of America that are referred to in the following paragraph — either because they or their property or because their relatives or their relatives' property has been adversely affected by those actions — may claim compensation before the Claims Commissions which the Ministry of Justice of the Republic of Cuba will create and establish, which will be empowered to rule on the validity and amount of claims and the responsibility of the Government of the United States of America.

The actions referred to in the preceding paragraph will include the deaths, injuries and economic losses caused by the torturers and assassins of the Batista tyranny and/or by saboteurs and other criminals at the service of U.S. imperialism against the Cuban nation ever since January 1, 1959.

The Ministry of Justice is empowered to control the handling of the claims referred to in this Article and to issue other provisions to this effect.

Article 13. The National Assembly of People's Power and the Government of the Republic of Cuba will cooperate and coordinate matters with other parliaments, governments and international agencies to promote as many actions as are considered necessary to prevent the application of the Helms-Burton Act.

Article 14. All of the people of Cuba are called upon to continue the thorough, systematic examination of the Government of the United States of America's annexationist, colonial plan that is included in the Helms-Burton Act, so as to ensure that the people in each territory, community, work place, study center and military unit fully understand the specific consequences which the implementation of that plan would entail for every citizen and to guarantee the active, aware participation of all in applying the measures required to defeat it.

Final Provisions

FIRST: The Government of the Republic of Cuba and the pertinent government agencies are empowered to issue as many provisions as may be necessary to carry out the provisions of this Law.

SECOND: All legal provisions and regulations that go counter to the provisions of this Law — which will go into effect as soon as it is published in the Official Gazette of the Republic — are hereby repealed.

National Assembly of People's Power
Havana, December 24, 1996

40

THE POPE'S VISIT

January 21-25, 1998

Throughout Cuba's history from the arrival of the conquistadores *five centuries ago (and their forcible imposition of a new faith) up to 1998, no Pope had ever visited Cuba. That wasn't exceptional in the long centuries during which the highest-ranking representatives of the Catholic Church seldom ventured outside Rome, but it became noticeable with the pontificate of John Paul II, a Pope who imbued the Vatican with great dynamism, developed a project of a new evangelism, which he carried to dozens of countries and vigorously projected the Church's social views on the most important current topics.*

Cuban Catholics and the rest of the people, as well, wanted Pope John Paul II, a world-renowned figure, to come to Cuba.

When the recently-elected Pope made his first trip abroad — to the Conference of Bishops in Puebla, Mexico, in 1978 — President Fidel Castro invited him to visit Cuba or at least to make a stopover there, but it wasn't possible at that time.

In the following years, the possibility of a Papal visit was postponed time and again for various reasons.

The tension in the relations between the Cuban Government and the Church hierarchy in Cuba, which dated from the period just after the triumph of the revolution, was renewed with the collapse of the European socialist countries, and the prospect of a visit became less probable. Thus, in spite of Cuba's good official relations with the Vatican and the admiration Cubans felt for Pope John Paul II on many counts, Cuba was one of the few countries in Latin America and the Caribbean that the Pope hadn't yet visited.

That situation changed in November 1996, when the Pope and Fidel Castro had their first, cordial meeting at the Holy See, when the Cuban President was in Rome to attend the World Summit on Food. The Cuban President reiterated his invitation and the Pope accepted, saying that he would travel to Cuba as soon as it was feasible to do so.

On January 21, 1998, the Pope kissed Cuban soil at Havana's José Martí International Airport, beginning a five-day visit that had an enormous international impact and highlighted the Cuban people's cultural maturity, organizational ability and sense of discipline.

In Cuba's specific situation, subjected to tremendous external pressures, Pope John Paul II's trip — in spite of the warm relations and sincere desire of both the Vatican and Havana that it be a success — was the object of insistent manipulation by some of the international press and by the inveterate enemies of the revolution. They attempted to inject politics and ideology into a visit that was, by definition, pastoral, and they did their utmost to portray the Pope's presence in Cuba as a kind of flaming thunderbolt that would do away with Cuban socialism.

All this turned the visit into a challenge, which Cuba took up with both grace and firmness, determined to make the Holy Father's trip to Cuba as near perfect as possible.

The Church mobilized its believers, and the masses of the people were also mobilized for every activity in which Pope John Paul II participated — welcoming him along the 12-mile (20-kilometer) route from the airport to the capital; attending the masses that were held in Santa Clara, Camagüey, Santiago de Cuba and Havana's José Martí Revolution Square and the meetings with the "world of grief" and the "world of culture"; witnessing his contacts with religious figures; and greeting him as he went through the streets. Throughout the visit, the people expressed their hospitality and affection for him as a spiritual leader with whom they agreed on many essential points and to whom they listened with respect, even on those topics on which they didn't share the same views.

All of the Pope's homilies and statements were broadcast in full over Cuban TV and in other media. The people themselves maintained order; during the Pope's visit, there were no armed police in the streets — and no unpleasant incidents, either.

The Pope's visit to Cuba may truly be described as a history-making event. It also had an important effect in Cuba, on both believers and nonbelievers, and it will be long remembered. It projected a vision toward the future, toward the universal struggle for a fairer world and toward Cuba's struggle to break its isolation against the efforts of powerful forces to strangle it. His Holiness's call to "globalize solidarity" and his plea that

Cuba open its doors to the world and that the world open its doors to Cuba bear this out.

The peoples of the world will eventually construct one human family...

(Farewell speech by Fidel Castro to His Holiness Pope John Paul II, January 25, 1998)

Your Holiness,

I believe we have given a good example to the world: you in visiting what some have called the last bastion of communism and ourselves in receiving a religious leader who is attributed with having brought about the destruction of communism in Europe. And there was no lack of those who foreboded apocalyptic events. There were even some who dreamed of them.

It was cruelly unjust that your pastoral journey should have been associated with mean hopes of destroying the noble aims and the independence of a small country subject to a blockade and submitted to a veritable economic war for the last nearly 40 years. Cuba, Your Holiness, is now in confrontation with the greatest power in all history, a kind of a new David, a thousand times smaller and who, with the same sling of biblical times, is struggling to survive against a huge Goliath of the nuclear age, one who is trying to prevent our development and make us submit through illness and hunger. If that story had not already been written, it would have to be written today. This monstrous crime cannot be ignored and there are no excuses for it.

Your Holiness: How many times have I heard or read the calumnies against my country and my people, invented by those who adore no other god than gold. I shall always recall the Christians of ancient Rome, so atrociously slandered, as I noted on the day of your arrival, and I shall remember, too, the fact that, throughout history, calumny has often been the great justification for the worst crimes against peoples. I also think of the Jews exterminated by the Nazis, or the four million Vietnamese who died under attacks by napalm, chemical weapons and explosives. Whether people are Christians, Jews or communists, nobody has the right to exterminate them.

Thousands of journalists have conveyed to thousands of millions of people around the world every detail of your visit and every word that has been pronounced. An infinite number of our citizens and foreigners have been interviewed all over the country. Our national television channels have transmitted live and directly to our people, all the masses, sermons and speeches. Never before, perhaps, have so many opinions and so much news about such a small nation been listened to, in such a short time, by so many people on our planet.

Cuba does not know fear, despises lies, listens with respect, believes in its ideas, unshakably defends its principles and has nothing to hide from the world.

I am moved by the effort Your Holiness has made to create a world that is more just. States will disappear, and their peoples will eventually constitute one human family. If the globalization of solidarity that you have proclaimed should reach to all corners of the earth, and the abundance of goods that humans can produce with their talent and their work were equitably shared amongst all human beings now inhabiting the planet, it might be possible to create a world that is really for all, without hunger or poverty, without oppression or exploitation, without humiliations or contempt, without injustice or inequalities, where everyone might live in full moral and material dignity, in true liberty — this would be a more just world! Your ideas on evangelization and ecumenism would not be in contradiction with this.

For the honor you have done us in visiting us, for all your expressions of affection toward the people of Cuba, for all your words, even those with which we may not agree, in the name of the entire population of Cuba, I wish to express our thanks to Your Holiness.

The restrictive economic measures imposed from outside the country are unjust and ethically unacceptable

(From the farewell speech of His Holiness John Paul II at the José Martí airport, 25 January 25, 1998)[1]

I ask God to bless and reward all those who have cooperated in bringing this long-desired visit about. Please accept my gratitude, Mr. President, and the authorities of this nation, for your presence here today and for the cooperation you have offered in the course of this visit, in which the greatest possible number of people have participated, whether it be attending the masses or following them through the public media. I would like to express my recognition of

---

[1] In *Cuba, te amo* (Cuba, I love you), by Alberto Michelini, (Italy: Ediciones Ares, 1998), 92-4.

the efforts and pastoral devotion with which my brother bishops here in Cuba have prepared my visit and carried out all their work amongst the people prior to it, the fruits of which were at once manifest in the warm welcome I have been given, and this must be continued somehow.

As successor to the Apostle Peter, and in keeping with the word of the Lord, I have come as a messenger of truth and hope, to confirm you in the faith and to leave behind me a message of peace and reconciliation in Christ. I, therefore, urge you to continue working together, urged on by the highest moral principles so that the well-known dynamism that distinguishes this noble people will produce abundant fruits of well-being and spiritual and material prosperity to the benefit of everyone.

Before leaving this capital, I should like to say goodbye, from the depths of my heart, to all the sons and daughters of this country — to those who live in the cities and in the countryside, to the children, the young and the old, to families and to each individual — trusting that you will continue to preserve and promote the most genuine values of the Cuban spirit that, true to the legacy of your elders, must know how to demonstrate, even amidst the difficulties, its trust in God, its Christian faith, its bond with the Church, its love of the culture and the traditions of this country, its desire for justice and freedom. In this process, all Cubans are called upon to contribute to the common good, in an atmosphere of mutual respect and with a profound sense of solidarity.

In our times, no nation can live alone. Thus the Cuban nation must not be deprived of its links with other peoples, which are necessary for economic, social and cultural development, and above all when isolation indiscriminately affects the population, increasing the difficulties of the most vulnerable amongst you in the basic aspects of their lives such as food, health and education. Everyone can and should take specific steps in order to bring about change in this regard. May other nations, in particular those which share the same Christian heritage and the same language, work effectively by extending the benefits of unity and harmony, by joining their efforts and overcoming obstacles so that the Cuban people, the leading player in its own history, can maintain international relations that will always work in favor of the common good. Thus it may be possible to overcome the anxiety caused by poverty, material and moral, amongst the causes of which may be unjust inequalities, the restriction of basic freedoms, depersonalization and the dispirited-ness of individuals, and the restrictive economic measures imposed from outside the country that are unjust and ethically unacceptable.

My dear Cubans, on leaving this beloved country, I take with me an indelible memory of my days here and a great confidence in the future of your country. Build it up with hope and enthusiasm, guided by the light of faith, with all the vigor of hope and the generosity of fraternal love and using your abilities to create an atmosphere of greater freedom and pluralism, and in the certainty that God loves you very dearly and remains true to His promises. The fact is, "For this end we toil and strive, because we have our hope set on the living God, who is the savior of all men, especially of those who believe" (I Tim. 4, 10). May He shower you with his blessings and may He let you feel His nearness to you at all times. Jesus Christ be praised!

A final word about the rain. Now it has stopped but earlier, during my visit to the Havana cathedral, it was raining quite heavily. I wondered why, after these hot days and after Santiago de Cuba where it was so hot, the rain should have come. This may be a sign: the sky of Cuba is weeping for the Pope is leaving us behind. This would be superficial hermeneutics. When we sing in the liturgy *"Rorate coeli desuper et nubes pluat justum,"* it is the Advent. This seems to me a more profound hermeneutics. This rain of the final hours of my stay in Cuba may mean an Advent. I would like to express my earnest desire that this rain is a good sign, that of a new Advent in your history. Thank you very much.

Also from Ocean Press

CUBA AND THE UNITED STATES
A Chronological History
By Jane Franklin
This chronology relates in detail the developments involving the two neighboring countries from the 1959 revolution through 1995.
ISBN 1-875284-92-3

AFROCUBA
An anthology of Cuban writing on race, politics and culture
Edited by Pedro Pérez Sarduy and Jean Stubbs
What is it like to be Black in Cuba? Does racism exist in a revolutionary society that claims to have abolished it? *AfroCuba* looks at the Black experience through the eyes of the island's writers, scholars and artists.
ISBN 1-875284-41-9

LATIN AMERICA: FROM COLONIZATION TO GLOBALIZATION
Noam Chomsky in conversation with Heinz Dieterich
An indispensable book for those interested in Latin America and the politics and history of the region.
ISBN 1-876175-13-3

CUBA — TALKING ABOUT REVOLUTION
Conversations with Juan Antonio Blanco by Medea Benjamin
One of Cuba's outstanding intellectuals discusses Cuba today, featuring an essay, "Cuba: 'socialist museum' or social laboratory?"
ISBN 1-875284-97-7

CAPITALISM IN CRISIS
Globalization and World Politics Today
By Fidel Castro
Cuba's leader adds his voice to the growing international chorus against neoliberalism and globalization.
ISBN 1-876175-18-4

CIA TARGETS FIDEL
The secret assassination report
Only recently declassified and published for the first time, this secret report was prepared for the CIA on its own plots to assassinate Fidel Castro.
ISBN 1-875284-90-7

PSYWAR ON CUBA
The declassified history of U.S. anti-Castro propaganda
By Jon Elliston
Secret CIA and U.S. Government documents are published here for the first time, showing a 40-year campaign by Washington to use psychological warfare and propaganda to destabilize Cuba.
ISBN 1-876175-09-5

Also from Ocean Press

FIDEL CASTRO READER
The voice of one of the 20th century's most controversial political figures — as well as one of the world's greatest orators — is captured in this new selection of Castro's key speeches over 40 years.
ISBN 1-876175-11-7

JOSE MARTI READER
Writings on the Americas
An outstanding new anthology of the writings, letters and poetry of one of the most brilliant Latin American leaders of the 19th century.
ISBN 1-875284-12-5

CHE GUEVARA READER
Writings on Guerrilla Strategy, Politics and Revolution
Edited by David Deutschmann
The most complete selection of Guevara's writings, letters and speeches available in English. An unprecedented source of primary material on Cuba and Latin America in the 1950s and 1960s.
ISBN 1-875284-93-1

SALVADOR ALLENDE READER
Chile's Voice of Democracy
Edited by James D. Cockcroft and Jane Carolina Canning
This new book makes available for the first time in English Allende's voice and vision of a more democratic, peaceful and just world.
ISBN 1-876175-24-9

CUBA AND THE MISSILE CRISIS
By Carlos Lechuga
For the first time Cuba's view of the most serious crisis of the Cold War is told by Carlos Lechuga, Cuban Ambassador to the United Nations in 1962.
ISBN 1-876175-34-6

FIDEL CASTRO ON THE BAY OF PIGS
By Fidel Castro
This book collects the Cuban leader's commentaries on the Bay of Pigs invasion from both the 1960s and his more recent reflections.
ISBN 1-876175-06-0

Spanish language edition of CUBAN REVOLUTION READER available as
LA REVOLUCION CUBANA
40 Grandes Momentos
ISBN 1-876175-28-1

Ocean Press, GPO Box 3279, Melbourne 3001, Australia
● Fax: 61-3-9329 5040 ● E-mail: info@oceanbooks.com.au
Ocean Press, PO Box 1186, Old Chelsea Stn., New York 10113-1186, USA

www.oceanbooks.com.au